# teach yourself

## beginner's french
catrine carpenter
**advisory editor**
paul coggle

For over 60 years, more than
40 million people have learnt over
750 subjects the **teach yourself**
way, with impressive results.

be where you want to be
with **teach yourself**

For UK order enquiries: please contact Bookpoint Ltd, 130 Milton Park, Abingdon, Oxon OX14 4SB. Telephone: +44 (0) 1235 827720. Fax: +44 (0) 1235 400454. Lines are open 09.00–18.00, Monday to Saturday, with a 24-hour message answering service. Details about our titles and how to order are available at www.teachyourself.co.uk

For USA order enquiries: please contact McGraw-Hill Customer Services, PO Box 545, Blacklick, OH 43004-0545, USA. Telephone: 1-800-722-4726. Fax: 1-614-755-5645.

For Canada order enquiries: please contact McGraw-Hill Ryerson Ltd, 300 Water St, Whitby, Ontario L1N 9B6, Canada. Telephone: 905 430 5000. Fax: 905 430 5020.

Long renowned as the authoritative source for self-guided learning – with more than 40 million copies sold worldwide – the **teach yourself** series includes over 300 titles in the fields of languages, crafts, hobbies, business, computing and education.

*British Library Cataloguing in Publication Data*: a catalogue record for this title is available from the British Library.

*Library of Congress Catalog Card Number*: on file.

First published in UK 1992 by Hodder Education, 338 Euston Road, London, NW1 3BH.

First published in US 1992 by Contemporary Books, a Division of the McGraw-Hill Companies, 1 Prudential Plaza, 130 East Randolph Street, Chicago, IL 60601 USA.

This edition published 2003

The **teach yourself** name is a registered trade mark of Hodder Headline.

Copyright © 1992, 2003 Catrine Carpenter

Typeset by Transet Limited, Coventry, England.
Printed in Great Britain for Hodder Education, a division of Hodder Headline, 338 Euston Road, London NW1 3BH, by Cox & Wyman Ltd, Reading, Berkshire.

Hodder Headline's policy is to use papers that are natural, renewable and recyclable products and made from wood grown in sustainable forests. The logging and manufacturing processes are expected to conform to the environmental regulations of the country of origin.

Impression number    10
Year                 2009 2008 2007 2006

iii

contents

about the course

*Teach Yourself Beginner's French* is the right course course for you if you are a complete beginner or wanting to make a fresh start. It is a self-study course which will help you to understand, read and speak most of the French you will need on holiday or a business trip.

## Two key elements

The book has two parts. The first ten units introduce you to the basic structures and grammatical points you'll need in everyday situations. Units 1–10 should be taken in order, as each builds on the previous one.

Units 11–19 deal with everyday situations such as shopping, eating, booking a room, travelling and give you the opportunity to put into practice the language you've acquired in the first part. These units may be taken in any order.

The course is best used together with the accompanying recording, but is not dependent upon it. You are recommended to obtain and use the recording if possible. The recorded dialogues and audio exercises give you plenty of practice in understanding the basic language; they will help you develop an authentic accent and increase your confidence in saying simple phrases. Readers without the recording will find that some units include one activity that cannot be done with the book alone, but in such cases the material is always adequately covered by the other activities in the unit.

## About Units 1–10

The first page of each unit tells you what you are going to learn and there is an easy exercise, *Essayez!* **Have a go!** which gets you speaking straight away.

**Key words and phrases** contain the most important words and phrases from the unit. Try to learn them by heart. They will be practised in the rest of the unit and the later units.

**Dialogue** Listen to the dialogue once or twice without stopping or read through it without looking anything up; try to get the gist of it. The notes underneath each dialogue will help you to understand it. Then, using the pause button, break the dialogue into manageable chunks and try repeating each phrase aloud. This will help you acquire a more authentic accent. Words and phrases listed in bold appear in the subsequent vocabulary box.

The sections marked with the ⓘ symbol provide cultural information or help you to develop your own 'techniques' to become a better learner, giving you tips on how to master the grammar, learn the vocabulary, improve your listening and reading skills and develop confidence in speaking.

**Grammar** In this section, you may want to start by reading the example(s) then work out the grammatical point, or you may prefer to read the **Grammar** section first and see how the rule applies. Once you feel confident about a particular grammar point, try to create your own examples.

**Activities** Each activity, in this section, allows you to practise one of the points introduced in the **Grammar** section. In some activities you will need to listen to the recording. It is not essential to have the recording in order to complete this course, as most of the activities are not dependent on it. However, listening to the recording will make your learning much easier.

**Mini-test** At the end of each unit you can test yourself on the last two or three units.

## About Units 11–19

The first page of each unit tells you what you are going to learn. There is also a checklist of structures which you have already learnt and will be practising in the unit. You'll also find in most units a short text in French about the topic.

**Key words and phrases** contains the basic vocabulary you'll need when coping, in real life, with practical situations such as checking into a hotel, ordering a snack, asking for a train timetable, going on an excursion.

**Dialogues** There are several short dialogues, each dealing with a different aspect of the topic. Remember to listen to the dialogues first and use the pause button to practise the new words and phrases out loud.

**Activities** The activities are mostly based on authentic French material. Here you can develop a feel for how things work in France, as well as practising your reading skills. You will then have more confidence to cope with the real situations.

**Mini-test** As in Units 1–10.

## Key to the exercises and tests

The answers to the questions on the **Dialogues** in Units 1–10, **Activities**, *Essayez!* **Have a go!**, *Pratiquez!* **Practise!**, Mini-tests, **Self-assessment tests** can be found at the back of the book.

## Be successful at learning languages

1 **Do a little bit every day,** between 20 and 30 minutes if possible, rather than two or three hours in one session.

2 **Try to work towards short-term goals,** e.g. work out how long you'll spend on a particular unit and work within this time limit.

3 **Revise and test yourself regularly** using the **Mini-test** at the end of each unit and the two **Self-assessment tests** at the back of the book.

4 **Make use of the tips** given in the book and try to say the words and phrases out loud whenever possible.

5 **Use every opportunity to speak the language.** Attend some classes to practise your French with other people, get some help from a French speaker or find out about French clubs, societies, etc.

6 **Don't worry too much about making mistakes.** The important thing is to get your meaning across and remember that making mistakes in French will not stop a French person understanding you. Learning can be fun particularly when you find you can use what you have learnt in real situations.

## At the back of the book

At the back of the book is a section which contains:

• A **Taking it further** section to direct you to further sources of French.

• Two **Self-assessment tests** based on Units 1–10 and 11–19 giving you an opportunity to assess your progress as you go along.

- Key to the exercises
- Numbers
- A **French–English vocabulary** list containing all the words in the course.
- An **English–French vocabulary** list with the most useful words you'll need when expressing yourself in French.
- An **Index** to enable you to look things up in the book.

## About symbols and abbreviations

▶ This indicates that the recording is needed for the following

ℹ This indicates cultural information or draws your attention to study tips and points to be noted.

(m)     masculine
(f)     feminine
(sing) singular
(pl)    plural
(lit.)  literally

**pronunciation guide**

The **Pronunciation guide** is on the recording at the end of Unit 1.

## ▶ 1 How to sound French

Here are a few rules that will help you to sound French right from the beginning:

1 In French, unlike in most English words, it is the last part of the word that bears a heavy stress:
res-tau-**rant**, o-**range**, ca-**fé**, té-lé-**phone**

2 French words that are spelt like English words are almost always pronounced differently:
**pardon, important, parking, sandwich, ticket**

3 In general, consonants at the end of a word such as **d g p s t x z**, and the letter **h**, are silent.
vous    anglais    nuit    dames    messieurs    hôtel

## ▶ 2 French sounds

Here is the list of the **French vowels** with a rough English equivalent sound. You'll see that an accent on an **e** or an **o** changes the way the letter is pronounced.

| letter | rough English sound | French example |
|---|---|---|
| a  à | cat | madame |
| e | 1 above | le ne |
|  | 2 best (before two consonants or x) | merci |
|  | 3 may (before z, r) | parlez |
| é | may | café |

| letter | rough English sound | French example |
|---|---|---|
| è ê | pair | père  fête |
| i î y | police | merci  dîner  typique |
| o | dot | olive |
| u | a sound not found in English – first say **oo**, but then keeping the lips in that position try saying **ee** | une  du |
| ai | as è ê above | lait |
| ô au eau | pronounced as **o** but with rounded lips | hôtel  autobus beaucoup |
| eu oeu | sir | leur  soeur |
| oi | the **wa** sound at the beginning of **one** | bonsoir |
| ou | moo | vous |

Many **consonants** are similar to English, with a number of exceptions and variations:

| letter | rough English sound | French example |
|---|---|---|
| ç | sit | ça  français |
| ch | shop | chic |
| g | leisure (before **i, e**) | Brigitte |
| gn | onion | cognac |
| h | not pronounced | hôtel  hôpital |
| j | leisure | je  bonjour |
| l ll | yes (often when **i** precedes **l, ll**) | fille  travail |
| qu | care | question |
| r | pronounced at the back of the throat with the tongue touching the bottom teeth | rat  Paris |
| s | desert (between vowels) | mademoiselle |
| t | (before **ion**) pass | attention |
| th | tea | thé |
| w | 1 what | whisky |
| | 2 van | wagon-restaurant |

Here are the **nasal sounds** formed usually with vowels followed by **m** or **n**. Speak through your nose when you pronounce them and listen carefully to the recording.

| ein im | { bang (stop before the g) } | frein  important |
|---|---|---|
| in ain | | vin  train |
| | | impossible |

| en an | long (stop before the g) | encore Jean restaurant |
| on | as above but with lips pushed forward | pardon on non |
| un um | similar to ein im in ain | parfum un |

## ▶ 3 How to link the sounds together

To make the words run more smoothly the final consonants of words which are usually silent are sounded when the next word starts with a vowel or h, e.g. très_important (trayzimportan). This is called a liaison. In some cases, as above, liaisons are essential; in other cases they are optional. To help you recognize when the liaisons are essential they'll be indicated with a linking mark (_) in Units 1–10.

When making liaisons all French people:

1 pronounce s and x like z: les_oranges   deux_heures

2 pronounce d and t like t, but the t of et (*and*) is never sounded: le grand_homme   c'est_ici   un café et une bière

3 link n in the nasal un when the next words starts with a vowel or a silent h: un_enfant   un_hôtel

## 4 A few tips to help you acquire an authentic accent

It is not absolutely vital to acquire a perfect accent. The aim is to be understood. Here are a number of techniques for working on your pronunciation:

1 Listen carefully to the recording or a native speaker or a teacher. Whenever possible repeat aloud imagining you are a native speaker of French.

2 Record yourself and compare your pronunciation with that of a native speaker.

3 Ask native speakers to listen to your pronunciation and tell you how to improve it.

4 Ask native speakers how a specific sound is formed. Watch them and practise at home in front of a mirror.

5 Make a list of words that give you pronunciation trouble and practise them.

6 Study the sounds on their own then use them progressively in words, sentences and tongue-twisters.

Try this one! **Panier-piano, panier-piano, panier-piano** (**panier** is a basket in French).

## ▶ 5 And now practise ...

Starting with **Paris** go round anti-clockwise saying each of the 14 towns out loud. Pause after each town and check your pronunciation with the recording.

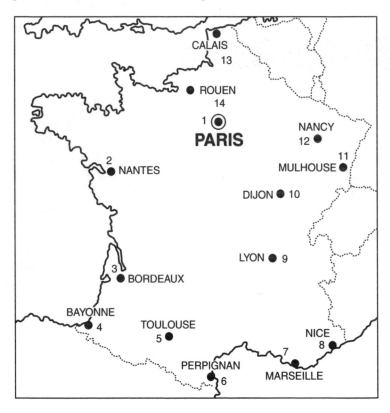

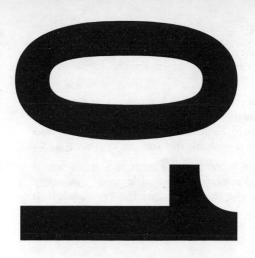

# 01

hello

## bonjour

**In this unit you will learn how to**
- say 'hello' and 'goodbye'
- exchange greetings
- observe basic courtesies
- ask people to speak more slowly

# Before you start

Read the **Introduction** to the course. This gives some useful advice on studying alone and how to make the most of the course.

Different people have different ways of learning: some need to know rules for everything, others like to feel their way intuitively. In this unit you'll be given the opportunity to find out what works best for you so look out for the symbol **i**.

Make sure you've got your recording **▶** next to you as you'll need it to listen to the **Pronunciation guide** and **Dialogues** sections. If you don't have the recording, use the **Pronunciation guide** in the book.

# **i** Study tips

Remember that studying for 20 minutes regularly is better than occasionally spending two hours in one go.

1 Listen to the **Dialogues** once or twice without the book (read them if you haven't got the recording).

2 Go over each one, bit by bit, in conjunction with the **Key words and phrases** and notes underneath the dialogues.

3 Read the **Grammar** section very carefully and study it.

4 Read the tips on **How to learn vocabulary** and **How to pronounce**.

5 Go back to the **Dialogues** and **Key words and phrases** for more listening and studying, this time using the pause button and repeating aloud after the recording.

6 Do the **Activities**, check your answers in the **Key to the exercises** and test yourself with the **Mini-test**.

*Essayez!* **Have a go!** Can you think of any French words you know such as the words for 'hello' and 'thank you'? Say them out loud, and then look at the sections **Key words and phrases** to check the answers.

# Key words and phrases

| | |
|---|---|
| bonjour | good morning/afternoon, hello |
| bonsoir | good evening (after 5.00pm) |
| bonne nuit | good night (when going to bed) |
| au revoir | goodbye |
| bonjour, Madame | good morning (Madam) |
| bonjour, Mademoiselle | good morning (Miss) |
| bonsoir, Monsieur | good evening (Sir) |
| au revoir, Messieurs-dames | goodbye ladies and gentlemen |
| oui | yes |
| non, merci | no, thank you |
| merci | thank you |
| merci beaucoup | thank you very much |
| s'il vous plaît | please |
| d'accord | OK |
| pardon | sorry (to apologize), excuse me |
| comment ça va? | how are things? |
| ça va | fine |
| très bien merci | very well thank you |
| et vous? | and you? |
| pardon? | sorry? (you want something repeated) |
| vous parlez_anglais? | do you speak English? |
| parlez plus lentement | speak more slowly |

When you see a linking mark '_' between two words, sound the last letter of the first word as though it were attached to the next word: vous **parlez_anglais?**

# ▶ Dialogues

*Listen to the recording and hear people practising saying 'hello' and greeting each other in French. Press the pause button after each sentence and repeat aloud.*

## Dialogue 1  Saying 'hello'

**Jane**    Bonjour, Messieurs-dames.

**Michel**  Bonjour, Mademoiselle.
**Jane**    Bonjour, Monsieur.

| Roger | Bonsoir, Madame. |
| Nathalie | Bonsoir, Monsieur. |

| Roger | Comment ça va, Jane? |
| Jane | Très bien, et vous? |
| Roger | **Moi aussi**, ça va bien. |

## Dialogue 2 Saying 'goodbye'

| Michel | Au revoir, Madame et … merci beaucoup. |
| Nathalie | Au revoir, Monsieur. |

## Dialogue 3 When things get difficult …

| Jane | Pardon, Monsieur, vous parlez_anglais? |
| Garçon | Ah, non, **je regrette** … |

| Garçon | Bonjour, Madame. **Qu'est-ce que vous désirez?** |
| Nathalie | Parlez plus lentement, s'il vous plaît. |
| Garçon | D'accord … Qu'est-ce que vous désirez? |

| moi | *me, I* |
| aussi | *also, too* |
| garçon | *waiter* |
| je regrette | *I'm sorry* |
| Qu'est-ce que vous désirez? | (lit.) *What do you wish?* but used in shops it means *Can I help you?* |

## ℹ How to pronounce …

- As a general rule don't pronounce **d g p s t x z** at the end of a word, e.g.: beaucou**p** vou**s** nui**t** plaî**t**.
- The letter **e** often gets swallowed as in **mad'moiselle**.
- The stress, in French, is on the last part of the word: par-d**on** mer-**ci** mad'-moi-**selle** mon-**sieur**.
- ç placed before **o**, **u**, **a** is pronounced **s** as in *sit*: garçon, ça va?
- The **s** in monsieur is pronounced as **ss** in *pass*.

# Grammar

## 1 Simple questions

The simplest way of asking something in French is to raise your voice on the last syllable (part of a word):

Vouz parlez anglais?   Pardon?   Ça va?

Now practise saying pardon? (to have something repeated) and

pardon (to apologize or attract someone's attention).

## 2 Refusing politely in French

If you want to refuse something in France, you can say **non merci** or **merci** on its own.

## 3 Calling the waiter's attention

Although **garçon** is the word for waiter, today you would usually say **Monsieur** to attract his attention. For a waitress, you say **Madame** or **Mademoiselle** as you think fit or just look expectant and say **s'il vous plaît**.

## 4 How to be courteous

In France when you're talking to someone you don't know very well, it's polite to add **Monsieur, Madame, Mademoiselle** particularly after short phrases like **oui, non, bonjour** or **merci**.

The French shake hands with good friends and acquaintances every time they meet or say goodbye. Kissing (on both cheeks) is reserved for family and close friends.

## 🛈 How to learn vocabulary

There are several ways of learning vocabulary. Find the way that works best for you; here are a few suggestions:

• Say the words out loud as you read them.
• Write the words over and over again.
• Listen to the recording several times.

- Study the list from beginning to end then backwards.

- Associate the French words with similar sounding words in English, e.g. **parlez** with *parlour*, a room where people chat.

- Associate the words with pictures or situations,
  e.g. **bonjour**, **bonsoir** with shaking hands.

- Use coloured pencils to underline/group the words in a way that will help you to remember them.

- Copy the words on to small cards or slips of paper, English on one side, French on the other. Study them in varying order giving the French word if the card comes out with the English on top, or vice versa.

## Activities

1 How would you say *hello* in the situations below? Remember to add **Monsieur, Madame, Mademoiselle**. Write your answer underneath each picture.

a_____    b_____    c_____

d_____    e_____    f_____

2 You're arriving late at a hotel one evening; greet the person behind the reception desk by choosing the right box below.

| | |
|---|---|
| Au revoir, Madame | Bonsoir, Monsieur |
| Pardon? | Bonjour, Messieurs-dames |

**3** A person at the bus stop asks you a question that you do not hear properly. What do you say? Choose **a**, **b** or **c**.

**a** s'il vous plaît  **c** pardon?
**b** non merci

**4** You are staying the night with some friends. It's late and you decide to go to bed. You say:

| Au revoir | Comment ça va? | Bonne nuit |

**5** You meet up with a French-speaking colleague. How do you ask: *How are you?*

C _ _ _ _ _ _   _ a v _ ?

The answer is *Very well, thank you.* What is it in French?

T _ _ _   b _ _ _   _ _ _ _ i

**6** Use the clues to complete the grid. When you've finished, the vertical word will be what you say if you step on someone's foot!

**a** The French translation for *please*
**b** Your answer to a friend who asks how you are
**c** *Goodbye*
**d** Calling the waitress's attention
**e** Greeting someone after 5pm
**f** Refusing politely

**7** Choose the appropriate word or group of words.

**a** How would you greet     **i** Bonjour Madame
several people?               **ii** Au revoir
                             **iii** Bonjour Messieurs-dames

**b** How would you refuse
politely?

   **i**   D'accord
  **ii**  Non merci
 **iii**  Pardon

**c** To ask someone if s/he
speaks English you say:

   **i**   Parlez plus lentement
  **ii**  Au revoir Messieurs-dames
 **iii**  Vous parlez_anglais?

**d** To wish someone
good night you say:

   **i**   Bonjour
  **ii**  Bonsoir
 **iii**  Bonne nuit

Remember to check your answers at the end of the book. If you have a number of wrong answers look back at the tips for learning vocabulary.

## Mini-test

You've arrived at the end of Unit 1. Now you know how to say 'thank you' and exchange greetings and you've also learnt a little about French sounds. How would you:

1 Say 'hello' to your friend?
2 Ask someone to slow down when speaking French? (Don't forget to add *please* at the end.)
3 Apologize as you step on someone's foot?
4 Say you agree?

You'll find the answers to the **Mini-test** in the **Key to the exercises and tests** at the end of the book. If they are correct you are ready to move to Unit 2. If you found the test difficult, spend more time revising Unit 1.

# 02

## c'est combien?

### how much is it?

**In this unit you will learn how to**
- count up to ten
- ask for something
- say how much you want
- ask the price

# Before you start

In this unit we will show you that it is nearly always possible to ask for what you want with just two words, **je voudrais** (*I would like*) and **s'il vous plaît** at the end.

The dialogue is short but there are a lot of new words including useful things you may need in France. Try to learn the words by heart using one of the techniques described in Unit 1 in the section **How to learn vocabulary**.

*Essayez!* **Have a go!** You are in a **pâtisserie** (*cake shop*) in France to buy a **baguette** (*French stick*). How would you greet the woman behind the counter? How would you ask for a French stick?

# Key words and phrases

*For you to say*

| | |
|---|---|
| un café | a coffee/a café |
| un thé | a tea |
| un coca-cola | a coca-cola |
| un_euro | a Euro |
| un journal | a newspaper |
| un plan | a map, plan |
| une baguette | a French stick |
| une bière | a beer |
| une chambre | a room |
| une pharmacie | a chemist's |
| une station-service | a petrol station |
| le timbre | the stamp |
| la carte postale | the postcard |
| la gare | the station |
| l'hôtel (m) | the hotel |
| l'hôpital (m) | the hospital |
| l'eau minérale (f) | the mineral water |
| l'addition (f) | the bill |
| les toilettes | the toilets |
| je voudrais | I would like |
| vous_avez ...? | do you have ...? |
| ça | this/that |
| du pain | some bread |
| du vin | some wine |

| | |
|---|---|
| de la limonade | *some lemonade* |
| de l'aspirine (f) | *some aspirins* |
| des sandwiches | *some sandwiches* |
| c'est combien? | *how much is it? (lit. it is how much?)* |
| un kilo | *one kilo* |
| un demi-kilo | *half a kilo* |
| un paquet | *one pack* |
| une bouteille | *one bottle* |
| une boite | *one tin, box* |

## For you to understand

| | |
|---|---|
| fermé | *shut* |
| je n'en_ai pas | *I haven't got any* |
| avec ça? | *will that be all? (lit. with that?)* |
| c'est tout? | *is that all?* |

## Numbers 1–10

| | | |
|---|---|---|
| 1 un | 4 quatre | 7 sept (the p is not pronounced) |
| 2 deux | 5 cinq | 8 huit |
| 3 trois | 6 six | 9 neuf |
| | | 10 dix |

## ▶ Dialogue

*Jane is in* une alimentation *(grocer's shop). What does she want to buy? Does she get what she wants? Listen to the recording first, answer the questions, then check your answers.*

| | |
|---|---|
| **Jane** | Vous_avez de la bière? |
| **Vendeuse** | Ah non, je regrette, je n'en_ai pas. |
| **Jane** | Et du vin? |
| **Vendeuse** | Euh oui. **Quel vin?** |
| **Jane** | Une bouteille de Muscadet. |
| **Vendeuse** | Oui, **voilà** … et avec ça? |
| **Jane** | Deux bouteilles d'eau minérale. |
| **Vendeuse** | Oui, **très bien**. C'est tout? |
| **Jane** | Oui, oui, **merci bien**. C'est combien? |
| **Vendeuse** | Pour le Muscadet, c'est 4,50 euros et pour l'eau minérale, 1 euro la bouteille. |

| la vendeuse | *the shop assistant (female)* |
| quel vin? | *which wine?* |
| voilà | *there you are* |
| très bien | *very well* |
| merci bien | *thank you* |

## ℹ How to pronounce ... *six et dix*

- when **six** and **dix** are on their own as numbers the **x** is pronounced as **s** and they rhyme with 'peace': **vous_avez des timbres? Oui, six.**

- when followed by a word starting with a consonant the **x** is not pronounced and they sound like 'dee' and 'see': **dix kilos, six bières.**

- when followed by a word starting with a vowel or **h** pronounce the **x** and **s** as **z**: **six_euros, dix_hôtels.**

# Grammar

## 1 Words for 'a, an': *un, une*

The word *a* or *an* is **un** in front of a masculine noun and **une** in front of a feminine noun. All French nouns belong to one of the two groups: masculine or feminine. Sometimes it is obvious as in **un Français** *a Frenchman*, **une Française** *a Frenchwoman* while other times it is not obvious as in **un café** but **une bière**.

There is no rule to tell you to which group a noun belongs, although the ending of a noun often acts as a guide. For example:

- words ending in -age, -ment are often masculine, as in **le village, le moment.**

- words ending in -lle, -tte, -ion, -ée are often feminine as in **une bouteille, une cigarette, une alimentation, une année.**

## 2 Words for 'the': *le, la, l', les*

There are four different ways of saying *the*:

| le with masculine nouns | le timbre |
| la with feminine nouns | la gare |

| l' with nouns starting with a vowel or an **h** | l'hôtel (m) l'eau (f) |
|---|---|
| **les** with plural nouns | **les** toilettes |

**i** Plural nouns usually take an **s** at the end. Make a habit of learning words together with **le** or **la** before them. If they start with a vowel or **h**, they are followed by (m) or (f) in **Key words and phrases** to indicate if they are masculine or feminine.

## 3 *Vous avez ...?* Do you have ...?

To check if they have what you want, start your request with **vous avez** (*do you have*). To indicate that it is a question raise the voice on the last syllable of the sentence.

**Vous_avez** une cham**bre?**    *Do you have a room?*

## 4 Words for 'some, any': *du, de la, de l', des*

When **de** (*of*) is used in combination with **le, la, l', les** it changes its form and can mean *some* or *any* according to the context:

| | |
|---|---|
| **de + le** becomes **du** | **de l'** remains unchanged |
| **de la** remains unchanged | **de + les** becomes **des** |

Compare the examples below:

| | |
|---|---|
| Je voudrais **du** vin. | *I would like some wine.* |
| Je voudrais **le** vin. | *I would like the wine.* |
| Vous_avez **de la** bière? | *Do you have any beer?* |
| Vous_avez **la** bière? | *Do you have the beer?* |
| Vous_avez **de l'**eau minérale? | *Have you any mineral water?* |
| Vous_avez **l'**eau minérale? | *Do you have the mineral water?* |
| Je voudrais **des** timbres. | *I would like some stamps.* |
| Je voudrais **les** timbres. | *I would like the stamps.* |

**i** In English we often omit the word *some*. In French, **de** + the definite article (**le, la, l'** or **les**) is almost always used.

## 5 *Un kilo de* A kilo/one kilo of

To ask for one of something use **un** with masculine nouns and **une** with feminine nouns.

**un** kilo de sucre       *one kilo of sugar* or
                          *a kilo of sugar*

une boîte de sardines

*one tin of sardines* or
*a tin of sardines*

## 6 *C'est combien?* How much is it?

You need only two words to ask for the price: **C'est combien?**
*How much is it?* (lit. it is how much) followed by whatever you
want to know the price of.

C'est combien la carte
postale?

*How much is the postcard?*

C'est combien la baguette?

*How much is the French
stick?*

### ℹ How to organize your learning

It may help you to remember the new vocabulary, pronunciation and
grammar rules that you learn in the book if you create your own
system to organize this information, perhaps using one or more of
the following ideas.

- You could group new words under:

  **a** generic categories, e.g. *food*, *furniture*.

  **b** situations in which they occur, e.g. under *restaurant* you can
  put *waiter*, *table*, *menu*, *bill*.

  **c** functions: greetings, parting, thanks, apologizing, etc.

- When organizing the study of pronunciation you could keep a
  section of your notebook for pronunciation rules and practise
  those that trouble you.

- To organize your study of grammar you may like to write your own
  grammar glossary and add new information as you go along.

## Activities

1 Look at the objects below, and write their names in French
preceded by **un**, **une** or **des**.

a

b

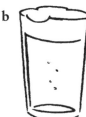

c

**2** You've arrived at a French hotel; you would like three things. What are they? You will find them hidden in the string of letters below:

> motunechambrepozowiuncafémoghttunjournaldfc

**3** Before you leave the hotel you want to buy a few things: how would you ask for them in French?

**a** I would like four cards, please.

.........................................................................................

**b** Do you have four stamps for England?

............................................................**pour l'Angleterre?**

**c** And some aspirin, please.

**et** ...................................................................................

**d** How much is it?

.........................................................................................

**4** All the numbers 'one' to 'ten' are listed in this wordsearch except for one. Which is missing? Read horizontally or vertically, either forwards or backwards.

| E | Y | Q | N | I | C |
|---|---|---|---|---|---|
| R | S | E | P | T | R |
| T | M | I | D | I | X |
| A | O | N | E | U | F |
| U | L | U | U | H | I |
| Q | S | H | X | I | S |

**5** Match the words in the left-hand column with the ones in the right.

| a deux bouteilles | | i chewing gum |
| b un kilo | de | ii vin |
| c une boîte | | iii sardines |
| d un paquet | | iv sucre |

▶ **6** Michel, sitting at a café, is ordering some drinks with his friends. He then asks for the bill. Using the words in the box, complete the script then check your version with the recording and/or the **Key to the exercises.**

**a** Garçon    Bonjour.................................

**b** Michel     Je voudrais un ......................
                et vous, Marie?

**c** Marie      Moi, une ...........................

**d** Sylvie     Je ...................... une limonade.

**e** Michel    Et je voudrais aussi l' ...........
                s'il vous plaît.

> café
> voudrais
> addition
> Messieurs-dames
> bière

▶ **7** As numbers are very important, here's another chance to practise them. Write your answers to the sums below (in words, not figures).

**a** deux + trois = ............      **e** dix    – huit = ..............
**b** cinq + quatre = ........      **f** sept   – trois = ..............
**c** neuf + un = ..............      **g** trois × trois = ..............
**d** six   + trois = ............      **h** quatre × deux = ..............

Check your answers by listening to the recording, **Activity 7.** If you do not have the recording, check them in the the **Key to the exercises,** then test yourself on Units 1 and 2 with **Mini-test.**

## Mini-test

**1** If a French friend said to you **Comment ça va?** what would you answer?

**2** You are speaking English to a French speaker. He says **Parlez plus lentement.** What does that mean?

**3** You have a headache. Stop at the chemist's and ask politely for what you need, then thank the chemist and say goodbye

**4** What's the word for *station*?

# 03 je m'appelle ... et vous?

my name is ... what's yours?

**In this unit you will learn how to**
- count up to 20
- talk about yourself and your family
- say that things are not so
- say how old you are

# Before you start

Speaking about yourself and your family in French is fairly easy once you know the vocabulary to describe your home and family and you know how to say what you do or don't have (**j'ai, je n'ai pas**) and what you are or aren't (**je suis, je ne suis pas**).

As we said in the introduction, to be successful at learning languages try to work towards short-term goals. In this unit concentrate on mastering **avoir** and **être**, the two most useful verbs in French. Keep practising them out loud: in the car, the bus, the bath. Aim at saying them without thinking.

*Essayez!* **Have a go!** You've just arrived in France. You stop at **une alimentation** to buy something to drink. How would you ask for two bottles of mineral water and one kilo of oranges? Je ...

# Key words and phrases

| | |
|---|---|
| **quel est votre nom?** | *what is your name?* |
| **vous_êtes français?** | *are you French? (to a man)/* |
| **...française?** | *(to a woman)* |
| **vous_êtes marié?** | *are you married? (to a man)/* |
| **...mariée?** | *(to a woman)* |
| **vous_avez des_enfants?** | *do you have any children?* |
| **des filles ou des garçons?** | *girls (or daughters) or boys?* |
| **vous_habitez (à) Londres?** | *do you live in London?* |
| **vous travaillez?** | *do you work?* |
| **où ça?** | *where abouts?* |
| **je m'appelle ... et vous?** | *my name is ... what's yours?* |
| **je suis_anglais/anglaise** | *I'm English (a man)/(a woman)* |
| **non, je ne suis pas marié** | *no, I'm not married (a man* |
| | *speaking)* |
| **je suis célibataire** | *I'm single* |
| **je n'ai pas d'enfants** | *I haven't got any children* |
| **oui, j'en_ai trois** | *yes, I have got three (children)* |
| **j'habite en_Angleterre** | *I live, I'm living in England* |
| **je suis de Vancouver** | *I am from Vancouver* |
| **avec ma famille** | *with my family* |
| **je travaille à Paris** | *I work in Paris* |
| **je suis secrétaire** | *I am a secretary* |

| je suis professeur/ professeure | I am a teacher (a man)/(a woman) |
| la fille | daughter, girl |
| le fils | son |
| la sœur | sister |
| je ne comprends pas | I do not understand |

## Numbers 11–20

| 11 | onze | 16 | seize |
|----|------|----|-------|
| 12 | douze | 17 | dix-sept |
| 13 | treize | 18 | dix-huit (weet) . |
| 14 | quatorze | 19 | dix-neuf |
| 15 | quinze | 20 | vingt (pronounced as French 'vin') |

conz.

# ▶ Dialogue

*Jane is sitting on the terrace of a café. She has struck up a conversation with a Frenchwoman. Listen to the recording or read the dialogue below. Does the Frenchwoman work? Has she got any children? Is Jane married?*

| Frenchwoman | Vous_êtes française? |
| Jane | Non, je suis_anglaise. |
| Frenchwoman | Vous_habitez Londres? |
| Jane | Non, Brighton, **dans le sud de l'Angleterre** et vous? |
| Frenchwoman | Moi, je suis **du nord de la France mais** j'habite Paris avec ma famille. |
| Jane | Vous_êtes mariée? |
| Frenchwoman | Oui, j'ai trois_enfants. |
| Jane | Des filles ou des garçons? |
| Frenchwoman | Une fille qui a dix_ans et deux garçons. **Ils_ont huit_ans et six_ans**. |
| Jane | Ah, très bien. |
| Frenchwoman | Et vous, vous_êtes mariée? |
| Jane | Non, je ne suis pas mariée mais j'ai **un petit_ami**. |
| Frenchwoman | C'est très bien. Et … vous travaillez? |
| Jane | Oui, **bien sûr**. Je suis dentiste, et vous? |
| Frenchwoman | Moi, je suis secrétaire. |

| dans le sud de l'Angleterre | *in the South of England* |
| du nord de la France | *from the North of France* |
| mais | *but* |
| ils_ont huit_ans et six_ans | *they are eight and six* |
| un petit_ami | *a boyfriend* |
| une petite amie | *a girlfriend* |
| bien sûr | *of course* |

## ℹ How to pronounce ...

- **nom** (*name*) is pronounced like **non** (*no*).

- **fille** is pronounced 'fee-ye' and **fils** is pronounced 'fee-sse'.

- Look at the **Key words and phrases** section and try to practise linking the words with a linking mark, e.g. **vous_êtes** (pronounce 'vou zêtes').

- To pronounce **secrétaire** French people will tend to pinch their lips for **se**, open the mouth up for **cré** and relax the mouth for **taire**. If you haven't got the recording check with the **Pronunciation guide**.

# Grammar

## 1 Regular verbs ending in -*er*, e.g. *parler*, to speak

In English *to speak* is the infinitive of the verb (this is the form of the verbs you find in the dictionary). In French the equivalent infinitive is **parler**. It follows the same pattern as many other verbs with infinitives ending in -**er**. Here is the present tense of **parler**.

| **parler** *to speak* | | |
|---|---|---|
| je | parle | *I speak, I'm speaking* |
| tu | parles | *you speak, you're speaking* |
| il/elle/on | parle | *he/she/one speaks, is speaking* |
| nous | parlons | *we speak, we're speaking* |
| vous | parlez | *you speak, you're speaking* |
| ils/elles | parlent | *they speak, they're speaking* |

**i** • The present tense in French makes no distinction between *I speak* and *I'm speaking*.

• Before a vowel or **h**, **je** becomes **j'**: **j'habite** *I live*.

• **On** is commonly used in French when people talk about themselves. In a general sense it is the equivalent of *one, you, we*.

• **Ils** is used when the group of people is mixed or all males.

• **Elles** is for an all-female group.

• Pronunciation: the **je tu il elle on ils elles** forms of the present tense of any regular **-er** verb sound the same. Do not pronounce the 3rd person plural ending **-ent**. If you do, people may not understand you.

*Pratiquez!* **Practise!** Can you work out the present tense of **travailler**? Write it down and read it aloud. Remember the pronunciation tips above.

## 2 Two important verbs: *avoir* to have; *être* to be

**Avoir** and **être** are irregular, i.e. they do not follow the normal pattern. They are the two most common verbs in French and need to be learnt individually.

| **avoir** *to have* | | **être** *to be* | |
|---|---|---|---|
| **j'ai** | *I have* | **je suis** | *I am* |
| **tu as** | *you have* | **tu es** | *you are* |
| **il/elle/on a** | *he / she /one has* | **il/elle/on est** | *he / she / one is* |
| **nous avons** | *we have* | **nous sommes** | *we are* |
| **vous avez** | *you have* | **vous êtes** | *you are* |
| **ils/elles ont** | *they have* | **ils/elles sont** | *they are* |

*Pratiquez!* **Practise!** Practise the verbs **avoir** and **être** in sentences using some of the key words you already know. Remember that for a question, you need to raise the voice on the last syllable. For example:

J'ai un_enfant.

Tu as des_enfants?
Il a trois frères.
Nous_avons ...

Je suis marié.

Tu es_anglaise?
Elle est professeure.

## 3 The negative form: *ne ... pas*

To say something is not so in French, you put **ne ... pas** round the verb: je **ne** comprends **pas** *I don't understand*.

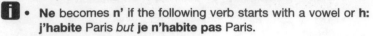

- **Ne** becomes **n'** if the following verb starts with a vowel or **h**: **j'habite** Paris *but* **je n'habite pas** Paris.

- After a negative form **du, de la ...** becomes **de**: J'ai **du** vin *but* je n'ai pas **de** vin.

## 4 Adjectives: how they agree

To describe things in detail or talk about yourself you need to add descriptive words (called adjectives) to nouns; an adjective describing a masculine noun has a masculine form, and one describing a feminine noun has a feminine form. As a general rule, feminine adjectives end in -e and the plural adjectives take an -s.

| | |
|---|---|
| J'ai un_ami américain. | *I have an American friend.* |
| J'ai une amie américaine. | *I have an American friend.* |
| Mes_amis sont_ américains. | *My friends are American.* |

## 5 Capital letters

In French, adjectives of nationality and names of languages are not written with a capital letter (unless they start a sentence).

| | |
|---|---|
| Vous parlez français? | *Do you speak French?* |
| Je suis canadien. | *I am Canadian.* |
| but: un(e) **Anglais(e)** | *an Englishman/woman* |
| un(e) **Américain(e)** | *an American* |
| un(e) **Français(e)** | *a Frenchman/woman* |

## 6 *Quel est votre nom?* What's your name?

**Quel,** meaning *what* or *which*, is a useful word to remember; it is always pronounced '*kel*' but it is spelt differently to agree with the noun to which it refers:

| | |
|---|---|
| Quel est votre **nom?** | *What's your name?* |
| **Nom** is a masculine noun. | |
| Quelle est votre **adresse?** | *What's your address?* |
| **Adresse** is a feminine noun. | |
| Quels **vins?** | *Which wines?* |
| **Vins** is a masculine plural noun. | |
| Quelles **bouteilles?** | *Which bottles?* |
| **Bouteilles** is a feminine plural noun. | |

## 7 Saying how old you are

Start with **j'ai** (not **je suis**), add your age followed by **ans** (*years*):
  Vous_avez quel âge?        *How old are you?*
  J'ai dix-sept ans.          *I am 17.*

## 8 When to use *tu* (you) and when to use *vous* (you)

The equivalent of *you* in French can be either **tu** or **vous**. French people use **tu** when speaking to children, teenagers, relations and close friends. They use **vous** in work and business situations or when speaking to senior or older people: **vous** is also used to address a group of people to whom one might say **tu** individually. The best advice is to say **vous** until you are addressed as **tu** or asked to use the **tu** form: **on se tutoie?** *shall we call each other tu?*

## ❢ Be active in your learning

As all language teachers will assure you, the successful learners are those students who overcome their inhibitions and get into situations where they must speak, write and listen to the foreign language. Here are some useful tips to help you practise French:

Rehearse in the foreign language.

- Hold a conversation with yourself, using the dialogues of the units as models and the structures you have learnt previously.
- After you have conducted a transaction with a salesperson, clerk or waiter in your own language, pretend that you have to do it in French, e.g. buying petrol, groceries, ordering food, drinks and so on.
- Look at objects around you and try to name them in French.
- Look at people around you and try to describe them in detail.

# Activities

▶ 1 On the recording, you will hear some numbers between 1 and 20. Repeat and write them down in figures.

a  ...................................        d  ...................................

b  ...................................        e  ...................................

c  ...................................        f  ...................................

g ............................................     i ..........................................

h ............................................     j ..........................................

2   This time practise these sums aloud and write the answers in words. (+ is **plus** in French and – is **moins**)

a   10 + 3 =  .......................      f   19 – 8 = .......................

b    7 + 8 =  .......................      g   11 – 6 = .......................

c   15 + 5 =  .......................      h   16 – 10 = .......................

d    4 + 9 =.......................      i   12 – 8 = .......................

e   13 + 6 =  .......................      j   15 – 3 = .......................

3   Look at the family tree below and fill in the sentences:

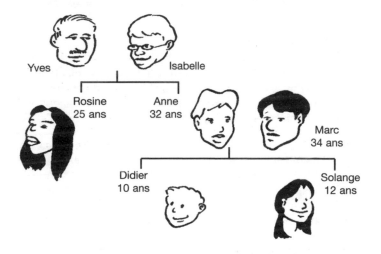

a   Isabelle .......... mariée avec Yves.

b   Ils .......... deux filles.

c   .......... s'appellent Rosine et Anne.

d   Anne et Marc ont deux .......... , une fille et .......... fils.

e   Rosine .......... .......... d'enfants.

f   Elle .......... .......... mariée.

g   Didier a .......... ans.

h   Solange .......... douze .......... .

**4** You are being very negative and answer **non** ... to all the following questions using **ne** ... **pas**:

**a** Vous_avez des timbres?    Non, je ........................................

**b** Elle a du café?    Non, elle ...........................................

**c** Il est marié?    Non, il ...............................................

**d** Elle est secrétaire?    Non, elle ..................................

**e** Vous_avez une chambre?    Non, je .........................

**f** Ils_ont quatre enfants?    Non, ils .............................

**g** Brighton est dans le nord de l'Angleterre?
Non, Brighton.....................................................................

**h** Vous parlez français?    Non, je ...............................

**i** Il a 18 ans?    Non, il ..............................................

▶ **5** As you listen to (or read if you haven't got the recording) the passage on **la famille Guise**, look back at the family tree in **Activity 3** to help you understand it better.

**La Famille Guise**

Monsieur et Madame Guise sont français. Ils_habitent Chaville, 15 rue de la Gare et travaillent_à Paris. Yves est dentiste, Isabelle est_artiste. Ils_ont deux filles, Rosine qui a vingt-cinq ans et qui est célibataire et Anne qui a trente-deux ans. Anne est secrétaire. Elle est mariée avec Marc qui est professeur de Math dans_une école. Ils_ont deux_enfants: une fille, Solange et un fils, Didier. Anne et Marc parlent_anglais.

**Rôle-play**

Now imagine you're Anne and that you've been asked to take part in a survey. What would you reply to the interviewer?

**a** Comment vous_appelez-vous?

**b** Vous_êtes célibataire?

**c** Vous_avez des_enfants?

**d** Des filles ou des garçons?

**e** Ils_ont quel âge?

**f** Où habitez-vous?

**g** Vous travaillez?

Merci beaucoup, Madame.

**6** This time you are the interviewer, questioning a man. Here are his replies. What were your questions?

**a** ..................................................    Oui, je suis marié.

**b** ..................................................    Non, je n'ai pas d'enfants.

c  ................................................  Oui, je suis professeur.

d  ................................................  Oui, j'habite Paris.

e  ................................................  Oui, j'ai deux frères
                                                    et une sœur.

f  ................................................  Ils ont 20 ans, 17 ans
                                                    et 12 ans.

g  ................................................  Non, je suis canadien.

h  ................................................  Oui, je parle anglais.

## Mini-test

1 How would you ask someone to speak more slowly?
2 **D'accord** means    **a** very much
                        **b** OK
                        **c** sorry
3 What does **je ne comprends pas** mean?
4 How would you ask for a bottle of wine? **Je** ........................
5 You want to know what something costs. What would you
  say?......................................................................................................
6 And now say in French: **a** my name is ...
                          **b** I am not married.
                          **c** I live in Brighton.

You'll find the answers in **Key to the exercises**. If most of the
answers are correct, you should congratulate yourself for doing
so well. Before going on to Unit 4 spend more time revising
Units 1, 2, and 3, to consolidate what you've already learnt. You
will learn more if you are able to revise regularly.

# 04

## vous habitez où?

where do you live?

**In this unit you will learn**
- numbers from 20 to 70
- simple and useful questions and their likely answers
- how to say that things are yours or someone else's
- how to understand prices

# Before you start

In this unit you will meet some simple questions which you will find useful when coping with everyday situations in France. Some are formed simply by raising the voice at the end of a statement, others by including a question word in the statement: c'est loin, la gare? *how far is the station?*, c'est combien, le billet? *how much is the ticket?*

*Essayez!* **Have a go!** At a party you meet a friend of a friend who only speaks French. You want to be friendly and try out your French. You know he/she is married and has a family. Can you think of at least four questions you could ask in French?

# Key words and phrases

| | |
|---|---|
| vous vous_appelez comment? | *what's your name?* |
| je m'appelle... | *my name is ...* |
| vous_habitez où? | *where do you live?* |
| le magasin est_ouvert? | *is the shop open?* |
| non, il est fermé | *no, it's closed* |
| c'est loin? | *is it far?* |
| c'est_au bout de la rue | *it is at the end of the street* |
| c'est près d'ici | *it is nearby* |
| c'est_à 50 mètres d'ici | *it is 50 metres away* (lit. 50 m from here) |
| c'est_à cinq minutes à pied | *it is five minutes away on foot* |
| c'est_une grande ville | *it is a big town* |
| c'est_une petite piscine | *it is a small swimming pool* |
| c'est gratuit, la brochure? | *is the brochure free?* |
| non, il faut payer | *no, you must pay* (lit. it's necessary to pay) |
| c'est combien, le billet? | *how much is the ticket?* |
| c'est où, l'arrêt d'autobus? | *where is the bus stop?* |
| c'est où, la station de métro? | *where is the tube (subway) station?* |
| c'est quand, le départ? | *when is the departure?* |
| c'est_à quel étage? | *what floor is it on?* |
| c'est_au premier étage | *it's on the first floor* |
| c'est cher/bon marché? | *it's expensive/cheap?* |
| il y a un car pour Caen? | *is there a coach for Caen?* |
| oui, il y en_a un | *yes, there is one* |

il y a un train direct pour Paris?   *is there a direct train to Paris?*
non, il n'y en_a pas   *no, there isn't any*
un restaurant dans l'hôtel   *a restaurant in the hotel*
beaucoup de ...   *a lot of ...*

**29**

where do you live?

**04**

## Numbers 20–70

| | | | |
|---|---|---|---|
| vingt | 20 | trente-deux | 32 |
| vingt_et un | 21 | quarante | 40 |
| vingt-deux | 22 | quarante et un | 41 |
| vingt-trois | 23 | quarante-deux | 42 |
| vingt-quatre | 24 | cinquante | 50 |
| vingt-cinq | 25 | cinquante et un | 51 |
| vingt-six | 26 | cinquante-deux | 52 |
| vingt-sept | 27 | soixante | 60 |
| vingt-huit | 28 | soixante et un | 61 |
| vingt-neuf | 29 | soixante-deux | 62 |
| trente | 30 | soixante-dix | 70 |
| trente et un | 31 | | |

# ▶ Dialogue

*Jane has been invited to an office party. She strikes up a conversation with one of her friend's colleagues. Does he work? Does he live near Paris? Is he married? Has he got any children?*

| | |
|---|---|
| **Jane** | Vous vous_appelez comment? |
| **Jean Durand** | Je m'appelle Jean Durand et vous? |
| **Jane** | Moi, Jane Wilson. Vous_habitez où? |
| **Jean Durand** | **Dans la banlieue** de Paris, à Chatou. |
| **Jane** | Et ... c'est loin Chatou? |
| **Jean Durand** | C'est_à 45 minutes en train. Il y a un train direct Paris–Chatou. |
| **Jane** | Et ... vous travaillez? |
| **Jean Durand** | Oui, je suis_**homme d'affaires** et vous? |
| **Jane** | Moi, je travaille en_Angleterre, à Brighton ... je suis dentiste. |
| **Jean Durand** | Et vous_êtes_**en vacances**? |
| **Jane** | Oui, je suis_ici **depuis deux semaines. J'aime** beaucoup Paris. Vous_êtes marié? |
| **Jean Durand** | Oui. |
| **Jane** | Vous_avez des_enfants? |
| **Jean Durand** | J'ai trois_enfants: deux garçons et une fille. |

| Jane | Il y a **une école** à Chatou? |
| Jean Durand | Oui. Il y en_a une à dix minutes à pied. |
| Jane | **Votre femme** travaille? |
| Jean Durand | Oui, elle est professeure à l'école de Chatou. |
| Jane | C'est_une grande ville, Chatou? |
| Jean Durand | Oui, c'est grand. Il y a beaucoup de magasins, deux banques, une pharmacie, **un parc** et une piscine. |
| Jane | Il y a un cinéma? |
| Jean Durand | Non, il n'y en_a pas. |

| | |
|---|---|
| **dans la banlieue** | *in the suburbs* |
| **un_homme d'affaires** | *a businessman* |
| **en vacances** | *on holiday* |
| **depuis deux semaines** | *for two weeks* |
| **j'aime** | *I like/love* |
| **une école** | *a school* |
| **votre femme** | *your wife* |
| **un parc** | *a park* |

## Grammar

### 1 How to ask simple questions

As you already know, the easiest way to ask a question is to make a statement and raise the voice on the last syllable:

**Vous_êtes marié?** *Are you married?*

### 2 *C'est ...?* Is it ...? Is that ...?

You can start the question with **c'est** (lit. *it is ...*) and raise the voice at the end of the sentence. To say that *it isn't* use **ce n'est pas**.

**C'est** loin? *Is is far?*
**Non, ce n'est pas** loin. *No, it isn't far.*

### 3 *Il y a ...?* Is there ...? Are there ...?

You can also start the question with **il y a** (*there is, there are*) and raise the voice at the end of the sentence. To say *there is no ...* or *there are no ...*, use **il n'y a pas de ...**

| Il y a un restaurant dans l'hôtel? | *Is there a restaurant in the hotel?* |
| Non, il n'y a pas de restaurant ici. | *No, there is no restaurant here.* |

## 4 Some likely answers: yes, there is; no, there isn't

To the question **il y a une banque près d'ici?** *is there a bank nearby?* most people in France would answer **oui, il y en_a une** *yes there is one* or **non, il n'y en_a pas** *no there isn't (one)*; **en** which means *one, some, of it, of them,* can be omitted in English but not French:

| Il y a une banque à Chatou? | *Is there a bank at Chatou?* |
| Oui, il y en_a une. | *Yes, there is one.* |
| Il y a une cabine téléphonique près d'ici? | *Is there a telephone box near here?* |
| Non, il n'y en_a pas. | *No, there isn't one.* |

## 5 More answers: yes, I have; no, I haven't

Similarly to the question **vous_avez un/une …** you will hear the answer **oui, j'en_ai un/une** or **non, je n'en_ai pas.**

| Vous_avez un timbre? | *Do you have a stamp?* |
| Oui, j'en_ai un. | *Yes, I have.* |
| Vous_avez une voiture? | *Do you have a car?* |
| Oui, j'en_ai une. | *Yes, I have.* |
| Non, je n'en_ai pas. | *No, I haven't.* |

## 6 Other questions

You can form other questions starting with **c'est** or giving a statement and adding the question word afterwards.

| C'est comment, le musée? | *What is the museum like?* |
| C'est combien, le billet? | *How much is the ticket?* |
| C'est où, l'arrêt d'autobus? | *Where is the bus stop?* |
| C'est quand, les vacances? | *When are the holidays?* |
| Les magasins ferment quand? | *When do the shops shut?* |
| Les magasins ouvrent quand? | *When do the shops open?* |

# 7 *Mon, ton, son* My, your, his

| Thing possessed | *my* | *your* | *his/her/its/ one's* | *our* | *your* | *their* |
|---|---|---|---|---|---|---|
| masc. sing. | mon | ton | son | notre | votre | leur |
| fem. sing. | ma | ta | sa | notre | votre | leur |
| masc. & fem. pl. | mes | tes | ses | nos | vos | leurs |

Like all adjectives in French, these agree with the noun they refer to:

| **mon mari** | *my husband* |
| **ma femme** | *my wife* |
| **mes enfants** | *my children* |

Take care when using **son** and **sa** to make them agree with the thing being owned, and not the owner:

**le fils de M. Durand** becomes **son fils** (*his son*)
**le fils de Mme Durand** becomes **son fils** (*her son*)
**la fille de M. Durand** becomes **sa fille** (*his daughter*)
**la fille de Mme Durand** becomes **sa fille** (*her daughter*)

## ℹ Create every opportunity to speak the language

- **Try to practise your French with other learners or French speakers.**
  Find out about French societies, clubs or circles in your area (the library is a good place to find out information). They provide an opportunity to meet other people with whom you can practise your newly acquired language.

- **Listen to some French regularly.**
  Not only will it sharpen your comprehension skills but it will help you improve your pronunciation.

- **Read something in French.**
  Buy a French magazine and see how many words you can recognize. Try to get the gist of short articles by concentrating on the words you know, getting clues from photographs if there are any and using some guesswork.

# Activities

1 Match the questions in the left-hand column with the answers on the right.

a C'est gratuit?
b C'est M. Martel?
c C'est_ouvert?

d Il y a des timbres?
e C'est loin?
f C'est cher?
g C'est combien?
h C'est près?

i Non, c'est Monsieur Durand.
ii Non, c'est bon marché.
iii Non, c'est_à dix minutes à pied.
iv Oui, c'est tout près.
v Non, il faut payer.
vi C'est 50,4 €.
vii Non, c'est fermé.
viii Non, il n'y en_a pas.

2 You've just arrived at an hotel. At the reception you find out about the hotel and the amenities in the area. Can you reconstruct the conversation?

a ...........................................................................
Non, Monsieur, il n'y a pas de restaurant dans l'hôtel.

b ...........................................................................
Oui, il y a une pharmacie au bout de la rue.

c ...........................................................................
Oui, il y a beaucoup de magasins près d'ici.

d ...........................................................................
Non, Monsieur, la banque est fermée maintenant.

e ...........................................................................
Oui, il y a un train direct pour Paris.

f ...........................................................................
Non, la gare n'est pas loin. Elle est_à cinq minutes à pied.

g ...........................................................................
Les toilettes sont_au premier étage.

3 That night you have a nightmare; you are in town doing some shopping but it is a very strange town. Using the example as a model describe what you see to your friend?

Example: Il y a des cartes postales mais il n'y a pas de timbres.

a .............. une pharmacie .................................. aspirine.
b .............. pâtisserie .................................. croissants.
c .............. une gare .................................. trains.
d .............. un arrêt d'autobus .......................... bus.
e .............. un bar .................................. bière.
f .............. une cabine téléphonique .................. téléphone.

4 You overhear one side of a woman's conversation in a café. These are the answers, but what were the questions?

  a Oui, je suis_en vacances.
  b Oui, je suis mariée?
  c Non, je n'ai pas d'enfants.
  d Non, je n'habite pas Londres, j'habite Manchester.
  e Je travaille comme secrétaire.

5 Fill in the gaps using one of the following question words: **où, quand, comment, combien.**

  a C'est ........... le journal?    C'est 1,11 €.
  b C'est ........... l'arrêt d'autobus? C'est_au bout de la rue.
  c C'est ........... les vacances?    C'est_en juin.
  d C'est ........... le Sacré-Cœur?  C'est_au nord de Paris.
  e C'est ........... la Pyramide?    C'est près du Louvre.
  f C'est ........... le film?      C'est super.

▶ 6 Listen to how much each item costs and fill in the price tags in Euros.

| a | b | c | d | e |
|---|---|---|---|---|
|   |   |   |   |   |

## Mini-test

1 Ask someone for his/her name.
2 Find out if he/she works.
3 Find out where he/she lives and say that you live in the suburbs of London.
4 Say how old you are.
5 Say that there is a bank nearby, at the end of the street.

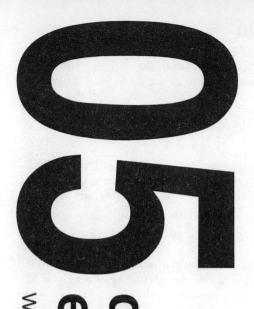

# 05 quelle heure est-il?

## what time is it?

**In this unit you will learn**
- the days of the week
- the months of the year
- some useful expressions of time
- numbers from 70 to 90
- how to say what you want to do
- how to ask what you can or cannot do
- how to ask for help
- the dates
- how to tell the time

# Before you begin

For a successful holiday or business trip in France you need to know when things are happening or when shops open. You also need to be able to say what you want to do, find out if it can be done and ask for help. You will be able to achieve all this with the few structures introduced in this unit. You'll also be introduced to quite a lot of vocabulary: days, dates and times.

*Essayez!* Have a go!

1 You are in **l'office du tourisme** (*tourist office*) in Paris. How would you ask for a street map? Ask if there are a bank and telephone box nearby? Can you think of other questions to ask?

2 Revise the following numbers: say them aloud.

41 – 22 – 68 – 15 – 5 – 55 – 14 – 29 – 31 – 47 – 60 – 11

▶ Check your answers and your pronunciation with the recording. If you do not have the recording, check with **Numbers** at the back of the book.

# Key words and phrases

| | |
|---|---|
| **à quelle heure ...** | *at what time ...* |
| **quand est-ce que l'avion part?** | *when does the aircraft leave?* |
| **quand est-ce que le bus arrive?** | *when does the bus arrive?* |
| **quand est-ce qu'on rentre?** | *when do we come back?* |
| **quand est-ce qu'on peut prendre le petit-déjeuner?** | *when can we have breakfast?* |
| **quand est-ce qu'il y a un métro?** | *when is there a (tube, subway) train?* |
| **quand finit le concert?** | *when does the concert finish?* |
| **quelle heure est-il?** | *what time is it?* |
| **il est ...** | *it's ...* |
| **qu'est-ce que vous faites dans la vie?** | *what's your job* (lit. what do you do in life?) |
| **dans dix minutes** | *in ten minutes' time* |
| **à dix heures du soir** | *at ten o'clock in the evening* |
| **je travaille ...** | *I work ...* |
| **tous les jours de la semaine** | *every day of the week* |
| **sauf le samedi et le dimanche** | *except Saturdays and Sundays* |
| **le lundi, le mardi et le mercredi** | *on Mondays, Tuesdays and Wednesdays* |

| le jeudi et le vendredi | on Thursdays and Fridays |
|---|---|
| jusqu'à midi/minuit | until lunch/midnight |
| depuis dix heures du matin | since ten in the morning |
| pendant l'après-midi | during the afternoon |
| je regarde la télévision ... | I watch TV ... |
| quelquefois | sometimes |
| souvent | often |
| toujours | always |
| aujourd'hui | today |
| demain | tomorrow |
| maintenant | now |

## ▶ Les mois de l'année *The months of the year*

| janvier | January |
|---|---|
| février | February |
| mars | March |
| avril | April |
| mai | May |
| juin | June |
| juillet | July |
| août | August |
| septembre | September |
| octobre | October |
| novembre | November |
| décembre | December |

## Numbers 70–90

| soixante-dix | 70 | quatre-vingts | 80 |
|---|---|---|---|
| soixante et onze | 71 | quatre-vingt-un | 81 |
| soixante-douze | 72 | quatre-vingt-deux | 82 |
| soixante-treize | 73 | quatre-vingt-trois | 83 |
| soixante-quatorze | 74 | quatre-vingt-quatre | 84 |
| soixante-quinze | 75 | quatre-vingt-cinq | 85 |
| soixante-seize | 76 | quatre-vingt-six | 86 |
| soixante-dix-sept | 77 | quatre-vingt-sept | 87 |
| soixante-dix-huit | 78 | quatre-vingt-huit | 88 |
| soixante-dix-neuf | 79 | quatre-vingt-neuf | 89 |
| | | quatre-vingt-dix | 90 |

# ▶ Dialogue

*Jane is asking Mme Durand about her working week. Listen to the recording several times. At what time does Mme Durand start in the mornings and finish in the evenings? Where does she go for lunch?*

| | |
|---|---|
| **Jane** | Mme Durand, qu'est-ce-que vous faites dans la vie? |
| **Mme Durand** | Je suis professeure de biologie. |
| **Jane** | Vous travaillez tous les jours? |
| **Mme Durand** | Oui, je travaille tous les jours sauf le dimanche. |
| **Jane** | A quelle heure est-ce que vous commencez le matin? |
| **Mme Durand** | **Ça dépend**, le lundi, le mercredi et le vendredi, je commence à huit heures et demie, mais le mardi et le jeudi je ne travaille pas le matin. |
| **Jane** | A quelle heure finissez-vous l'après-midi? |
| **Mme Durand** | Je finis à cinq heures et demie le lundi, le mardi, le jeudi et le vendredi. Le mercredi après-midi je ne travaille pas **mais je reste** dans mon **bureau**. Le samedi, l'école finit à midi et c'est le week-end jusqu'au lundi matin. |
| **Jane** | Où est-ce que vous déjeunez à midi? |
| **Mme Durand** | Mes_enfants et moi, nous déjeunons_à l'école. Il y a une caféteria **qui est_ouverte** toute la journée de neuf heures à cinq heures. |
| **Jane** | Et le week-end, qu'est-ce que vous faites? |
| **Mme Durand** | Ah, le week-end c'est **formidable** mais_**il passe trop vite**. Samedi après-midi je regarde souvent le football à la télévision avec mon **mari** et mes_enfants. Dimanche **on va** toujours à la piscine de Chatou. |

| | |
|---|---|
| **ça dépend** | *it depends* |
| **mais je reste** | *but I stay* |
| **le bureau** | *the office* |
| **qui est_ouverte** | *which is open* |
| **formidable** | *great* |
| **il passe trop vite** | *it goes too quickly* |
| **mari** | *husband* |
| **on va** | *we go* |

# Grammar

## 1 Saying what you want / want to do

Instead of saying **je veux** (*I want*), it's more polite to start with **je voudrais** (*I would like*). To say what you want to do, put the infinitive next. (**Je veux** and **je voudrais** are part of the verb **vouloir**.)

| | |
|---|---|
| Je voudrais_une chambre pour ce soir. | *I would like a room for tonight.* |
| Je voudrais_acheter un timbre pour l'Angleterre. | *I would like to buy a stamp for England.* |

## 2 Asking what you can do; asking for help

To ask if you can do something use **je peux** or **on peut** followed by the infinitive describing what you want to do. To ask for someone's help use **vous pouvez**. (**Je peux, on peut, vous pouvez,** are part of the verb **pouvoir**.)

| | |
|---|---|
| Je peux changer de l'argent? | *Can I change some money?* |
| On peut prendre le petit déjeuner à quelle heure? | *At what time can I / we have breakfast?* |
| Vous pouvez répéter? | *Can you repeat that?* |

## 3 Three different ways to ask a question

a By giving a questioning tone to what is really a statement:

Tu es française?         *Are you French?*

b By leaving the verb as it is and using **est-ce que** (pronounced *esker*) which is the equivalent of the English *do, does,* in sentences such as *do you speak English?*

| | |
|---|---|
| Est-ce que tu travailles? | *Do you work?* |
| Où est-ce que tu habites? | *Where do you live?* |

c By turning the verb round and joining the two parts with a hyphen:

Travailles-tu?         *Do you work?*

**i** Out of the three different ways of asking a question, the safest one is **b** as there are no situations in which **est-ce que** cannot be used; **a** is common in conversation but less so in written French; **c** is not usually used with **je**.

# 4 Questions starting with *Qu'est-ce que ...?* What ...?

Many questions start with **qu'est-ce que ...?** *what ...?*

| | |
|---|---|
| Qu'est-ce que c'est? | *What's that?* |
| Qu'est-ce que vous désirez? | *What would you like?* (in a shop) |
| Qu'est-ce que vous faites dans la vie? | *What's your job?* (lit. what do you do in life?) |

# 5 Verbs ending in *-ir* and *-re*

There are three main groups of regular verbs in French:

| | |
|---|---|
| verbs ending in -er | e.g. **travailler** |
| verbs ending in -ir | e.g. **finir** |
| verbs ending in -re | e.g. **attendre** |

To work out the present tense of **-ir** and **-re** verbs, knock the **-ir** and **-re** off the infinitives and then add the following endings:

| **finir** *to finish* | | **attendre** *to wait* | |
|---|---|---|---|
| je | fin**is** | j' | atten**ds** |
| tu | fin**is** | tu | atten**ds** |
| il/elle/on | fin**it** | il/elle/on | atten**d** |
| nous | fin**issons** | nous | atten**dons** |
| vous | fin**issez** | vous | atten**dez** |
| ils/elles | fin**issent** | ils/elles | atten**dent** |

| | |
|---|---|
| **A quelle heure finissez-vous?** | *At what time do you finish?* |
| **Je finis à 5h.30.** | *I finish at 5.30.* |
| **L'école finit à midi.** | *School finishes at lunchtime.* |
| **J'attends le train de 7h.30.** | *I'm waiting for the 7.30 train.* |
| **Elle attend son petit_ami.** | *She's waiting for her boyfriend.* |

**i** Remember not to pronounce the last letters in: finis/finit/finissons/finissent; attends/attend/attendons/attendent.

# 6 Giving the date

The English talk about the 1st, 2nd, 3rd, 4th, etc. ... of the month. The French say 'the 1st' (**le premier** or **1er**) but 'the two', 'the three', 'the four', etc. ... of the month.

| Quelle est la date? | What's the date? |
| Nous sommes le 1er_octobre. | It's the 1st October. |
| Aujourd'hui c'est le deux_avril. | Today is the 2nd of April. |

## 7 Telling the time

a The 24-hour clock is used widely in France to distinguish between a.m. and p.m.

| il est treize heures | it's 1 p.m. |
| il est quatorze heures quinze | it's 2.15 p.m. |
| il est quinze heures trente | it's 3.30 p.m. |
| il est seize heures quarante-cinq | it's 4.45 p.m. |
| il est dix-sept heures cinquante | it's 5.50 p.m. |
| il est dix-huit heures cinquante-deux | it's 6.52 p.m. |
| il est dix-neuf heures cinquante-cinq | it's 7.55 p.m. |

b The 12-hour clock. To reply to the question **Quelle heure est-il?** *What time is it?*, one is more likely to use the 12-hour clock.

a il est dix heures
b il est dix heures cinq
c il est dix heures dix
d il est dix heures et quart
   (*lit. ten hours and a quarter*)

e il est dix heures vingt
f il est dix heures vingt-cinq
g il est dix heures et demie
   (*lit. ten hours and half*)

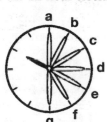

h il est onze heures moins vingt-cinq
   (*lit. eleven hours minus twenty-five*)

i il est onze heures moins vingt
j il est onze heures moins le quart
   (*lit. eleven hours minus the quarter*)

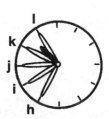

k il est onze heures moins dix
l il est onze heures moins cinq

To distinguish between 9 a.m. and 9 p.m. people say:

| | |
|---|---|
| il est neuf heures **du matin** | *it's 9 a.m.* |
| il est neuf heures **du soir** | *it's 9 p.m.* |

**i** Pronounce the **f** of **neuf** as a **v** when it is followed by a vowel or an **h**.

Noon and midnight are however distinguished from each other:

| | |
|---|---|
| **il est midi** | *it's (12 p.m.) midday* |
| **il est minuit** | *it's (12 a.m.) midnight* |

## 8 *Faire* to do/to make

**Faire** is an irregular verb as it does not follow the pattern of **attendre**. It is used in a number of expressions in French (can you think of a recent one you've seen?). Here is a new one: **faire la cuisine** *to do the cooking*.

| | |
|---|---|
| **je fais** | **nous faisons** |
| **tu fais** | **vous faites** |
| **il/elle/on fait** | **ils/elles font** |

## 9 *Prendre* to take

**Prendre** is also an irregular verb and needs to be learnt on its own. **Apprendre** *to learn* and **comprendre** *to understand* follow the same pattern as **prendre**.

| | |
|---|---|
| **je prends** | **nous prenons** |
| **tu prends** | **vous prenez** |
| **il/elle/on prend** | **ils/elles prennent** |

## **i** Experiment while learning

### Get a feel for the language

Learning a language is like learning any other skill. Take swimming for example: it is only when you go into the water and put into practice what you've read or been told, that real learning starts.

- Experiment with grammar rules: sit back and reflect on some of the rules you've been learning. See how they compare with your own language or other languages you may already speak. Try to find out some rules on your own and be ready to spot the exceptions. By doing this you'll remember the rules better and get a feel for the language.

- Experiment with words: use the words that you've learnt in new contexts and find out if they are correct. For example, you've learnt that **passe** can mean *go* in the context of time, e.g. **le dimanche passe trop vite**. Experiment with **passe** in new contexts. **Les vacances passent trop vite; la semaine passe ...** etc. Check the new phrases either in this book, a dictionary or with French speakers.

# Activities

1 See how many sentences you can make using the verbs in the boxes below and adding a few words.

| je voudrais<br><br>je peux<br>on peut<br>vous pouvez | **+** | déjeuner .........................<br>habiter .........................<br>prendre .........................<br>acheter .........................<br>finir...............................<br>commencer .....................<br>apprendre ...................... |
| --- | --- | --- |

2 Put the correct endings to the verbs in brackets.

   a Le matin je (prendre) le train à 7h.30.
   b Mes enfants (commencer) l'école à 8h.30.
   c Le train (arriver) à huit heures du matin.
   d Il (apprendre) le français depuis deux mois.
   e A midi on (déjeuner) à la cafétéria.
   f Qu'est-ce que vous (prendre) pour le petit-déjeuner?
   g De huit heures à neuf heures je (faire) la cuisine.
   h Quelle heure (être)-il?
   i Le mercredi, la journée (finir) à midi.
   j Qu'est-ce que vous (faire) dans la vie?
   k Nous (attendre) à l'arrêt d'autobus.
   l Ils (comprendre) l'anglais.

3 Complete the questions by selecting the appropriate endings.

   a Comment
   b Quel âge
   c C'est où
   d Qu'est-ce que
   e Il y a
   f A quelle heure
   g Vous avez

   i vous faites dans la vie?
   ii une banque près d'ici?
   iii vous appelez-vous?
   iv commencez-vous le matin?
   v la cabine téléphonique?
   vi combien d'enfants?
   vii ont-ils?

4 Below is M. Durand's timetable for a typical day. However the lines got muddled up. Can you put them in the right order, starting with the sentence in bold type?

a Il arrive au travail à 9 heures.
b Le soir, il regarde la télévision jusqu'à 22 heures.
c Il travaille de 9h.15 jusqu'à 13h.
d Il finit la journée à 17h.30.
e Il prend le train à 7 heures du matin.
f **Il prend le petit-déjeuner à 6h.30 du matin.**
g A midi il déjeune au restaurant avec ses collègues.
h Il rentre à la maison vers 19h.15.

5 Using the pictures to help you, fill in the missing words.

a Je .......... le petit-déjeuner.

b Ils .......... le train.

c Elle .......... le travail à 9h.

d Il .......... jusqu'à midi.

e A midi il .......... à la cafétéria.

f Le soir il .......... le travail à 17h.30.

g Elle .......... la cuisine.

h Ils .......... la télévision.

**6** Give the following dates in French:

> 1st May    10th June    3rd February    13th October
> 21st March    30th September    15th July    6th August

▶ **7** Listen to the recording. Michel is talking about what he's going to do this week. Fill in the gaps with the correct day of the week in French (**aller** = *to go*).

a ...............    je déjeune au restaurant avec Sophie
b ...............    je prends le train pour Manchester
c ...............    je regarde la télévision avec ma famille
d ...............    je réserve une chambre à l'Hôtel Nelson
e ...............    j'achète trois bouteilles de vin
f ...............    je voudrais_aller au cinéma avec mes_enfants
g ...............    je travaille au bureau toute la journée

**8** What time is it? Write out your answers in full, using the 12-hour clock. To differentiate between a.m. and p.m. you can use **du matin/de l'après midi/du soir**. Use also **midi** and **minuit** to distinguish between the middle of the day and the middle of the night.

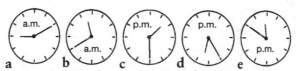

▶ **9** Listen to the recording and fill in the clock faces below with times spoken:

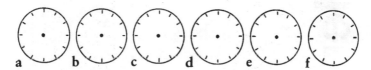

# Mini-test

1 Say the days of the week in reverse order starting with Sunday.
2 How would you ask 'When does the bank shut?'
3 Ask the ticket collector in Calais 'Is there a train for Lille?'
4 How would you ask if you can have breakfast in the hotel?
5 Give the date and the time.

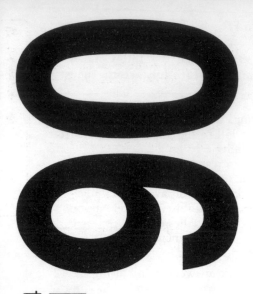

# 06

## pour aller à ...?
the way to ...?

**In this unit you will learn**
- how to count from 90 upwards
- how to ask for and understand directions
- useful verbs to describe what you do every day

# Before you start

In **Key words and phrases**, Unit 4, you learnt to say how far somewhere is and how long it takes to go somewhere on foot and by car. Revise these structures as you will need them to understand the dialogue in this unit.

You now know how to ask where things are: **Où est ...?** or **C'est où ...?** Asking the way is also very simple; you start your question with the phrase **pour aller à** and raise the voice at the end of the statement.

Understanding the answer can be more tricky and you'll need to pick out the few essential words such as **tout droit, à gauche, à droite** out of the flow of other words.

As people give you directions, repeat after them, to make sure you have understood. If you do not understand, ask them to repeat or slow down.

*Essayez!* **Have a go!**

1 Ask someone:
   **a** to speak more slowly
   **b** to repeat
2 Talk about your typical day. Use the verbs in the box below to make it exciting and busy.

---

je reste ..........     je travaille ..........

je regarde ..........

je pars ..........     je finis ..........

je commence ..........     je rentre ..........

je prends le déjeuner ..........

---

# Key words and phrases

## To go straight on

| | |
|---|---|
| **pour_aller à ...** | *the way to ...* |
| **(vous) allez tout droit** | *(you) go straight on* |
| **continuez** | *carry on* |
| **descendez la rue** | *go down the street* |
| **montez l'avenue** | *go up the avenue* |

| | |
|---|---|
| passez le magasin | *go beyond the shop* |
| traversez la place | *cross the square* |
| prenez la route de ... | *take the road to ...* |

## To turn

| | |
|---|---|
| (vous) tournez_à gauche | *(you) turn left* |
| tournez_à droite | *turn right* |
| vous_allez prendre ... | *you're going to take ...* |
| la première rue à droite | *the first street on the right* |
| la deuxième sur votre gauche | *the second on your left* |

## Where it is

| | |
|---|---|
| la place du marché est située ... | *the market place is ...* |
| au coin de la rue | *at the corner of the street* |
| à côté du supermarché | *next to the supermarket* |
| en face de la boulangerie | *opposite the baker's* |
| au centre ville | *in the town centre* |
| sur votre gauche | *on your left* |
| sur, sous | *on, under* |
| devant, derrière | *in front of, behind* |
| dans | *in, inside* |
| entre | *between* |
| il faut combien de temps? | *how long does it take?* |
| il faut_environ 25 minutes | *you need about 25 minutes* |

## Numbers 90...

| | | | |
|---|---|---|---|
| quatre-vingt-dix | 90 | cent | 100 |
| quatre-vingt-onze | 91 | cent un | 101 |
| quatre-vingt-douze | 92 | cent deux | 102 |
| quatre-vingt-treize | 93 | cent vingt trois | 123 |
| quatre-vingt-quatorze | 94 | cinq cent trente-quatre | 534 |
| quatre-vingt-quinze | 95 | mille | 1000 |
| quatre-vingt-seize | 96 | mille neuf cent quinze | 1915 |
| quatre-vingt-dix-sept | 97 | deux mille | 2000 |
| quatre-vingt-dix-huit | 98 | | |
| quatre-vingt-dix-neuf | 99 | | |

## ▶ Dialogue

**Jane passe la journée chez les Durand. L'après-midi, elle décide d'aller au centre ville de Chatou.**

*Jane is spending the day with the Durands. She decides to go to the town centre in the afternoon.*

*While you listen to the recording, look at the street map (**le plan de ville**) of Chatou on page 54. How do you get from M. Durand's house to the park and how long does it take to walk there?*

| | |
|---|---|
| Jane | M. Durand, avez-vous un plan de Chatou? Je voudrais_aller **d'abord** au parc et puis, **si j'ai le temps**, dans les magasins ... |
| M. Durand | **Voici** le plan. Vous pouvez **le garder** car j'en_ai deux. |
| Jane | Merci beaucoup. Où est le parc de Chatou? |
| M. Durand | **Voyons**, nous sommes_ici sur le plan. Vous tournez_à gauche **en sortant de la maison**, vous_allez jusqu'au bout de la rue Vaugirard, vous tournez_à droite dans la rue Vincennes et puis c'est sur votre gauche à 200 mètres. |
| Jane | Bon, alors, à gauche en sortant puis je tourne à droite et c'est sur ma gauche ... C'est loin à pied? |
| M. Durand | Non, pas très loin; il faut_environ 25 minutes. |
| Jane | Oh là là, c'est trop loin pour moi. Euh, on peut_y aller en_autobus? |
| M. Durand | Oui, oui. L'arrêt d'autobus est situé juste au coin de la rue Vaugirard. C'est très pratique et il y a un autobus toutes les dix minutes. |
| Jane | Je voudrais_aussi **faire des_achats** pour moi et acheter quelques souvenirs pour ma famille en Grande-Bretagne et au Canada. |
| M. Durand | Eh bien, vous pouvez_aller au **centre commercial**. Il est sur la place du marché à côté de la gare. Vous_avez un_autobus direct. Il va du parc au centre commercial. |
| Jane | Bon, je pars tout de suite ... j'ai beaucoup de choses à acheter et ... je voudrais rentrer vers 19 heures. |

| | |
|---|---|
| **d'abord** | *firstly* |
| **si j'ai le temps** | *if I have the time* |
| **voici** | *here is ...* |
| **le garder** | *keep it* |
| **voyons** | *let's see* |
| **en sortant de la maison** | *as you leave the house* |
| **faire des_achats** | *to do some shopping* |
| **le centre commercial** | *the shopping centre* |

# Grammar

## 1 Asking the way and giving directions

Pour_aller à (*to get to*) is a very useful structure to remember.
Used in a questioning tone it means *How do I/we get to ...?*

| | |
|---|---|
| Pardon, Monsieur, pour_aller à Gordes? | *Excuse me, Sir, how do we get to Gordes?* |
| Pour_aller à Gordes, prenez la route pour St. Saturnin. | *To get to Gordes, take the road to St. Saturnin.* |

## 2 *Aller* to go *partir* to leave

Here are two very useful verbs. Both verbs are irregular, and
**aller** is particularly useful as it is used when speaking about the
future (explained in Unit 10).

| **aller** *to go* | **partir** *to leave* |
|---|---|
| **je vais** | **je pars** |
| **tu vas** | **tu pars** |
| **il/elle/on va** | **il/elle/on part** |
| **nous allons** | **nous partons** |
| **vous allez** | **vous partez** |
| **ils/elles vont** | **ils/elles partent** |

| | |
|---|---|
| Vous_allez jusqu'au bout de la rue. | *You go to the end of the road.* |
| Je voudrais_aller à la banque. | *I would like to go to the bank.* |
| Je pars tout de suite. | *I'm leaving immediately.* |

## 3 Understanding directions

Understanding directions can be more tricky than asking the
way as the directions can sound complicated, so it is important
to pick out the essential words:

**a** As an answer to your question, you'll probably hear one of
the following constructions:

| **prenez** | **descendez** | **tournez à** | **allez** | **montez** |
|---|---|---|---|---|
| *take* | *go down* | *turn* | *go* | *go up* |

| Il faut prendre … | You have to (lit. it's necessary to) take … |
| Il faut descendre … | You have to go down … |
| Il faut tourner … | You have to turn … |
| Il faut_aller … | You have to go … |
| Il faut monter … | You have to go up … |

**b** The **t** in **droite** *right* is sounded but it is not in **droit** *straight*. **Droit** is usually preceded by **tout**: **tout droit** *straight on*. **Droite** is preceded by **à** or **sur la**: **à droite, sur la droite**:

| Il faut_aller tout droit. | *You have to go straight on.* |
| La gare est sur la droite. | *The station is on the right.* |

**c** You may be unlucky when asking directions and find that you are asking a tourist! His answer would be **je ne sais pas** (*I don't know*), or **je ne suis pas d'ici** (*I am not from here*).

**d** If you don't understand the information, e.g. the address, the street name, or the number of the building you are given, use the structure **c'est quel(le) …?** (Unit 3) to have the information repeated:

| C'est quelle rue? | *Which street is it?* |
| C'est quel numéro? | *Which number is it?* |
| C'est quelle adresse? | *Which address is it?* |

## 4 When to use *à*; when to use *en*

To say that you are in town or you are going / want to go to a town always use **à** (with an accent to differentiate it from **a** *has*). Study the examples below:

| Je suis_à Bordeaux. | *I'm in Bordeaux.* |
| Nous_allons_à Bordeaux. | *We're going to Bordeaux.* |

To say that you are in a country or you're going to a country, use **en** with feminine countries (often finishing with an **-e**) and **au/aux** with the others.

| Je suis_en_Australie. | *I am in Australia.* |
| Je vais_en_Angleterre. | *I'm going to England.* |
| Vous_allez_au Canada. | *You're going to Canada.* |

**i** The country is preceded by its article in sentences such as:

| **Je connais bien la Suisse.** | *I know Switzerland, quite well.* |
| **J'aime beaucoup le Portugal.** | *I like Portugal a lot.* |

## 5 When à (at, to, in, on) is followed by *le, la, l', les* ...

The preposition à followed by a definite article (le, la, l', les) changes its form in the following way:

| | | |
|---|---|---|
| à + le | becomes | **au** |
| à + la | remains | **à la** |
| à + l' | remains | **à l'** |
| à + les | becomes | **aux** |

Pour_aller **au musée** du
Louvre, s'il vous plaît?

Nous_allons à **l'église** St. Paul.

Il arrive **à la gare** à huit heures
du matin.

Il va **aux_États-Unis** deux
fois par mois.

*Which way to the Louvre
Museum please?*

*We are going to St Paul's
Church.*

*He arrives at the station at
eight o'clock in the morning.*

*He goes to the United
States twice a month.*

## 6 Locating the exact spot

Remember that when **de** is used in a combination with **le, la, l', les** in expressions such as **en face de** *opposite*, **à côté de** *next to*, **au coin de** *at the corner of*, **près de** *near*, you need to change its form (Unit 2).

au coin **du parc**
près **des grands magasins**
en face **de la piscine**
à côté **de l'office** du
tourisme

*at the corner of the park*
*near the department stores*
*opposite the swimming pool*
*next to the tourist office*

## 7 *Premier, deuxième, troisième* first, second, third

If you are directed to the 3rd floor, the 2nd street and so on, the numbers end in -ième.

| | | | |
|---|---|---|---|
| **deuxième** | *second* | **quatrième** | *fourth* |
| **troisième** | *third* | **dixième** | *tenth* |

But, first is **premier** before all masculine nouns, and **première** before all feminine nouns.

Vous montez au **premier**
étage.

*You go up to the first floor.*

| | |
|---|---|
| C'est la **première** porte. | *It is the first door.* |
| Vous prenez la **deuxième** à gauche. | *You take the second on the left.* |
| C'est le **troisième** bâtiment. | *It's the third building.* |

## ℹ Self-evaluation

- How well are you doing with speaking French? The revision of the last six dialogues, at the end of this unit, will give you the opportunity to test your overall speaking performance. If you experience some difficulties, look back at the last five units. They give advice on how to organize the study of vocabulary and grammar and how to create opportunities to practise your French.

- How well are you doing with understanding: are you listening to some French every day? Look at pages 86–7 and read about the various ways in which you can improve your understanding. If you have the recording, listen to the dialogues again and again pausing and repeating until you feel familiar with the passages. When listening to a passage, pick out the most important key words.

# Activities

1 You are Jane, visiting Chatou for the first time. How would you ask a passer-by the way to:

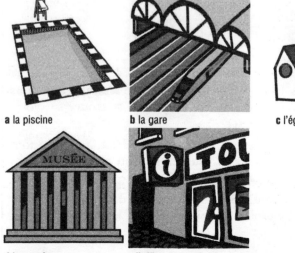

**a** la piscine  **b** la gare  **c** l'église St. Paul

**d** le musée  **e** l'office du tourisme

▶ 2 Now listen to the replies of the passers-by on the recording and work out which letter on the map represents each of these places. If you haven't got the recording, read the replies below:

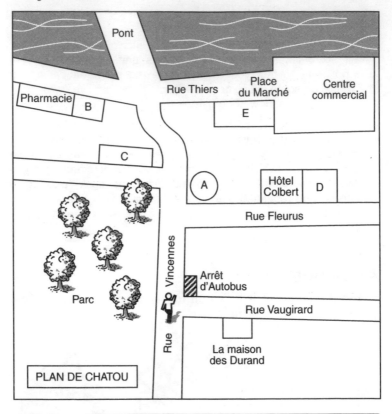

a C'est très facile. Vous montez la rue Vincennes et vous prenez la première à gauche. La piscine se trouve sur votre droite, en face du parc.

b Bon, pour la gare, continuez tout droit, toujours tout droit. Juste avant le pont, tournez_à droite et vous_êtes dans la rue Thiers. La gare est à côté du centre commercial.

c L'église St. Paul? Eh bien, c'est tout droit, à 100 mètres d'ici, sur votre droite, au coin de la rue Fleurus.

**d** Euh – attendez voir – Il faut tourner tout de suite à droite puis descendez la rue Fleurus et le musée est_à 10 minutes à pied sur votre gauche à côté de l'Hôtel Colbert.

**e** Vous_allez tout droit jusqu'au pont. Juste avant le pont tournez_à gauche et l'office du tourisme se trouve à côté d'une pharmacie.

3 Now it's your turn to practise giving directions. Use the text above as a model but you don't have to answer exactly like it; for example instead of **vous montez/descendez la rue** you can say (vous) **allez/continuez tout droit.** (The answers are not given in **Key to the exercises.**) Here are the questions:

**a** Pardon Monsieur, pour_aller à la piscine?

**b** S'il vous plaît Madame, je voudrais_aller au musée; pouvez-vous me dire où il se trouve?

**c** Pardon Monsieur, savez-vous où est l'office du tourisme?

**d** Pardon Mademoiselle, je ne suis pas d'ici ... euh, il y a un centre commercial à Chatou?

4 Choose the right answer.

Jane habite      à Brighton?
            en Brighton?
            de Brighton?

Elle et son petit_ami passent leurs vacances en France
                                    au France
                                    France

mais_ils préfèrent Allemagne.
                l'Allemagne.
                en Allemagne.

Jane est restée une semaine à Berlin  et trois jours Bonn.
                              Berlin              au Bonn.
                              en Berlin           à Bonn.

Cet_été (*this summer*) elle va  au Danemark    où elle a des_amis.
                              Danemark
                              en Danemark

Son petit_ami va souvent en_États-Unis   et au Japon.
                        aux_États-Unis   en Japon.
                        les_États-Units  Japon.

Il est_homme d'affaires (*businessman*) et travaille en Londres.
à Londres.
Londres.

5 Look at the **centre commercial de Chatou** and fill in the blanks using the words from the list below.

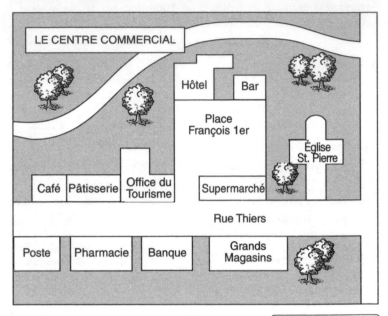

a La poste est ............... café.
b Le café est ............... pâtisserie.
c L'office du tourisme est ............... la place François 1er.
d La pharmacie est ............... la poste et la banque.
e L'église est ............... la rue Thiers.
f Les ............... sont en face du supermarché.
g Le ............... est à côté de l'hôtel.
h La ............... est entre le café et l'office du tourisme.
i La pharmacie est ............... Thiers.
j Le supermarché est ............... François ler.

à côté de la

en face du

dans la rue

entre

grands magasins

pâtisserie

sur la place

au coin de

au bout de

bar

## 6 Numbers

Test yourself. Pick numbers from the box below and say them aloud in French. Check your answers at the back of the book where all the numbers are listed. Repeat the exercise over a number of days and see if you can improve your performance.

|    | 72 | 24 | 80 | 92 | 65 | 43 | 75 | 61 |    |
|----|----|----|----|----|----|----|----|----|----|
| 76 |    | 68 |    | 15 | 66 | 17 | 96 | 87 | 70 |
|    | 19 | 21 | 49 | 55 | 65 | 56 | 13 | 77 |    |

# Test

In this unit, **Mini-Test** is replaced by a revision of the last six dialogues: try translating the dialogues from Units 1 to 6 into English and then from English retranslate them orally into French. Check your answers with the book. You might like to record yourself, imagining that you're French. If you have the original recording, compare your own recording with it. How different is yours from the original? Try in your recording to match the speed, the accent and intonations on the original recording.

# 07

## c'est comment?

what is it like?

**In this unit you will learn**
- how to describe things and people
- how to say precisely what you want
- how to compare people and objects
- colours

# Before you start

In Unit 2 you've already seen how to ask for things using just a few words. Getting precisely what you need may involve giving a few more details. This unit will provide you with some of the keywords you'll need to describe what you are looking for, specifying colours, materials, quantities, prices, etc. There is a lot of new vocabulary in this unit, appearing in the sections **Key words and phrases**, **Grammar** and **Activities**. It will be useful to you when doing Unit 11 which concentrates on the topic of shopping in France.

*Essayez!* **Have a go!** Fill in the blanks in the sentences below with some of the prepositions you met in the last unit.

1 Les fleurs sont ............... (*in*) le vase.
2 Le croissant est ............... (*on*) l'assiette.
3 Le journal est ............... (*between*) le vase et l'assiette.
4 Le jus d'orange est ............... (*next to the*) journal.
5 La carte postale est ............... (*under*) l'assiette.
6 Les clefs sont ............... (*in front of*) le jus de fruit.
7 Les aspirines sont ............... (*behind*) le vase.

# Key words and phrases

## For you to say

| | |
|---|---|
| faire des achats, des courses, du shopping | to do some shopping |
| qu'est-ce que vous_avez comme ... souvenirs/cadeaux? | what do you have in the way of ... souvenirs/presents? |
| qu'est-ce que c'est? | what is it? |
| vous_avez autre chose? | do you have anything else? |
| ça fait combien? | how much is it? |
| c'est de quelle couleur? | what colour is it? |
| je cherche quelque chose ... | I'm looking for something ... |
| grand/moyen/petit | big/medium/small |
| un peu plus grand | a little bigger |
| un peu moins cher | a little less expensive |
| meilleur marché | cheaper |
| spécial/différent | special/different |
| pour réparer, ouvrir | to repair, open |
| je vais prendre le plus petit | I'll take the smallest |
| rouge, blanc, vert, marron/brun, bleu, jaune | red, white, green, brown, blue, yellow |
| qui est-ce? | who is it? |
| c'est_une personne sympathique | he/she is a nice person |
| c'est_un jeune homme français | he's a young Frenchman |
| c'est_une jeune fille anglaise | she's a young English girl |
| c'est quelqu'un de grand/petit/ gros/mince | it's someone tall/small/ big/thin |
| il porte des lunettes de soleil | he wears/is wearing sunglasses |
| il a les cheveux noirs et raides | he has black, straight hair |
| elle porte une chemise unie | she wears/is wearing a plain shirt |
| elle a les yeux marron | she has brown eyes |

## For you to understand

| | |
|---|---|
| je vais vous montrer | I'll show you |
| et avec ceci (ça)? | is that all? (lit. and with this?) |
| on s'occupe de vous? | are you being served? |
| il vaut mieux prendre | you should take (lit. it is better to take) |

# ▶ Dialogue

Jane fait des courses dans un grand magasin de Chatou.

*Jane is shopping in a department store in Chatou. She is looking for something special to bring back to her mother in the UK.*

*Listen to the recording once or read the dialogue in the book: What does Jane buy? How much is it? Listen a second time: What was the price of the other items? Describe what Jane buys.*

| | |
|---|---|
| **Vendeuse** | Vous désirez? |
| **Jane** | Je cherche un souvenir ... euh quelque chose de spécial pour ma mère en_Angleterre. |
| **Vendeuse** | Oui, très bien. Je peux vous montrer des **foulards en soie** avec des **scènes typiquement** françaises. (*the shop assistant gets them out*) |
| **Jane** | Oh, ils sont très **jolis** et les couleurs sont vraiment superbes. C'est combien? |
| **Vendeuse** | Alors, ça fait 68,50 €, 53 € et 46 € pour les petits. |
| **Jane** | Je peux voir **ceux qui** sont_à 46 €? |
| **Vendeuse** | Mais bien sûr. **Certains** sont jaunes et bleus, **d'autres** représentent les monuments **célèbres** de Paris. |
| **Jane** | Je préfère les grands mais_ils sont trop chers (*she hesitates*). Je vais prendre **ce petit** à 46 € avec les Champs-Elysées. **Je crois que** ma mère **sera** très **contente**. Vous pouvez me **faire un paquet-cadeau**, s'il vous plaît? |
| **Vendeuse** | Oui, un instant ... **si vous voulez bien me suivre?** (*after a while ... when the present is wrapped up*) Et maintenant vous **payez_à la caisse**. |
| **Jane** | Ah bon, merci bien, Madame. |

| | |
|---|---|
| **foulard** (m) | *scarf* |
| **en soie** | *made of silk* |
| **scène** (f) | *scene* |
| **typiquement** | *typically* |
| **joli(e)** | *pretty* |
| **ceux qui ...** | *the ones which ...* |
| **certains ... d'autres** | *some ... others* |
| **célèbres** | *famous* |
| **ce petit** | *this small one* |
| **je crois que** | *I believe that* |
| **sera contente** | *will be pleased* |

| faire un paquet-cadeau | *to gift-wrap* |
| si vous voulez bien me suivre | *would you come this way?* |
| payer à la caisse | *pay at the till* |

## Grammar

### 1 *Ce, cet, cette, ces* this, that, these, those

Ce, cet, cette all mean *this* or *that*; ces means *these* or *those*. Ce comes before masculine singular nouns, cet before masculine singular nouns beginning with a vowel or silent **h**, cette before feminine singular nouns and ces before plural nouns.

|  | *masculine* | *masc. (before a vowel or silent **h**)* | *feminine* |
|---|---|---|---|
| *singular* | ce | cet | cette |
| *plural* | ces | ces | ces |

| ce foulard | *this/that scarf* |
| cet_homme | *this/that man* |
| cette femme | *this/that woman* (**femme**, *pronounced 'fam', also means 'wife'*) |
| ces_enfants | *these/those children* |

### 2 Saying precisely what you want

You already know how to ask for something (Unit 5), e.g. **je voudrais cette bouteille**. This is the most general way of asking for things, but you may want to give more information.

**a How much?** Expressions of quantity are linked with **de**:

| Combien d'enfants? | *How many children?* |
| beaucoup d'enfants? | *lots of children* |
| un verre de vin | *a glass of wine* |
| une boîte de haricots | *a tin of beans* |

**b Made of what?** You can use **de** or **en** to say what things are made of:

| une chemise de coton | *a cotton shirt* |
| une robe en soie | *a silk dress* |

c **What kind?** Add adjectives to describe in more detail:

| | |
|---|---|
| un verre de vin **rouge** | *a glass of red wine* |
| une boîte de **petits** pois français | *a tin of French peas* |
| un kilo de raisins **noirs** | *a kilo of black grapes* |

d **What's in/on it?** Special features such as patterns, flavours or key ingredients are linked with **à**:

| | |
|---|---|
| un yaourt **à** l'abricot | *an apricot yoghurt* |
| un sandwich **au** fromage | *a cheese sandwich* |
| une glace **à la** vanille | *a vanilla ice cream* |
| une tarte **aux** pommes | *an apple pie* |

Don't forget to change the **à** to **au** or to **aux** if the following noun is masculine or plural.

e **With/without.** Put **avec** (*with*) or **sans** (*without*) in front of what you want or don't want:

| | |
|---|---|
| une chambre **avec** télévision | *a room with (a) television* |
| un hôtel **sans** parking | *a hotel without car park* |

## 3 How adjectives work

As explained in Unit 3 adjectives change according to what they are describing; they may take masculine, feminine or plural forms.

| | masculine | feminine |
|---|---|---|
| *singular* | petit | petite |
| *plural* | petits | petites |

| | |
|---|---|
| ce **petit** foulard | *this little scarf* |
| c'est_une **bonne** école | *it's a good school* |
| les **petits** pois sont **verts** | *peas are green* |
| avec des scènes **françaises** | *with French scenes* |

a Adding an **-e** to the masculine (if it has not already got an **-e**) to form the feminine, often changes the pronunciation as in **petit** (m), **petite** (f), but not always, e.g. **noir** (m), **noire** (f), **bleu** (m), **bleue** (f). The **-s** in the plural is not sounded.

b **Brun** is used almost exclusively to refer to the colour of someone's hair, complexion or brown ale (**bière brune**). For most brown objects, use **marron**, which is an invariable form.

**c** A few adjectives have two masculine forms: the second one is used in front of nouns beginning with a vowel or silent **h**:

| | |
|---|---|
| le **nouveau** garçon | *the new boy* |
| le **nouvel**_élève | *the new pupil* |
| le **vieux** port | *the old harbour* |
| le **vieil**_hôtel | *the old hotel* |

**d** Here are some common adjectives with irregular endings. You will pick up others as you go along.

| masc.  masc. 1   masc. 2 | *fem.* | *masc. pl.* | *fem. pl.* |
|---|---|---|---|
| beau       bel | belle | beaux | belles |
| nouveau  nouvel | nouvelle | nouveaux | nouvelles |
| vieux       vieil | vieille | vieux | vieilles |

**e** Adjectives are usually placed after the noun:

| | |
|---|---|
| un café **noir** | *a black coffee* |
| une bière **brune** | *brown ale* |

except with common ones such as: **petit** (*small*), **bon(ne)** (*good*), **beau** (*beautiful*), **grand** (*tall*), **jeune** (*young*), **vieux** (*old*), **mauvais** (*bad*), **joli** (*beautiful*), **tout** (*all*).

| | |
|---|---|
| un **grand** café | *a large coffee* |
| une **bonne** bière | *a good beer* |

**f** If there are two or more adjectives after the noun they are linked with **et**:

| | |
|---|---|
| un homme **grand et mince** | *a tall, slim man* |
| des cheveux **blonds et longs** | *long, blonde hair* |

## 4 Making comparisons

To say that something is *more ... than* or *less ... than* use:

| | |
|---|---|
| **plus ... que** | *more ... than* |
| **moins ... que** | *less ... than* |

Le train est **plus rapide que** la voiture.
*The train is faster than the car.*

Il est **moins grand que** moi.
*He's less tall than I.*

**i** The **-s** of **plus** is not pronounced except in the following cases:

- before a vowel or silent **h**, **-s** is sounded **z**: **plus_âgé**

- whenever the word means *plus* (+), **-s** is sounded **s**:

  Il y a du beurre **plus** du lait dans la recette.
  *There is some butter plus some milk in the recipe.*

- when it is followed directly by **que** to produce **plus que** *more than*, (**-s** is sounded **s**):

  Il travaille **plus que** moi.
  *He works more than I.*

### Saying 'better'

To say that something/someone is *better*, use **meilleur (e)**; to say that you do something *better* use **mieux**:

Le film est meilleur que le livre.
*The film is better than the book.*

Elle parle français mieux que moi.
*She speaks French better than I.*

## **i** Learning to cope with uncertainty

- **Don't over-use your dictionary.**
  When reading a text in the foreign language, don't be tempted to look up every word you don't know. Underline the words you do not understand and read the passage several times, concentrating on trying to get the gist of the passage. If after the third time there are still words which prevent you from getting the general meaning of the passage, look them up in the dictionary.

- **Don't panic if you don't understand.**
  If at some point you feel you don't understand what you are told, don't panic or give up listening. Either try and guess what is being said and keep following the conversation or, if you cannot, isolate the expression or words you haven't understood and have them explained to you. The speaker might paraphrase them and the conversation will carry on.

- **Keep talking.**
  The best way to improve your fluency in the foreign language is to talk every time you have the opportunity to do so: keep the conversation flowing and don't worry about the mistakes. If you get stuck for a particular word, don't let the conversation stop; paraphrase or replace the unknown word with one you do know, even if you have to simplify what you want to say. As a last resort use the word from your own language and pronounce it in the foreign accent.

# Activities

**1** **A la gare routière:** fill in the blanks with **ce, cet, cette** or **ces**. To check if the words are masculine or feminine look at the **French–English vocabulary**.

| | |
|---|---|
| **Touriste** | Pardon Monsieur, ..... autobus va à Quimper? |
| **Homme** | Oui, Madame, tous ..... autobus vont à Quimper. |
| **Touriste** | Je voudrais partir ..... matin. A quelle heure partent les_autobus? |
| **Homme** | Bon, ..... deux_autobus partent pour Quimper ..... matin. Le premier part à 8h.30 et arrive à 12h et le deuxième part à 9h.15 et arrive à 13h.15 ..... après-midi. |
| **Touriste** | Très bien. Je veux rentrer ..... nuit. A quelle heure rentre le dernier_autobus de Quimper? |
| **Homme** | Alors ..... semaine, le dernier bus quitte Quimper à 20h.30. |

▶ **2** Using the grid below and M. Durand's description as a model, write down in a few sentences what Mme Durand and Jane look like. Make sure that the adjectives agree with the nouns they describe. Check the vocabulary with the drawings below or in the vocabulary list at the back of the book. Then write a few sentences describing yourself.

| | **M. Durand** | **Mme Durand** | **Jane** |
|---|---|---|---|
| sexe | homme | femme 35 ans | femme |
| âge | 40 ans | blonds/longs | 23 ans |
| cheveux | noirs/raides | verts | bruns/courts |
| yeux | marron | 1,70 mètre | bleus |
| taille | 1,78 mètre | 65 kg | 1,62 mètre |
| poids | 79 kg | lunettes | 55 kg |
| signes particuliers | moustache | rondes ensemble | – |
| vêtements | costume bleu marine, cravate jaune, chaussures noires | vert uni, chemise blanche, chaussures légères | jean bleu pâle, pull-over blanc, bottes noires |

Monsieur Durand a 40 ans. Il a les cheveux noirs et raides et les yeux marron; il fait 1 mètre 78 et pèse 79 kg. Il a une moustache. Il porte un costume bleu marine, une cravate jaune et des chaussures noires.

Look in the **Key** at the back of the book and check that what you've written is correct. Using as a model **M. Durand's** description on the recording, read aloud what you've written.

3 How would you ask for all the items on the list? The words in the box will help, though they aren't all there!

| | |
|---|---|
| baba (m)    vanille (f) | **a** *a tin of French peas* |
| petits pois (m) | **b** *an apple tart* |
| vin (m) | **c** *a rhum baba* |
| pommes (f)    fromage (m) | **d** *a vanilla ice cream* |
| citron (m) | **e** *a lemon sorbet* |
| sucre (m) | **f** *a big glass of red wine* |
| sandwich (m)    poulet (m) | **g** *a white coffee without sugar* |
| verre (m)    lait (m) | **h** *a chicken at 6,80 €* |
| tarte (f)    rhum (m) | **i** *a small black coffee* |
| glace (f) | **j** *a cheese sandwich* |
| café (m)    sorbet (m) | **k** *a bottle of milk* |
| boîte (f)    boutcille (f) | |

4 Sally is spending Christmas and New Year in France with a French family. She writes to her friend Isabelle. Can you fill the gaps with the words from the box overleaf? You may have to look up some of the words in the **Vocabulary** at the back of the book.

(a) .......... Isabelle,

Je suis depuis une semaine avec la (b) .......... Guise. Ici (c) .......... le monde est très (d) .......... et je passe de très (e) .......... vacances. La maison est (f) .......... et (g) .......... . Je fais de (h) .......... promenades presque tous les (i) .......... . La cuisine française est (j) .......... que la cuisine (k) .......... et je mange trop. Je parle (l) .......... le français maintenant. Je retourne chez moi la semaine (m) .......... .

Joyeux Noël et Bonne Année
Sally

| | | | | |
|---|---|---|---|---|
| meilleure | longues | tout | jours | confortable |
| prochaine | famille | bonnes | grande | anglaise mieux |
| | Chère | sympathique | | |

5 You are in a **café** with four of your friends. The waiter arrives and you order (**vous commandez**):

| Garçon | Bonjour, Messieurs-Dames. Qu'est-ce que vous désirez? |
|---|---|
| **a** *You* | *A large black coffee.* |
| Garçon | Un grand café, oui... |
| **b** *You* | *Two draught beers* |
| Garçon | Oui. |
| **c** *You* | *And a small white coffee.* |
| Garçon | Alors un grand crème, deux limonades et un petit café noir, c'est ça? |
| **d** *You* | *No. Two draught beers, a small white coffee and a large black coffee.* |
| Garçon | Bon très bien. Excusez-moi. |
| **e** *You* | *Have you got some croissants?* |
| Garçon | Vous_en voulez combien? |
| **f** *You* | *Say you want four.* |
| Garçon | Très bien, Monsieur. |

## Mini-test

Now test yourself and see how well you remember the information in Units 6 and 7.

1 How would you say:
  a at the end of the street
  b take the road to Lille

2 **Il faut prendre** means:
   a you can take
   b you must take
   c you take

3 **Vous_allez tout droit** means:
   a you go straight on
   b you turn right
   c you take the second on the left

4 How would you say:
   Do you have anything else?
   What colour is it?
   I'll take the smallest.

# 08

## vous aimez le sport?

### do you like sport?

In this unit you will learn
how to
- ask and talk about likes and
  dislikes
- say what you and others do
  as a hobby
- talk about the weather

# Before you start

Once you know a French person well enough you'll find yourself wanting to express your likes and dislikes and talk about your hobbies; here are the structures you'll need:

| | |
|---|---|
| j'adore | *I adore, I love* |
| j'aime beaucoup | *I like very much* |
| je n'aime pas | *I don't like* |
| je déteste | *I hate* |
| je joue | *I play* |
| je fais | *I do* |

Talking about the weather is a particularly important aspect of the British way of life; you may find it useful to enquire about the weather forecast if you are planning some kind of outdoor activity.

*Essayez!* **Have a go!** You are in a shop in France looking for a corkscrew. However you don't know the French word for it. How would you say that you're looking for something to open bottles of wine?

**You** ..................................................................................

**Shopkeeper** Ah! Vous voulez un tire-bouchon (a corkscrew)?

# Key words and phrases

### *For you to say*

| | |
|---|---|
| qu'est-ce que vous faites/ pratiquez comme sport? | *what sport do you do?* |
| qu'est-ce que vous faites pendant vos loisirs? | *what hobbies do you have?* |
| vous_aimez faire du sport? | *do you like doing sport?* |
| quelle est votre cuisine préférée? | *which cooking do you prefer?* |
| j'adore aller au restaurant | *I love going to the restaurant* |
| mon sport préféré est la natation | *swimming is my favourite sport* |
| j'aime (beaucoup) ... | *I like (very much) ...* |
| jouer au squash | *playing squash* |
| la cuisine française | *French cooking* |
| écouter de la musique | *listening to music* |
| regarder la télévision | *watching television* |

| je n'aime pas … | I don't like … |
|---|---|
| la planche à voile | windsurfing |
| la musique classique | classicial music |
| me promener à pied | going for a walk |
| je déteste faire la cuisine | I hate cooking |
| je joue au tennis | I play tennis |
| je joue du piano | I play the piano |
| je préfère l'équitation | I prefer riding |

## *For you to understand*

| moi, ce que j'aime c'est | what I really like is going out |
|---|---|
| sortir avec mes_amis | with my friends |
| moi, ce que je déteste c'est | what I really dislike is |
| la viande saignante | rare meat |

## Le temps *The weather*

| quel temps fait-il? | what's the weather like? |
|---|---|
| il fait beau, mauvais | the weather is fine, bad |
| il fait chaud, froid | it is hot, cold |
| le soleil brille | the sun shines |
| il pleut | it's raining |
| il neige | it's snowing |

# ▶ Dialogue

Jane parle de sports et de loisirs avec les Durand.

*Jane and the Durands are talking about sport and hobbies.*

*Listen to the recording or read the dialogue once and then answer the following questions: What's Mrs Durand's favourite hobby? What sports does Mr Durand do? Listen or read a second time: What does Mrs Durand like to cook? How many times a week does Mr Durand play squash?*

| Jane | Mme Durand, qu'est-ce que vous faites pendant vos loisirs? |
|---|---|
| Mme Durand | Moi, j'adore faire la cuisine, **surtout** la cuisine française. |
| Jane | Et dans la cuisine française, quels sont vos **plats favoris**? |

| Mme Durand | Eh bien, j'aime beaucoup faire tous les plats_en sauce, en particulier **le boeuf bourguignon** ou **le coq au vin. Vous savez**, mon mari aime bien manger et bien **boire**; il est très gourmet et **il apprécie** ma cuisine … alors **ça fait plaisir**! |
|---|---|
| Jane | Et vous, Monsieur Durand, vous_aimez faire la cuisine? |
| M. Durand | Moi, **je laisse la cuisine** à ma femme. Elle la fait très bien. Je préfère le sport. |
| Jane | Quels sports **pratiquez**-vous? |
| M. Durand | Je joue au squash deux fois par semaine après mon travail et **quand j'ai le temps**, je fais de la natation avec les_enfants le samedi, à la piscine de Chatou. |
| Mme Durand | Tu aimes bien aussi faire de la planche à voile **en_été**. |
| M. Durand | Oui, **c'est vrai**. J'aime beaucoup la planche à voile surtout quand_il y a du **vent**, mais je déteste en faire quand_il fait froid ou quand_il pleut. |
| Mme Durand | Et vous Jane, qu'est-ce que vous faites comme sport? |
| Jane | Oh moi, je pratique un peu tous les sports: le badminton, le tennis et quelquefois l'équitation, mais je n'ai pas beaucoup de temps pour faire du sport. |

| | |
|---|---|
| **surtout** | *mainly* |
| **plats favoris** | *favourite dishes* |
| **le boeuf bourguignon** | *beef stew with wine* |
| **le coq au vin** | *chicken cooked in wine* |
| **vous savez** | *you know* |
| **boire** | *to drink* |
| **il apprécie** | *he appreciates* |
| **ça fait plaisir** | *it is a pleasure* |
| **je laisse la cuisine** | *I leave the cooking* |
| **pratiquer** | *to do* |
| **quand j'ai le temps** | *when I have the time* |
| **en_été** | *in summer* |
| **c'est vrai** | *it's true* |
| **le vent** | *the wind* |

# Grammar

## 1 Asking and saying what you do as a hobby

In French to answer questions such as **qu'est-ce vous faites comme sport?** *what do you do in the way of sport?* or **qu'est-ce que vous faites pendant vos loisirs?** *what are your hobbies?* use **je fais de ...** or **je joue à ...** if it is a game. If you play a musical instrument use **je joue de.**

Je fais **de la** natation et **du** surf.
*I swim and I surf.*
Je joue **au** tennis et **à la** pétanque.
*I play tennis and petanque* (kind of bowls played in the South of France).
Je joue **du** piano et **de la** trompette.
*I play the piano and the trumpet.*

## 2 Likes and dislikes

To express your tastes and feelings, you can use **aimer** (*to like, to love*) or the two extremes **adorer** and **détester**:

| | |
|---|---|
| **j'adore** | aller au restaurant |
| **j'aime (beaucoup)** | jouer au squash |
| | cuisiner |
| | écouter des disques |
| | regarder la télé |
| **je n'aime pas** | la planche à voile |
| | la musique classique |
| | me promener à pied |
| **je déteste** | faire la cuisine |

To say what you like/dislike doing, add the infinitive after **j'aime, j'adore, je déteste, je préfère: je déteste faire de la bicyclette:** *I hate cycling.*

Include the article **le, la, les** when making generalizations.

J'aime **les** fromages français.    *I like French cheese.*
L'histoire est plus_intéressante    *History is more interesting*
    que **la** géographie.    *than geography.*

When stating likes/dislikes you will often hear French people use the following structures:

Moi, ce que j'aime c'est sortir avec mes_amis.
Moi, ce que je déteste c'est la viande saignante.

# 3 Pronouns: *le, la, les* it, him, her, them

The pronouns **le** (*it, him*), **la** (*it, her*), **les** (*them*) are used to avoid unnecessary repetitions of nouns; they are placed before the verb to which they refer.

| | |
|---|---|
| Vous connaissez M. Durand? | *Do you know Mr Durand?* |
| Oui, je **le** connais. | *Yes, I know **him**.* |
| Vous prenez la carte postale? | *Are you taking the postcard?* |
| Oui, je **la** prends. | *Yes, I'm taking **it**.* |
| Vous_achetez ces foulards? | *Are you buying these scarves?* |
| Oui, je **les**_achète. | *Yes, I'm buying **them**.* |
| Vous_aimez le thé? | *Do you like tea?* |
| Oui, je **l'**aime. | *Yes, I like **it**.* |

**i** **L'** replaces **le** or **la** when the next word starts with a vowel or silent **h**. In a negative sentence, **l'**, **le**, **la**, **les** come between the **ne** or **n'** and the verb:

| | |
|---|---|
| Vous préférez le tennis? | *Do you prefer tennis?* |
| Non, **je ne le préfère pas.** | *No, I don't prefer it.* |

# 4 More negatives

You saw in Unit 3 how to make a statement negative in French, using **ne ... pas**:

| | |
|---|---|
| Je **n'**ai pas d'cnfants. | *I have no children.* |

There are other negatives you can use:

| | |
|---|---|
| **ne ... plus** | *no more/no longer* |
| **ne ... rien** | *nothing* |
| **ne ... jamais** | *never* |
| **ne ... que** | *only* |

| | |
|---|---|
| Je **n'**ai **plus** de vin. | *I have no more wine.* |
| Il **ne** veut **rien**. | *He wants nothing.* |
| Il **n'**a **jamais** d'argent. | *He never has any money.* |
| Je **n'**ai **que** dix_euros. | *I've only got ten Euros.* |

# 5 'To know': when to use *savoir*, when to use *connaître*

There are two verbs for *knowing*: **savoir** and **connaître**.

**a** Use **savoir** (on its own) to say that you *know* or *don't know* a fact.

| | |
|---|---|
| **Je sais à quelle heure part le train.** | *I know when the train leaves.* |

| | |
|---|---|
| Je ne sais pas où est l'arrêt d'autobus. | *I don't know where the bus stop is.* |

b Use **savoir** followed by the infinitive to say that you *know how to do* something:

| | |
|---|---|
| Je sais faire la cuisine. | *I know how to cook.* |
| Vous savez faire du ski? | *Do you know how to ski?* |

c **Connaître** is used to say that you *know people and places.*

| | |
|---|---|
| Je connais Paris. | *I know Paris.* |
| Depuis combien de temps est-ce que vous le connaissez? | *How long have you known him?* |

## 6 *Quel temps fait-il?* What's the weather like?

The easiest way to talk about the weather is to start with **il fait**:

| | |
|---|---|
| il fait beau, mauvais | *it's fine, the weather is bad* |
| il fait froid, chaud | *it's cold, hot* |
| il fait du vent | *it's windy* |
| il fait du brouillard | *it's foggy* |
| il pleut | *it's raining* |
| il neige | *it's snowing* |
| le soleil brille | *the sun is shining* |

*Pratiquez!* Practise!

How would you answer the question:
Quel temps fait-il aujourd'hui? **Aujourd'hui il ...**

## ℹ Learn from your errors

- Don't let errors interfere with getting your message across. Making errors is part of any normal learning process, but some people get so worried that they won't say anything unless they are sure it is correct. This leads to a vicious circle as the less they say, the less practice they get and the more mistakes they make.

- Note the seriousness of errors. Many errors are not serious as they do not affect the meaning; for example if you use the wrong article (**le** or **la**) or wrong pronouns (**je l'achète** for **je les achète**) or wrong adjective ending (**blanc** or **blanche**). So concentrate on getting your message across and learn from your mistakes.

# Activities

▶ 1 Roger Burru has agreed to take part in a survey and is ready to talk about himself. Can you ask him in French the questions on the right? Then listen to the whole survey on the recording and check your answers (or check them in the **Key to the exercises**).

| | | |
|---|---|---|
| a Nom | Roger Burru | *What's your name?* |
| b Âge | 35 | *How old are you?* |
| c Marié(e) | oui | *Are you married?* |
| d Enfant(s) | non | *Have you any children?* |
| e Profession | professeur | *What's your job?* |
| f Depuis ... | 10 ans | *Since when?* |
| g Adresse | Lille | *Where do you live?* |
| h Sport | natation | *What sport do you do?* |
| i Loisir | faire la cuisine | *What are your hobbies?* |

Now it's your turn to take part in a survey. Can you answer in French the same questions? (the answers are not included in **Key to the exercises**).

▶ 2 On the recording you will hear Cloé talk about her likes and dislikes. Listen carefully and put a tick in the appropriate box below:

| | adore | aime beaucoup | n'aime pas | déteste |
|---|---|---|---|---|
| a Playing volleyball | ☐ | ☐ | ☐ | ☐ |
| b Working on Sundays | ☐ | ☐ | ☐ | ☐ |
| c Going out in the evenings | ☐ | ☐ | ☐ | ☐ |
| d Watching TV | ☐ | ☐ | ☐ | ☐ |
| e Listening to music | ☐ | ☐ | ☐ | ☐ |
| f Shopping | ☐ | ☐ | ☐ | ☐ |
| g Eating out | ☐ | ☐ | ☐ | ☐ |
| h Cooking | ☐ | ☐ | ☐ | ☐ |

Now it's your turn to tell Cloé what you like and dislike. Can you think of any more likes/dislikes you could add to the list?

3 Answer the following questions using the example as a model. You may have to revise the verbs ending in -er (page 20), -ir and -re (page 40), **prendre** (page 42) and **faire** (page 42).

a Vous_achetez les oranges?     Oui nous les_achetons.
b Vous prenez le train?     Oui, je ...
c Je connais M. Durand?     Oui, vous ...
d Elle a les timbres?     Oui, elle ...
e Vous_avez l'adresse de Claude?     Oui, je ...
f Ils_aiment le coq au vin?     Oui, ils ...
g Vous faites la cuisine?     Oui, je ...
h Vous_attendez l'autobus?     Oui, nous ...
i Il regarde la télé?     Oui, il ...
j Vous_écoutez les disques?     Oui, nous ...

4 Find the right ending for each sentence:

a Il ne va ...     i jamais de sport.
b Il n'écoute ...     ii plus de viande. Il est végétarien.
c Elle ne veut ...     iii pas du piano.
d Il ne mange ...     iv rien faire.
e Elle ne boit ...     v qu'une fille.
f Je ne regarde ...     vi plus comme secrétaire.
g Il ne joue ...     vii jamais de musique.
h Elle ne travaille ...     viii pas dans les musées.
i Il n'a ...     ix que de l'eau.
j Elle ne fait ...     x plus la télé.

▶ 5 Listen to the weather report while looking at the map; some of the statements below are true (**vrai**), others are false (**faux**). Put an x in the appropriate boxes.

| | vrai | faux |
|---|---|---|
| a Il fait beau à Newcastle. | ☐ | ☐ |
| b A Brighton, il pleut. | ☐ | ☐ |
| c Il pleut à Calais. | ☐ | ☐ |
| d Le soleil brille à Nice. | ☐ | ☐ |
| e Il pleut à Strasbourg. | ☐ | ☐ |
| f Il fait froid en Espagne. | ☐ | ☐ |
| g Il fait du vent à Malaga. | ☐ | ☐ |
| h Il fait très chaud en Italie. | ☐ | ☐ |
| i Il fait du vent à Rome. | ☐ | ☐ |
| j **En Suisse il fait chaud.** | ☐ | ☐ |

k  Il neige à Ostende.  ☐  ☐
l  Le soleil brille à Bruxelles.  ☐  ☐

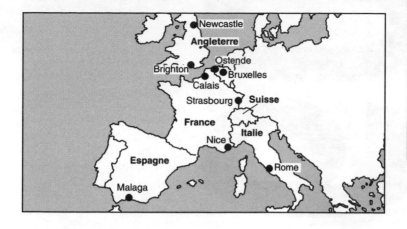

## Mini-test

Check how well you've understood and remembered Units 7 and 8 with this test. How would you say:

1  I play squash better than Fabrice.
2  France is bigger than England.
3  She has glasses and long hair.
4  I'm looking for something to mend my car.
5  I like squash but I prefer playing tennis.
6  I like French cooking very much.

**i** Remember that French people talk about **le** squash, **la** France, **l'**Angleterre, **la** cuisine française, while the English do not use the article.

# 09

## qu'est-ce qu'il faut faire?

what should I do?

**In this unit you will learn**
- a few useful linking words
- how to ask for assistance
- how to use **pouvoir** and **vouloir**
- how to give and understand instructions

# Before you start

This unit prepares you to cope with difficulties you may encounter in France. It gives you the few structures you need to let people know that you're having a problem: **je suis perdu, je ne comprends pas, la machine ne marche pas**, and also to ask for help: **vous pouvez me montrer? qu'est-ce qu'il faut faire?** (see **Key words and phrases**).

*Essayez!* **Have a go!**

1 How would you ask someone politely to:
  a repeat
  b speak more slowly
2 How would you answer the question:
  **Quel temps fait-il aujourd'hui?**

# Key words and phrases

### *For you to say*

| | |
|---|---|
| **pardon Monsieur, Madame ...** | *excuse me* |
| **je suis perdu** | *I'm lost* |
| **je ne sais pas ...** | *I don't know ...* |
| **je ne comprends pas ...** | *I don't understand ...* |
| **vous pouvez m'aider, s'il vous plaît?** | *can you help me please?* |
| **qu'est-ce qu'il faut faire?** | *what must I/we do?* |
| **la machine ne marche pas** | *the machine does not work* |
| **excusez-moi de vous déranger** | *sorry to disturb you* |
| **d'abord** | *firstly* |
| **et puis** | *and then* |
| **après ça** | *after that* |
| **finalement** | *finally* |

### *For you to understand*

| | |
|---|---|
| **il faut_introduire ...** | *you must insert ...* |
| **il faut vérifier le niveau d'huile** | *you have to check the oil level* |
| **vous devez composter le billet** | *you must date-stamp the ticket* |
| **je vais m'en_occuper** | *I'll attend to it* |
| **ne pas déranger** | *do not disturb* |
| **en dérangement/en panne** | *out of order (machine, telephone)* |
| **hors de service** | *out of order* |

# 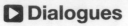 Dialogues

Jane est au garage. Elle demande au mécanicien de vérifier le moteur de son auto qui fait un drôle de bruit.

*Jane is at the garage, asking the mechanic to check the engine of her car which is making a strange noise.*

| | |
|---|---|
| **Jane** | Ah, bonjour Monsieur. Voilà … Depuis ce matin il y a un drôle de bruit dans le moteur de ma voiture. Je ne sais pas ce que c'est. Je ne comprends pas, la voiture marche bien mais … |
| **Mécanicien** | Oui, bien sûr! Avez-vous vérifié le niveau d'huile? Le niveau d'eau? Il fait très chaud aujourd'hui et peut-être que **le moteur chauffe trop**. |
| **Jane** | Euh … non. Je ne sais pas ce qu'il faut faire. Vous pouvez vérifier tout ça, s'il vous plaît? |
| **Mécanicien** | Bon, allez … d'accord, **repassez** dans trois_heures, je m'en_occupe. |

| | |
|---|---|
| **le moteur chauffe trop** | *the engine is heating up too much* |
| **repassez** | *come back* |

Jane est sur le quai de la gare. Elle essaie de composter son billet pour le valider mais sans succès. Elle arrête une passante.

*Jane is on the platform at the station. She is trying to date-stamp her ticket but she is having difficulties. She stops a passer-by:*

| | |
|---|---|
| **Jane** | Pardon, Madame, je ne sais pas comment marche cette machine. Vous pouvez m'aider, s'il vous plaît? |
| **Passante** | Mais oui, Mademolselle, c'est très facile; il faut introduire votre billet sous **la flèche verte**. |
| **Jane** | **C'est ce que j'ai fait** et ça ne marche pas. |
| **Passante** | Alors il faut peut-être tourner le billet **dans l'autre sens**? |
| **Jane** | (*she hears a click*) Ah, bien, mon billet est maintenant composté. Merci, Madame, et excusez-moi de vous avoir dérangée. |
| **Passante** | **De rien**, Mademoiselle. |

| | |
|---|---|
| **la flèche verte** | *the green arrow* |
| **c'est ce que j'ai fait** | *that's what I've done* |
| **dans l'autre sens** | *the other way round* |
| **de rien** | *don't mention it* (lit. *for nothing*) |

# Grammar

## 1 Asking for assistance

There are several ways of asking a favour, depending on how polite you want to be and how well you know the person.

The easiest but perhaps least polite way of asking is to use the verb in the 2nd person plural (i.e. **vous** person) deleting the **vous**.

| | |
|---|---|
| Faites le plein, s'il vous plaît. | *Fill the car up with petrol, please* (lit. make the full, please). |

A more polite way of asking is to start with **vous pouvez** (*can you*) and raise the voice on the last word:

| | |
|---|---|
| **Vous pouvez** me montrer, s'il vous plaît? | *Can you show me, please?* |

Some likely answers:

| | |
|---|---|
| Oui, avec plaisir | *Yes, with pleasure* |
| Certainement | *Certainly* |
| D'accord | *OK* |
| Bien sûr | *Of course* |

Like the verbs **aimer, détester, adorer** (Unit 8), **vous pouvez** is followed by a verb in the infinitive:

| | |
|---|---|
| **Vous pouvez vérifier** le niveau d'huile, s'il vous plaît? | *Can you check the oil level, please?* |

## 2 Two very useful verbs: *pouvoir* to be able to, *vouloir* to want

**Pouvoir** and **vouloir** are two verbs used very frequently in French:

| **pouvoir** *to be able to, can* | **vouloir** *to want* |
|---|---|
| **je peux** | **je veux** |
| **tu peux** | **tu veux** |
| **il/elle/on peut** | **il/elle/on veut** |
| **nous pouvons** | **nous voulons** |
| **vous pouvez** | **vous voulez** |
| **ils/elles peuvent** | **ils/elles veulent** |

## 3 Giving and understanding instructions

**a** The simplest and most commonly used way to give instructions is to use the **vous** or **tu** forms of the present tense:

Pour téléphoner en Angleterre,
  **vous composez** le 00,
  **vous attendez** la tonalité,
  **vous faites** le 44 puis
  l'indicatif de la ville.

*To phone England,*
*dial 00, wait for the*
*dialling tone, dial 44 then*
*the local code.*

**b** In written instruction a verb is often in the infinitive:

**Introduire** votre billet sous
  la flèche verte, le **glisser** vers
  la gauche jusqu'au déclic;
  si la mention 'tournez votre
  billet' apparaît, **présenter**
  l'autre extrémité.

*Insert your ticket under the*
*green arrow and slide it to*
*the left until there is a click;*
*if the sign 'turn your ticket'*
*appears, insert the*
*other end.*

**c Qu'est-ce qu'il faut…?** To find out what needs to be done use **qu'est-ce qu'il faut** followed by the appropriate verb in the infinitive:

**Qu'est-ce qu'il faut faire**
  pour composter son billet?

*What do you have to do to*
*date-stamp your ticket?*

**d Il faut + a verb.** Followed by a verb in the infinitive, **il faut** (which is only used in the 3rd person) means any of the following, depending on the context: *it is necessary, I/we/you have to, must, one has to, must*:

**Il faut** décrocher l'appareil.
**Il faut** attendre la tonalité.

**Il faut** composter le billet.

*You must lift the receiver.*
*One must wait for the*
*dialling tone.*
*You must date-stamp*
*your ticket.*

**e Il faut + a noun.** Followed by a noun, **il faut** means *you need/one needs/I need*.

**Il lui faut** une télécarte
  pour téléphoner.
**Il me faut** un passeport
  pour aller en France.

*He needs a phone card*
*to phone.*
*I need a passport to go*
*to France.*

## Activities

1 Using the words in the box, say what is needed in each case. Practise the questions and answers aloud:

**Qu'est-ce qu'il faut**

a pour ouvrir une bouteille?
b pour prendre le train?
c pour envoyer une lettre?
d pour faire une omelette?
e pour jouer au tennis?
f pour jouer de la musique?
g pour apprendre le français?
h pour aller en France?
i pour acheter de l'essence?

i une station-service
ii le livre *Teach Yourself Beginner's French*
iii une raquette et des balles
iv un passeport
v un tire-bouchon
vi des_oeufs
vii un billet
viii un_instrument
ix un timbre

2 Below is a list of things you need to do to keep fit **pour être en pleine forme**. Match them up with the appropriate verbs on the left. You may need to look up some of the words in the vocabulary list at the back of the book.

**Pour être en pleine forme il faut**

a boire
b manger
c pratiquer
d dormir
e diminuer

f aimer

i un sport
ii les sucreries et le sel
iii son travail
iv peu d'alcool
v beaucoup de légumes et de fruits
vi huit heures par jour

3 Here is a recipe from a children's cookery book. Match the instructions with the corresponding drawings overleaf then answer the questions:

### Omelette
### *(pour quatre personnes)*

*a D'abord tu bats sept oeufs dans un grand bol.*

*b Puis tu poivres et tu sales.*

*c Ensuite tu fais fondre dans la poële 30 grammes de beurre.*

*d Quand le beurre est chaud, tu verses les oeufs.*

e *Après trois ou quatre minutes, tu mélanges avec une fourchette.*

f *Finalement, quand l'omelette est cuite, tu sers immédiatement.*

i How many eggs are needed?
ii What do you do after beating the eggs?
iii What do you melt in the frying pan?
iv When is the egg mixture poured into the bowl?
v What do you use to mix the mixture?

## ⓘ Learn to guess the meaning

Here are three tips to help your general listening and reading comprehension:

- **Imagine the situation.**
  When listening to the recording try to imagine where the scene is taking place and who the main characters are. Let your experience of the world help you guess the meaning of the conversation, e.g. if a dialogue takes place in a snack bar you can predict the kind of vocabulary that is being used.

- **Concentrate on the main part.**
  When watching a foreign film you usually get the meaning of the whole story from a few individual shots. Understanding a foreign conversation or article is similar. Concentrate on the main parts to get the message and don't worry about individual words. When conversing with French speakers look out for clues given by facial expressions and body language; they can tell you a lot about the mood and atmosphere of the conversation.

- **Guess the key words; if you cannot, ask.**
  When there are key words you don't understand, try to guess what they mean from the context. If you're listening to a French speaker and cannot get the gist of a whole passage because of one word or phrase, try to repeat that word with a questioning tone; the speaker will probably paraphrase it, giving you the chance to understand it. If for example you wanted to find out the meaning of the word **voyager** (*to travel*) you would ask **Que veut dire voyager?**

*Pratiquez!* Practise! The notice below is situated in the grounds of a museum of sculptures in Paris. There are strict rules about what you can and cannot do! What are they? (Check your answers with the translation in **Key to the exercises**.)

---

**IL EST EXPRESSÉMENT DÉFENDU:**

- de photographier avec pied ou flash
- de dégrader les sculptures, vases
- de cueillir des fleurs ou des fruits
- d'escalader les sculptures
- de marcher sur le gazon et de monter sur les bancs
- de déjeuner hors de la zone réservée à la cafétéria
- d'introduire des animaux
- de circuler à bicyclette
- de jouer avec des balles et ballons
- de déposer ou de jeter des ordures ailleurs que dans des corbeilles à papier

---

# Mini-test

1 Say in French: Today it is cold but it's not raining.
2 How would you ask for what needs to be done?
3 How would you say that you need a phone card to phone?
4 Imagine that you are in Paris. Ask someone to help you with three things starting with:
   a Vous pouvez me montrer ...?
   b Vous pouvez me dire ...?
   c Vous pouvez me donner ...?

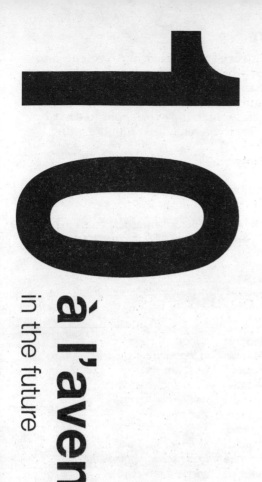

# 10 à l'avenir

in the future

**In this unit you will learn**
- how to say what you usually do
- how to say what you need
- how to talk about your future plans
- how to use the pronoun **y**
- two useful verbs **sortir** and **venir**

# Before you start

Talking about the future is very easy in French. All you need to do is to use **je vais** followed by the infinitive form of whatever you're going to do. For example to say that you intend to play tennis tomorrow you would say: **demain je vais jouer au tennis**. In this unit you'll learn useful words and expressions to describe your typical day and say what you intend to do in the future.

*Essayez!* Have a go!

1 If you see on a telephone box a notice saying **En dérangement** what does it mean?

2 You want to use the Internet (**utiliser l'Internet**) from a post office in France. How would you ask: *What must I do to use the Internet?*

# Key words and phrases

| | |
|---|---|
| demain | *tomorrow* |
| à l'avenir | *in the future* |
| qu'est-ce que vous_allez faire? | *what are you going to do?* |
| je vais ... | *I'm going to ...* |
| visiter les monuments_historiques | *visit old buildings* |
| rendre visite à mes_amis | *visit my friends* |
| voyager | *to travel* |
| faire de longues promenades | *to go for long walks* |
| faire du tourisme | *to do some sightseeing* |
| passer quelques jours ... | *spend a few days ...* |
| partir pour une semaine ... | *go for a week ...* |
| au bord de la mer | *to the seaside* |
| à la campagne | *to the countryside* |
| à la montagne | *to the mountains* |
| en_été, en_automne, en_hiver | *in summer, in autumn, in winter* |
| au printemps | *in spring* |
| l'année prochaine | *next year* |
| en mars | *in March* |
| pendant le mois d'août | *during the month of August* |
| j'ai besoin de ... | *I need ...* |
| j'ai chaud, froid | *I'm hot, cold* |
| j'ai soif, faim | *I'm thirsty, hungry* |
| comment passez-vous votre journée? | *how do you spend your day?* |

| | |
|---|---|
| **généralement** | *generally* |
| **je me lève** | *I get up* |
| **je m'habille** | *I get dressed* |
| **je me lave** | *I wash* |
| **je prends le petit-déjeuner** | *I have breakfast* |
| **je pars de la maison** | *I leave the house* |
| **j'emmène les_enfants à l'école** | *I take the children to school* |
| **je vais chez mes_amis** | *I go to my friends' house* |
| **je fais des courses** | *I do some shopping* |
| **je prépare le déjeuner** | *I prepare lunch* |
| **je vais chercher Jean à la gare** | *I go and fetch John from the station* |
| **le soir, je vais_au cinéma** | *in the evening I go to the cinema* |
| **je me couche/je vais_au lit** | *I go to bed* |
| **louer** | *to rent* |
| **se baigner** | *to go for a swim* |
| **surtout** | *mainly* |
| **se reposer** | *to rest* |
| **lire** | *to read* |
| **sortir** | *to go out* |
| **à la maison** | *at home* |

# ▶ Dialogue

Les Durand parlent de leurs projets pour les vacances d'été.

*The Durands talk about their summer holiday plans.*

*Listen or read at least twice. How long are they going on holiday for? Where are they going? Note down at least three things M. and Mme Durand intend to do. Does their daughter Rosine enjoy sightseeing?*

| | |
|---|---|
| **Jane** | Monsieur et Madame Durand, qu'est-ce que vous_allez faire pour vos vacances cet_été? |
| **M. Durand** | Nous_allons prendre quatre semaines de vacances: une semaine au bord de la mer au mois de juillet et trois semaines à la montagne en_août. |
| **Jane** | Vous_allez rester à l'hôtel ou vous_allez louer une maison? |
| **Mme Durand** | Nous_allons d'abord passer quelques jours chez nos_amis au bord de la mer. Ils_habitent à 50 km de Nice. Après ça nous_allons dans notre maison de campagne dans le petit village de Puy-St.-Pierre près de Briançon. |

| Jane | Et comment allez-vous passer vos vacances? |
|---|---|
| Mme Durand | Au bord de la mer, je vais me baigner tous les jours. A Puy-St.-Pierre, je voudrais jouer au tennis, faire de longues promenades et visiter les monuments historiques de la région. |
| M. Durand | Moi, je vais surtout me reposer, lire et faire un peu de sport comme le tennis ou jouer à la pétanque avec les_enfants. Le soir, j'espère sortir quelquefois pour voir un bon film ou même aller au restaurant. |
| Rosine | Moi, cette année je ne veux pas faire de tourisme. Je préfère rester à la maison ou sortir avec mes_amis. |

# Grammar

## 1 Saying what you usually do using some reflexive verbs

When describing your typical day you can't avoid using reflexive verbs, i.e. verbs describing things you do to or for yourself such as se lever (*to get oneself up*), s'habiller (*to get dressed*). While in English the *myself, yourself, himself*, etc... is often dropped, in French the me, te, se, etc ... must be kept. Here is the pattern followed by all reflexive verbs in the present.

---

**se laver** *to wash (oneself)*

| Je me lave | *I wash (myself)* |
|---|---|
| tu te laves | *you wash (yourself)* |
| il/elle/on se lave | *he/she/it/one washes (himself, etc...)* |
| nous nous lavons | *we wash (ourselves)* |
| vous vous lavez | *you wash (yourself/selves)* |
| ils/elles se lavent | *they wash (themselves)* |

---

ℹ️ Perhaps the most useful reflexive verbs is **s'appeler** (lit. to call oneself).

Comment vous_appelez-vous? Je m'appelle ...
Comment t'appelles-tu? (friendly form) Je m'appelle ...
Comment s'appellent_ils? Ils s'appellent ...

*Pratiquez!* **Practise!** To check that you understand reflexive verbs: try to write out **s'habiller** (*to get dressed*). The **me, te, se,** will be shortened to **m', t', s'** as **habiller** starts with an **h**.

## 2 Saying what you need: *j'ai besoin de ...*

To say what item you need, use **j'ai besoin de (d')** followed by a noun:

| | |
|---|---|
| **J'ai besoin d'un passeport pour la France.** | *I need a passport for France.* |
| **Il a besoin d'un timbre de 50 centimes pour envoyer sa lettre.** | *He needs a 0,50€ stamp to send his letter.* |

To say what you need to do, use **j'ai besoin de (d')** followed by a verb in the infinitive:

| | |
|---|---|
| **J'ai chaud; j'ai besoin de boire** un verre d'eau. | *I'm hot; I need to drink a glass of water.* |
| **Elle n'a plus d'argent. Elle a besoin d'aller** à la banque. | *She has no money left. She needs to go to the bank.* |

- **J'ai chaud/froid/faim/soif** use **avoir** (not **être!**).
- **Pour** is used before verbs in the infinitive to translate the idea of *in order to*: **Pour** envoyer sa lettre il a besoin d'un timbre.

## 3 Stating your intentions

Just as you use **je voudrais** to say what you would like to do, use **je vais** to say what you are going to do followed by the verb in the infinitive.

| | |
|---|---|
| **Je vais** *I'm going* | **me lever** à huit heures. *to get up at eight o'clock.* |
| **Tu vas** *You're going* | **prendre** le petit-déjeuner à neuf heures. *to have breakfast at nine o'clock.* |
| **Il/Elle va** *He/She is going* | **partir** de la maison. *to leave the house.* |
| **Nous_allons** *We're going* | **faire** des courses à midi. *to do some shopping at lunchtime.* |
| **Vous_allez** *You're going* | **chercher** Jean à la gare. *to fetch John from the station.* |
| **Ils/Elles vont** *They're going* | **se coucher** vers 11 heures. *to go to bed around 11 o'clock.* |

## 4 The pronoun *y*

To replace an expression of place preceded by à, use the pronoun y (*there*):

| | |
|---|---|
| Vous_allez à Paris? | *Are you going to Paris?* |
| Oui, j'y vais. | *Yes, I'm going there.* |
| Il va travailler à la pharmacie? | *Is he going to work at* |
| Oui, il va y travailler. | *the chemist's? Yes, he's going to work there.* |

**i** Like other pronouns, e.g. **en, le, la, les,** etc. (Unit 8), **y** is placed just before the verb to which it refers, e.g. **il faut y aller** *we must go there.*

## 5 *Sortir* to go out, *venir* to come

Here are two useful verbs to describe daily activities.

| **sortir** *to go out* | **venir** *to come* |
|---|---|
| **je sors** | **je viens** |
| **tu sors** | **tu viens** |
| **il/elle/on sort** | **il/elle/on vient** |
| **nous sortons** | **nous venons** |
| **vous sortez** | **vous venez** |
| **ils/elles sortent** | **ils/elles viennent** |

## 6 Using capital letters

The months, seasons and days of the week do not take a capital letter in French unless they begin a sentence (Unit 3): **en juillet, en_été, le mardi.**

## 7 When to use *visiter* (to visit) in French

French people talk about visiting museums, old buildings or interesting places but they do not visit the cinema or their relations! They **go** to the cinema or the pub and they **pay a visit** or **see** their relations or friends:

| | |
|---|---|
| Je vais_aller **visiter** le Louvre l'été prochain. | *I'm going to visit the Louvre next summer.* |
| Ce week-end je vais **rendre visite** à ma grand-mère. | *This weekend I'm going to visit my grandmother.* |

| | |
|---|---|
| Ils vont **voir** leurs_amis dans le sud de la France. | *They are going to visit their friends in the south of France.* |

## ℹ️ Assess yourself and keep up with grammar

Having reached the end of the Grammar section it may be useful to find out how well you're doing with grammar, ways to practise it and, in Units 11–20 of the book, how to build on what you already know.

- **How well are you doing with grammar?**
  Look at the **Index** with grammar terms and decide which functions you feel are particularly important. Test yourself on two or three of these at a time using the **Activities** of Units 1–10. If you find the exercises difficult, revise the **Grammar** carefully studying the examples.

- **Test yourself in a practice activity.**
  Once you've completed successfully all the activities in Units 1–10 of *Teach Yourself Beginner's French* you may feel that you need to test yourself with another book of grammar exercises with the answers at the back. To test yourself you can read the explanations first and do the exercises or try the questions first, check the answers and work out the rule.

- **Build up a 'pattern bank'.**
  Using the material from Units 11–20 of the book and any other French material, collect examples that can be listed under the structures you've already met. Seeing the structures in various contexts will help you assimilate them.

## Activities

1 Imagine you're the man or woman whose typical day is illustrated on page 96. Write underneath the pictures what you do during the day but first have a go at saying it aloud.

2 Repeat Exercise 1. This time pretend that you are describing your friend's, brother's or sister's typical day. Start the sentences with **il ...** or **elle ...** .

**a** D'abord je …  **b** puis je …  **c** ensuite …

**d** A 8h.30 j'…  **e** ensuite …  **f** à midi …

**g** L'après-midi …  **h** ou je …  **i** ou je …

**j** Le soir je …  **k** ou j' …  **l** enfin …

3  Your friends Robert and Jeanine have just planned their holidays for this summer. You ask them about it:

a  What does Robert say?
b  What does Jeanine tell you?

|  | Robert | Jeanine |
|---|---|---|
| Tu va partir quand? | in August | on 21st June |
| Pour combien de temps? | three weeks | ten days |
| Où vas-tu aller? | to Oxford in England | to Anglet near Biarritz in the South of France |
| Comment vas-tu passer tes vacances? | • learn English<br>• visit old buildings<br>• see some friends<br>• go out in the evening<br>• play tennis | • go swimming<br>• read a lot<br>• watch a bit (un peu) of TV<br>• go for long walks<br>• go to bed early (tôt) |

Practise the exercise several times and try memorizing the questions.

4  What questions would you ask Robert and Jeanine if you said vous to them?

5  Jane has received a letter from a French friend who is about to visit her in Brighton. Fill in the gaps using each of the words in the box on page 98.

Chère Jane,

Merci (a)........ pour ta gentille lettre.

Oui, mon (b)........, mon fils et moi allons bientôt te rendre visite en (c)........ . Marc (d)........ l'école le 27 juin donc nous pensons quitter Paris le (e)........ 30 juin à midi pour arriver à Gatwick à deux heures de (f) l' ........

Nous pensons (g)........ avec toi quelques (h)........, puis nous voulons faire un peu de tourisme à Londres pour (i)........ les monuments historiques. Ensuite nous voulons aller à

Oxford où (j)........ nos amis Green. Tu n'as pas (k)........ d'aller nous chercher à Gatwick. Nous pouvons très bien (l)........ le train jusqu'à Brighton et puis un taxi jusqu'à chez toi. A très bientôt. Amicalement.

| prendre | jours | mari | Grande-Bretagne | | |
|---|---|---|---|---|---|
| finit | habitent | samedi | rester | visiter | |
| beaucoup | | besoin | | après-midi | |

▶ **6** Michel has a lot of things planned for tomorrow. Listen to the recording and try to find out what's he's going to do. He has a list of nine things. If you haven't got the recording, look at the answers in the **Key to the exercises** to find out about Michel's plans.

## Mini-test

1 You cannot date-stamp your ticket at the machine.
   **a** Ask someone to help you?
   **b** You are told what to do but you don't understand. What do you say?
2 Finish the following sentences with an appropriate ending following the example:
   **Tu vas en France? Tu as besoin d'un passeport.**
   **a** Il a soif? Il a besoin de _____
   **b** Nous n'avons pas d'argent. Nous _____
   **c** Ils ont faim? Ils _____
   **d** Je suis malade. J'_____
3 Fill in the blanks with the right endings of the verb **aller**:
   M. et Mme Durand (**a**) ........ prendre quatre semaines de vacances. M. Durand (**b**) ........ lire et faire du sport. Mme Durand et Rosine (**c**) ........ se baigner tous les jours. Et toi qu'est-ce que tu (**d**) ........ faire? Moi? Je (**e**) ........ rester chez moi. Mais le samedi après-midi moi et mon petit_ami (**f**) ........ regarder un match de football à la télé.

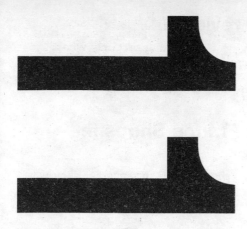

# 11

**shopping**

# les courses

**In this unit you will**
- find out about shops in France
- practise buying groceries
- practise buying something to wear

# Before you start, revise

- numbers (page 227)
- asking what's available (page 13)
- *some* and *any* (page 13)
- asking the price (page 14)

- saying precisely what you want (page 63)
- *less ...*, *more ...* (page 65)
- colours (page 61)

## *Les magasins en France* Shops in France

To find out about French shops read the passage below. Answering the questions in **Activity 1** will help you to understand it.

**i** Les magasins, en France, restent ouverts en général jusqu'à 19 heures ou 20 heures. Beaucoup ferment entre 12 heures et 14 heures. Le lundi ils sont souvent fermés dans les petites villes.

La boulangerie ouvre très tôt, vers sept heures du matin, et ferme tard car beaucoup de Français achètent leur pain deux fois par jour. Le dimanche matin, beaucoup de magasins comme les pâtisseries et les charcuteries restent ouverts.

Dans toutes les grandes villes il y a un marché presque tous les jours et souvent le dimanche. Dans les petites villes ou villages il y a un marché une fois par semaine: le jour du marché. Au marché, on peut acheter **des légumes**, des fruits, **du poisson**, **de la viande** et même **des vêtements**.

| | | | |
|---|---|---|---|
| **les légumes** | *vegetables* | **la viande** | *meat* |
| **le poisson** | *fish* | **les vêtements** | *clothes* |

## Activity 1

**a** Until what time do shops generally stay open during the week?
**b** Are they usually open or shut at lunchtime?
**c** What day of the week do they often shut?
**d** Which shops are often open on Sunday morning?

## Activity 2

Now read the passage several times and then, without looking at it, try to say aloud in French what you know about French shops. Check back with the passage.

**i** • The **-s** at the end of the plural nouns is not pronounced.

• The **-nt** at the end of the verbs such as **ferment, restent** is not pronounced so **ferment** sounds like 'fairm' and **restent** like 'rest'.

## Key words and phrases

With the key words below you should be able to cope with most buying situations. A good way to test yourself once you've learnt the **Mots-clés** is to hide the left side of the page, look at the English and say the French aloud.

| | |
|---|---|
| où est la boulangerie la plus proche s'il vous plaît? | where is the nearest bakery please? |
| où est le supermarché le plus proche? | where is the nearest supermarket? |
| où est-ce que je peux acheter/ trouver un/une/des ... | where can I buy/find a/some ... |
| je voudrais/il me faut un/une/des ... | I would like/I need a/some ... |
| un paquet/une plaquette de ... | a pack of ... |
| une tranche de ... | a slice of ... |
| un morceau de ... | a piece of ... |
| vous avez autre chose? | do you have anything else? |
| c'est trop grand/petit/cher | it's too big/small/expensive |
| je cherche quelque chose de différent | I'm looking for something different |
| vous avez quelque chose de plus grand/petit/moins cher? | have you got anything bigger/smaller/cheaper? |
| je vais prendre une tranche/ un kilo/une livre de plus/ 500 grammes de moins | I'll take a slice/a kilo/a pound more/500 grams less |
| un demi-kilo | half a kilo |
| c'est combien? | how much is it? |
| c'est tout, merci | that's all, thank you |

# *Acheter des provisions* Food shopping

## À la boucherie (*butcher's*), on achète:

| | |
|---|---|
| du veau | *veal* |
| du boeuf | *beef* |
| du porc | *pork* |
| des saucisses | *sausages* |
| un poulet | *chicken* |

## À la charcuterie (*delicatessen*), on achète:

| | |
|---|---|
| du jambon | *ham* |
| du saucisson | *salami-type sausage* |

## À la boulangerie/pâtisserie (*baker's*), on achète:

| | |
|---|---|
| une baguette | *French 'stick'* |
| un pain complet | *wholemeal loaf* |
| des petits pains | *soft bread rolls* |
| une tarte aux fraises | *strawberry tart* |
| des croissants | *croissants* |

## À l'épicerie (*grocer's*), au libre-service (*self-service*), à l'alimentation (*foodstore*), on achète:

| | |
|---|---|
| du thé | *tea* |
| du café | *coffee* |
| du beurre | *butter* |
| du lait | *milk* |
| des oeufs (rhyming with deux) | *eggs* |
| du fromage (de chèvre) | *(goat's) cheese* |
| de la lessive | *washing powder* |
| des pommes | *apples* |
| des pommes de terre | *potatoes* |
| une laitue | *lettuce* |
| des yaourts à la fraise | *strawberry yoghurts* |
| des boissons (jus de fruit, vins, etc.) | *drinks (fruit juice, wine, etc.)* |

## Activity 3

There is no supermarket around; say in French which shops sell:

a  chicken
b  bread rolls
c  pork
d  washing powder

e  milk
f  salami
g  wine

## Activity 4

Below is a dialogue between a grocer and a client. See if you can put the lines in their correct order starting with **Bonjour Madame.**

a  Une douzaine (*a dozen*), s'il vous plaît.
b  Voilà, Madame, ça fait 6,85 euros.
c  **Bonjour Madame.**
d  Non, il me faut aussi du jus de fruit.
e  Oui ... voilà une douzaine d'oeufs, c'est tout?
f  Bonjour Monsieur, je voudrais des oeufs, s'il vous plaît.
g  Qu'est-ce que je vous donne: jus de pomme, orange ou ananas (*pineapple*)?
h  Vous en voulez combien?
i  Je vais prendre le jus d'orange.

## ▶ Dialogue 1: *Au marché* At the market

Un client achète des provisions pour un pique-nique.

*At the market a customer buys some food for a picnic.*

*Listen to the recording (read the dialogue if you haven't got the recording) then without looking back at the text try Activity 5.*

| | |
|---|---|
| **Client** | Bonjour, mademoiselle. Je voudrais du beurre, s'il vous plaît? |
| **Vendeuse** | Une plaquette comme ça? |
| **Client** | Non, quelque chose de plus petit. Et qu'est-ce que vous avez comme fromages? |
| **Vendeuse** | Brie, fromage de chèvre, gruyère. Qu'est-ce que je vous donne? |
| **Client** | Du gruyère. |

| Vendeuse | Un morceau comme ça? |
|---|---|
| Client | Ah non… ça c'est un peu trop gros. Vous pouvez m'en donner un peu moins, s'il vous plaît? C'est pour notre pique-nique. |
| Vendeuse | Ah bon, d'accord. Voilà … 300 grammes. Et avec ça? Qu'est-ce qu'il vous faut? Des fruits, des yaourts, des biscuits? |
| Client | Euh, je vais prendre aussi des fruits. |
| Vendeuse | Alors nous avons des fraises, des bananes, des pommes, des pêches et du melon. |
| Client | Elles sont bonnes les fraises? |
| Vendeuse | Délicieuses. Je vous en mets un demi-kilo? |
| Client | 500 grammes! Non, c'est un peu trop. Une demi-livre c'est assez. Ah oui, je voudrais aussi 2 grandes bouteilles d'eau minérale … Voilà, c'est tout, c'est combien? |
| Vendeuse | Alors, ça vous fait 17,83 €. |
| Client | Et pour acheter du pain? |
| Vendeuse | Vous trouverez une boulangerie à 200 mètres sur votre gauche. Et … bon pique-nique Monsieur. |

## Activity 5

Look at the three columns below. Can you pick out four items bought by the customer?

| | | |
|---|---|---|
| a du poulet | e des pommes | i du lait |
| b du beurre | f du melon | j du vin |
| c du saucisson | g des fraises | k de la bière |
| d du fromage | h des pêches | l de l'eau minérale |

## Activity 6

Pretend that you're a customer. Using the dialogue above and the **Key words and phrases** on pages 101–2 practise buying a small packet of butter, 300 grams of cheese and half a pound of strawberries. Don't forget to find out where you can buy some bread. (The answers are not given in the **Key to the exercises**.)

# *Acheter autre chose* Shopping for other things

## Activity 7

Here is a list of the shops and services in the town of Cauterets.

| CAUTERETS et ses COMMERCES |
| :---: |
| Alimentation Générale – Primeurs – **Ets. Vaud** |
| Bijouterie – **Angélique** |
| Boulangerie – «Le Croissant» |
| Brasserie – *«Au bon acceuil»* |
| Boucherie – Charcuterie – Bon et fils |
| Cave – Marchand de Vin – *Veuve de Bonnet* |
| Chaussures – *Saint-Etienne* |
| Coiffeur – Esthéticienne – *Élégance* |
| Confection – MariSol |
| Confiserie – «Au bon chocolatier» |
| Droguerie – *Sans souci* |
| Electricien – Ets. Dufour |
| Fleuriste – **Sandrine** |
| Garage – Service Station – **Bernay** |
| Généraliste – Dr LeGrand |
| Informatique – **infocom** |
| Kinésithérapeute – *Mlle Chantal* |
| Librairie – *Blanchard* |
| Lingerie – Vêtements – «Chez Madame» |
| Magasin du sport – **Interaventure** |
| Médecins Thermaux – **«Thermed»** |
| Meubles Hi-Fi – *La maison en bois* |
| Pharmacie – Sain et sauf |
| Peintre – *Michel* |
| Plombier – **Au courant** |
| Photographe – *Etoile* |
| Pressing – *A votre service* |
| Restauration rapide - *chez jacques* |
| Traiteur – bonne bouche |
| Souvenirs – Cadeaux – **Souvex** |

Can you identify the French words for:

a  Sweet shop / candy store      b  Florist
c  Fashion boutique              d  Dry-cleaner's
e  General practitioner          f  Book shop
g  Hairdresser's – Beautician    h  IT
i  Jewellery                     j  Physiotherapist

---

## À la droguerie (*hardware shop*)

| | |
|---|---|
| **une brosse à dent** | *toothbrush* |
| **un savon** | *soap* |
| **un peigne** | *comb* |
| **de l'huile pour bronzer** | *suntan lotion* |
| **des kleenex** | *tissues* |
| **un ouvre-boîte** | *tin opener* |
| **un tire-bouchon** | *corkscrew* |

## Au bureau de tabac (*newsagent's*)

| | |
|---|---|
| **un carnet de timbres** | *book of stamps* |
| **des journaux** | *newspapers* |
| **du chewing gum** | *chewing gum* |
| **une carte postale** | *postcard* |
| **des magazines** | *magazines* |

## Au magasin de vêtements (*clothes shop*)

| | |
|---|---|
| **un pull-over** | *pullover* |
| **un pantalon** | *trousers* |
| **une chemise** | *a shirt* |
| **une paire de chaussures** | *shoes* |
| **un maillot de bain** | *swimming costume* |
| **une robe** | *dress* |
| **une jupe** | *skirt* |
| **un jean/des jeans** | *jeans* |

---

## ▶ Dialogue 2: *Dans un magasin de vêtements* In a clothes shop

For this dialogue, you need to understand two new questions:

**1  Quelle taille?** (*What size?*) when you're buying clothes. (42 is the European equivalent to the woman's size 14 in Britain and

12 in America, 44 is equivalent to size 16 in Britain and 14 in America, etc.). **Quelle pointure?** means *What size shoes?* Size 5 in Britain or 7 in America = 38, size 6 in Britain and 8 in America = 39, etc.

**2 Je peux essayer?** (*Can I try?*) when you want to try something on.

**Cliente**    Bonjour, Madame, je cherche une jupe noire.
**Vendeuse**   Noire ... euh oui d'accord. **Vous faites quelle taille?**
**Cliente**    40 ... 40/42, **ça dépend du modèle.**
**Vendeuse**   J'ai ce modèle-ci en 40 et 42. C'est une jupe en coton. En 40, je n'ai pas de noir; j'ai du rouge, du gris mais pas de noir.
**Cliente**    Elles font combien ces jupes?
**Vendeuse**   50 euros.
**Cliente**    Vous n'avez pas quelque chose de moins cher?
**Vendeuse**   Euh non, sauf ces jupes **en solde** à 29 euros mais elles sont grises.
**Cliente**    Non, il me faut du noir. Bon, eh bien, je vais essayer la jupe à 50 euros.
**Vendeuse**   (*pointing to a changing room*) Vous avez **la cabine d'essayage** là-bas.
               (*after a while*)
**Vendeuse**   Elle vous va bien?
**Cliente**    Ça va; elle est un peu large mais je crois que je vais la prendre car j'en ai besoin pour ce soir. Vous acceptez les cartes de crédit?
**Vendeuse**   Mais bien sûr, Madame.

| | |
|---|---|
| **vous faites quelle taille?** | *what size are you?* |
| **ça dépend du modèle** | *it depends on the style* |
| **en solde** | *on sale* |
| **la cabine d'essayage** | *changing room* |
| **là-bas** | *over there* |

# ▶ Activity 8

Listen to the recording again and try to spot the French version of the following phrases, then write them down:

**a** I'm looking for a black skirt .................................................
**b** What's your size? ..................................................
**c** something cheaper ..................................................

**d** I shall try ..................................................................
**e** the skirt at 50 Euros ........................................................
**f** How does it fit? ...............................................................

## Activity 9

You're at the **bureau de tabac** (the **c** in **tabac** is not sounded) and wish to buy a newspaper, stamps, cards and a magazine for your wife.

**Vendeur** Bonjour, Monsieur, vous désirez?

**a** *You* *Say you would like a newspaper. Ask him what English newspapers he's got.*

**Vendeur** Comme journaux anglais? Nous avons le Times, le Guardian et le Daily Telegraph.

**b** *You* *Say that you will take* The Times *and these three postcards. Ask how much a stamp for England is.*

**Vendeur** Un timbre pour l'Angleterre? C'est le même prix que pour la France: 50 centimes.

**c** *You* *Say that you will take eight stamps.*

**Vendeur** Voilà, Monsieur; huit timbres à 50 centimes. C'est tout?

**d** *You* *Say that you'll also buy the magazine* Elle *for your wife.*

**Vendeur** Très bien, Monsieur. Ça vous fait 11,27€.

## ▶ Activity 10

On the recording you will hear Michel shopping. Listen to the conversation several times and then answer the questions below, in English.

**a** What does he want to buy?
**b** What colours does he ask for?
**c** What's wrong with the first garment?
**d** What's wrong with the second garment?
**e** How much is the one he buys?

## Mini-test

How do you say in French:

1 I need some tissues.
2 I would like something bigger, please.
3 Do you have anything else?
4 That's all.
5 Do you accept credit cards?

# 12
## se reposer, dormir
resting, sleeping

**In this unit you will**
- find out about accommodation in France
- find out how to ask for information at the tourist office
- practise booking into a hotel and a campsite
- complain about things missing/not working
- learn to spell your name
- write a letter to book accommodation

## Before you start, revise

- saying what you want (page 62)
- asking what you can do (page 39)
- different ways to ask a question (page 39)
- asking the price (page 14)
- recognizing 'first', 'second', 'third', etc. (page 52)
- saying that there isn't any (page 31)
- dates (page 40)

# *Choisir un hôtel* Choosing a hotel

Les offices du tourisme et syndicats d'initiative:

- L'office de tourisme à Paris: www.paris-touristoffice.com
- FNOTSI (Fédération Nationale des Offices de Tourisme et Syndicats d'Initiative): www.tourisme.fr

Les Maisons de la France:

- en France: www.franceguide.com
- en Grande-Bretagne: www.fr-holidaystore.co.uk

**i** En France, les offices du tourisme (appelés aussi 'syndicats d'initiative') donnent gratuitement des brochures avec la liste des hôtels et des restaurants de la région. Ils peuvent aussi faire une réservation dans l'hôtel de votre choix. À Paris, l'office du tourisme est situé au 127, avenue des Champs Elysées – 75008.

**À l'étranger**, les Maisons de la France vous donneront toutes sortes de brochures et d'informations sur Paris et la France: Grande-Bretagne: 178 Piccadilly, London W1V 0AL; États-Unis: 444 Madison Avenue, Level 16, New York, NY 10022-6903; Australie: 25 Bligh Street, level 22, Sydney NSW 2000

Les hôtels sont **homologués** par le gouvernement **d'une étoile** ★ (hôtel simple) à quatre étoiles luxe ★★★★L (très grand confort, palace). Vous pouvez choisir entre **pension complète** et **demi-pension**. Il faut demander si le petit-déjeuner est **compris** dans le prix de la chambre. Il est souvent **en supplément**.

| | | | |
|---|---|---|---|
| **à l'étranger** | *abroad* | **la demi-pension** | *half board* |
| **homologué** | *classified* | **compris** | *included* |
| **une étoile** | *star* | **en supplément,** | *extra* |
| **la pension complète** | *full board* | **en sus** | |

## Activity 1

a Are **offices du tourisme** the same as **syndicats d'initiative**?
b Do you have to pay for tourist brochures?
c What are the **offices du tourisme** prepared to do for you?
d Is breakfast usually included in the price list of a hotel?

## How to pronounce ...

Practise reading out loud the French key words in the table below.

- **baignoire** and **WC** are pronounced as 'bé-noir' and 'vais-c'est'.
- pronounce the words: **radio**, **télévision** and **bar** the French way. Check their pronunciation in the **Pronunciation guide**.
- **ascenseur** is pronounced as 'as-cen-soeur'.

### CHOISIR SON HÔTEL

| Le confort dépend du nombre d'étoiles | ★ | ★★ | ★★★ | ★★★★ | ★★★★L |
|---|---|---|---|---|---|
| l'eau courante chaude et froide au lavabo | ✓ | ✓ | ✓ | ✓ | ✓ |
| une douche | # | ✓ | ✓ | ✓ | ✓ |
| un bidet | ● | # | ✓ | ✓ | ✓ |
| une baignoire | ● | # | ✓ | ✓ | ✓ |
| un W.C. dans la chambre | ● | # | # | ✓ | ✓ |
| le téléphone intérieur | ● | # | # | ✓ | ✓ |
| le téléphone extérieur | ● | ● | ● | # | ✓ |
| la radio | ● | ● | ● | # | ✓ |
| la télévision | ● | ● | ● | # | ✓ |
| un bar privé | ● | ● | ● | # | ✓ |
| l'ascenseur | # | ✓ | ✓ | ✓ | ✓ |

✓ = oui toujours
# = oui le plus souvent
● = non

## ▶ Activity 2

Look carefully at the table before listening to the recording – if you haven't got it, read Kate's assertions below and say whether they are true or false. Correct the false ones:

| | True | False |
|---|:---:|:---:|
| a  Il y a plus de confort dans un hôtel à deux étoiles que dans un hôtel à quatre étoiles. | ☐ | ☐ |
| b  Un hôtel de luxe peut avoir jusqu'à six étoiles. | ☐ | ☐ |
| c  Tous les hôtels ont de l'eau courante chaude et froide au lavabo. | ☐ | ☐ |
| d  Il n'y a pas de baignoire dans les chambres d'un hôtel à une étoile. | ☐ | ☐ |
| e  On a souvent dans un hôtel à une étoile une chambre avec douche. | ☐ | ☐ |
| f  Il y a toujours un ascenseur dans les hôtels à une étoile. | ☐ | ☐ |
| g  Dans les hôtels à deux étoiles, les chambres ont la télévision. | ☐ | ☐ |
| h  Pour avoir un bar privé dans la chambre, il faut réserver une chambre dans un hôtel à quatre étoiles luxe. | ☐ | ☐ |

# Key words and phrases

| | |
|---|---|
| **est-ce que vous avez ...?** | *have you ...?* |
| **je cherche ...** | *I'm looking for ...* |
| **un emplacement pour une tente/** | *a site for a tent/* |
| **pour une caravane** | *for a caravan* |
| **une chambre simple/double** | *a single/double room* |
| **à deux lits** | *with two single beds* |
| **avec un grand lit** | *with a double bed* |
| **avec douche et WC** | *with shower and WC* |
| **avec salle de bains** | *with bathroom* |
| **avec cabinet de toilette** | *with basin and bidet partitioned off* |
| **avec demi-pension** | *with half board* |
| **avec pension complète** | *with full board* |
| **pour ... personne(s)** | *for ... person(s)* |
| **pour ... nuit(s)** | *for ... night(s)* |
| **le petit déjeuner est compris?** | *is breakfast included?* |
| **non, c'est en supplément/en plus** | *no, it's extra* |
| **c'est à quel nom?** | *in whose name?* |
| **c'est complet** | *it's full up* |
| **l'arrondissement\* (m)** | *district in large towns* |

\*Paris is divided into 20 **arrondissements** which spiral out from the city centre clockwise like a conch shell.

# ▶ Dialogue 1: *À la recherche d'un hôtel* Looking for a hotel

À l'office du tourisme une touriste accompagnée de son mari se renseigne sur les hôtels à Paris.

*At the tourist office, a tourist accompanied by her husband inquires about hotels in Paris.*

**Touriste** Bonjour Madame. Je viens d'arriver à Paris et je cherche une chambre. Vous avez une liste d'hôtels, s'il vous plaît?

**Hôtesse** Oui Madame, voilà.
*(the tourists look at the brochure)*

**Touriste** Pouvez-vous me réserver une chambre, s'il vous plaît?

**Hôtesse** Oui, bien sûr. Vous choisissez quel hôtel?

**Touriste** Un hôtel à deux étoiles, l'Hôtel Victor Hugo, dans le 16ème arrondissement.

**Hôtesse** C'est pour combien de personnes?

**Touriste** Euh, pour mon mari et moi …

**Hôtesse** Et pour combien de nuits?

**Touriste** Pour deux nuits.

**Hôtesse** Bien. Une chambre à deux lits ou un grand lit?

**Touriste** Un grand lit. Nous voulons une douche également.

**Hôtesse** Bon, alors une chambre pour deux nuits, pour deux personnes avec un grand lit et douche. Très bien, je vais téléphoner et je vous réserve ça tout de suite.

**Touriste** J'espère que l'hôtel n'est pas complet!

**Hôtesse** Je crois qu'en cette saison, il y aura de la place.

## Activity 3

Listen to the dialogue as often as you need and spot the French version of the following phrases:

a  Do you have a list of hotels? .......................
b  Can you book me a room? ........................
c  Which hotel are you choosing? ......................
d  in the 16th district ................................
e  I hope the hotel is not full! .......................
f  There will be some room. ..........................

# ▶ Dialogue 2: *À l'hôtel* In the hotel

À la réception: les Wilson arrivent à leur hôtel.

*At reception: the Wilsons arrive at their hotel.*

| | |
|---|---|
| **Touriste** | Bonjour, Monsieur. Nous avons une réservation au nom de Wilson. |
| **Réceptionniste** | Ah oui, vous êtes les Anglais qui ont téléphoné cet après-midi! |
| **Touriste** | Oui, c'est ça. |
| **Réceptionniste** | Bon, vous avez la chambre 43 au deuxième étage. C'est une chambre très agréable avec grand lit, douche et WC. |
| **Touriste** | Le petit-déjeuner est compris dans le prix de la chambre? |
| **Réceptionniste** | Ah non, Madame, c'est en plus: quatre euros par personne. |
| **Touriste** | Et à quelle heure servez-vous le petit-déjeuner? |
| **Réceptionniste** | À partir de 8 heures jusqu'à 9h.30. |
| **Touriste** | Vous servez le petit déjeuner dans la chambre? |
| **Réceptionniste** | Mais oui, Madame, bien sûr. |
| **Touriste** | Très bien. Pouvez-vous nous apporter le petit-déjeuner à 8h.30, s'il vous plaît? |
| **Réceptionniste** | C'est entendu, Madame. |
| **Touriste** | Et est-ce qu'il y a un ascenseur dans l'hôtel? Nos valises sont très lourdes. |
| **Réceptionniste** | Oui, au fond du couloir à droite. |
| **Touriste** | On peut prendre un repas dans l'hôtel? |
| **Réceptionniste** | Non, je regrette, nous ne servons que le petit-déjeuner mais il y a beaucoup de bons restaurants tout près d'ici. |

## Activity 4

Answer the following statements with **vrai** or **faux**:

| | vrai | faux |
|---|---|---|
| **a** Room 43 is on the third floor. | ☐ | ☐ |
| **b** Breakfast is included in the price. | ☐ | ☐ |
| **c** Breakfast is served from eight o'clock. | ☐ | ☐ |
| **d** Their suitcases are heavy. | ☐ | ☐ |
| **e** The lift is at the end of the corridor on the left. | ☐ | ☐ |
| **f** They serve only breakfast. | ☐ | ☐ |
| **g** There are a lot of restaurants nearby. | ☐ | ☐ |

## Activity 5

By surfing the Internet you found a central hotel in the 5th **arrondissement**. Judging from its description, it seems quiet and comfortable, which is just what you are looking for. You make your way there to book a room for two.

---

HOTELS UNIS
*de Paris*

# *Hôtel Relais*
# *Saint-Jacques*

★★★★

*3, rue de l'Abbé de l'Epée, 75005 Paris*
*Metro: Saint-Michel (4)*
*Luxembourg (RER B)*
*Tél: 33.(0) 1.53.73.26.00   Fax: 33.(0) 1.43.26.17.81*

HOTELS UNIS
*de Paris*

*A deux pas des Jardins du Luxembourg,*
*de la Sorbonne, du Panthéon, et de la*
*rue Mouffetard, sur une petite place calme,*
*cet hôtel de pur style Haussmannien fréquenté*
*jadis par le célèbre écrivain autrichien*
*Rilke, conjugue harmonieusement: luxe, confort,*
*raffinement, spiritualité.*

---

| | |
|---|---|
| **Vous** | *Say 'good evening' and ask if they have a room.* |
| **Réceptionniste** | Oui, qu'est-ce que vous voulez comme chambre? Une chambre pour une personne? |
| **Vous** | *Say 'no, a double room with two beds and a bathroom'.* |
| **Réceptionniste** | C'est pour combien de nuits? |
| **Vous** | *It's for three nights.* |
| **Réceptionniste** | Oui, j'ai une chambre avec salle de bains. |
| **Vous** | *How much is it?* |
| **Réceptionniste** | 96 €. |
| **Vous** | *Ask if breakfast is included.* |
| **Réceptionniste** | Oui, le petit-déjeuner est compris. |
| **Vous** | *Ask what time breakfast is served.* |
| **Réceptionniste** | Entre huit heures et dix heures. |
| **Vous** | *Ask if you can have a meal in the hotel.* |

**Réceptionniste**    Mais oui, bien sûr. Le restaurant est au premier
étage.

***Vous***    *Ask who Haussmann is.*

**Réceptionniste**    Il a transformé la ville de Paris au 19e siècle.

## *Se plaindre* Complaining

Things aren't always as they ought to be and you may have to
complain about things not working … **ne marche(ent) pas** or
things that are missing **il n'y a pas de ….** If the situation is really
bad you can always ask to speak to the **directeur** (manager).

### Activity 6

How would you explain to the **directeur** that some objects in
your room are not working (those in the square boxes) and
some are missing (those in the circles)?

l'eau chaude     le savon     les couvertures

le radiateur     la douche

la lampe     la télévision

les serviettes

## Au camping-caravaning At the caravan-campsite

**ℹ** Les offices du tourisme ont la liste des campings; ils peuvent vous aider à réserver un emplacement pour votre tente ou votre caravane.

## ▶ Dialogue 3

Un touriste vient d'arriver dans un camping-caravaning.

*A tourist has arrived at a caravan-campsite.*

| | |
|---|---|
| **Touriste** | Bonjour Madame. **Auriez-vous** un emplacement pour une voiture et une caravane … pour huit jours? |
| **Femme** | Pour huit jours? Oui, c'est possible. |
| **Touriste** | Il nous faut **un branchement électrique**. |
| **Femme** | Oui, sans problème. Vous avez **la carte du campeur** ou **une pièce d'identité**? |
| **Touriste** | J'ai mon passeport. |
| **Femme** | Excellent. J'en ai besoin pour noter votre nom et votre adresse. |
| **Touriste** | Le voilà. C'est combien la nuit? |
| **Femme** | Alors pour le forfait emplacement, 8,70 € la nuit. |
| **Touriste** | Forfait emplacement? |
| **Femme** | Oui, **c'est-à-dire** le prix pour l'emplacement de 90 m2; donc pour une voiture, une caravane et deux personnes. |
| **Touriste** | Il faut payer pour l'électricité? |
| **Femme** | Oui, c'est en plus: 1,70 € par nuit. Mais **par contre** pas de supplément pour l'eau chaude … **ni** pour les douches. |
| **Touriste** | C'est bien … On peut voir l'emplacement? |
| **Femme** | Bien sûr. **Il me reste** un **emplacement à l'ombre**, vous le voulez? |

| | |
|---|---|
| **auriez-vous …?** | *would you have?* |
| **branchement électrique** | *electric connection* |
| **la carte du campeur** | *camping carnet* |
| **la pièce d'identité** | *identification* |
| **c'est-à-dire** | *which means* |
| **par contre** | *on the other hand* |
| **(ni…) ni** | *(neither…) nor* |
| **il me reste …** | *I have got … left* |
| **l'emplacement à l'ombre** | *pitch in the shade* |

# L'alphabet français The French alphabet

When booking accommodation or tickets you may be asked to give your name: **votre nom?** or **(c'est) à quel nom?** and to spell it: **ça s'écrit comment?** or **vous pouvez épeler?**

## Activity 7

Read the alphabet below several times and practise spelling your name and your address.

| A | B | C | D | E | F | G |
|---|---|---|---|---|---|---|
| ah | bé | cé | dé | eux | eff | j'ai |
| H | I | J | K | L | M | N |
| ahsh | ee | j'y | kah | elle | emm | enne |
| O | P | Q | R | S | T | U |
| oh | pé | ku | erre | ess | té | u* |
| V | W | X | Y | Z | | |
| vé | doubl'vé | eeks | ee grec | zed | | |

*as in **du**

- To spell double consonants the French will say **deux** .... For example, to spell **mallet** they'll say: emm - ah - *deux - elle* - eux - té; and to spell **poussin**: pé - oh - u - *deux ess* - ee - enne
- Be particularly careful when spelling the French letters **e, i, g** and **j** as they can be confusing for English speakers.

## Activity 8

Michael Rice has just received a brochure on campsites from the tourist office in Cauterets in the Hautes-Pyrénées. He likes the look of 'Le Cabaliros' (page 119). Read its description, then fill in the statements below with one of the words in the box.

> meeting place  mountains  hot water  children
> forest  advisable  river

**a** The camping is near a _____ and a _____.
**b** It is surrounded by _____.
**c** You can have free and unlimited _____ in all washbasins, showers and other points.

**d** There is a playing area for _____ and a _____ with fireplace, television, phone.

**e** It is _____ to reserve during July and August.

## LE CABALIROS**
### Pont de Secours 65110 CAUTERETS
### Tel. 05 62 92 55 36
### Fax 05 62 92 55 36
### Camping Qualité Plus

Directeur : M. BOYRIE Jean

Situé en bordure de rivière et de forêt, dans un environnement de montagne, tout le confort : eau chaude pour tous les lavabos, douches et point de puisage (à volonté et en permanence). Emplacements confort 3 points. Congélation, jeux pour enfants, salle de rencontre (cheminée, télévision, points phone), baby-change, cabine handicapé, camping-car. Réservations juillet-août conseillées.

| | |
|---|---|
| Date d'ouverture | 01/06/03 → 30/09/03 |
| Caravaneige | |
| Nombre emplacement | 100 |
| Bibliothèque | • |
| Machine à laver | • |
| Repassage | • |
| Caravane à louer | |
| Emplacement à l'année | |

# *Écrire des lettres* Writing letters

## *Réserver une chambre* Booking accommodation

**i** Si vous avez l'intention de faire du camping ou de réserver un hôtel en France, il vaut mieux (*it's better*) réserver longtemps à l'avance surtout pendant les périodes de vacances. Si vous réservez par téléphone, le gérant/la gérante de l'hôtel vous demandera de confirmer par écrit (*confirm by writing*) et de verser des arrhes ou un acompte (*and ask you for an advance*).

## Activity 9

Mrs Osborne writes to Mme Noguère, the owner of the Hotel 'Les Edelweiss', to book a two-night stay for herself and her husband in Cauterets. Read her letter as well as Mme Noguère's answer below and answer the questions on page 121.

Madame,

Je voudrais réserver une chambre double avec douche en 1/2 pension pour deux pour les nuits du 8 et 9 juillet prochains. Serait-il possible d'avoir une chambre avec vue sur le jardin et une place dans votre parking pour notre voiture?

Je vous prie de bien vouloir m'indiquer vos prix et de me confirmer la réservation par écrit.

Dans l'attente de vous lire, recevez, Madame, mes salutations les meilleures.

*Susan Osborne*

*Madam,*

*I would like to book a double room with shower, half board, for the nights of 8 and 9 July. Would it be possible to have a room looking on to the garden as well as a space in the car park?*

*I would be grateful if you would let me know your charges and send me a written confirmation of the booking.*

*Looking forward to hearing from you,*

*Yours faithfully,*

*Susan Osborne*

HOTEL "LES EDELWEISS" ★★ N.N.
M. et Mme Jean-Claude Noguère

7, BOULEVARD LATAPIE-FLURIN - 65110 CAUTERETS
TEL. : 05 62 92 52 75  -  FAX : 05 62 92 62 73

14 Sydney Street
Brighton BN1 4EH
East Sussex – UK

Cauterets, le 25 avril 2003

<u>A l'attention de Madame Susan Osborne.</u>

Madame,

Pour faire suite à votre demande, nous vous confirmons votre réservation pour les nuits du 8 et 9 juillet 2003.

Nous vous proposons une chambre double avec douche, WC, T.V. et téléphone, au deuxième étage, avec balcon donnant sur le jardin. En chambre + petit-déjeuner: 112€ pour le séjour, pour les deux personnes. En demi-pension: 168€ pour le séjour, pour les deux personnes. Taxe de séjour en plus 1€ par jour et par personne. Une place de parking (gratuit) de l'hôtel sera réservée pour votre voiture.

Nous vous demandons de nous faire parvenir un chèque d'arrhes international de 11€ pour confirmer cette réservation.

Avec nos remerciements, nous vous prions d'agréer, Madame, l'expression de nos meilleurs sentiments.

*V. Noguère*

a  Does Mrs Osborne obtain what she requested?
b  What is the total amount that she will have to pay?
c  What does Mme Noguère ask Mrs Osborne to do?

## Mini-test

How do you say in French:

1  I'm looking for a two-star hotel.
2  Can you book a room for me?
3  Is breakfast included?
4  There's no telephone in the room.
5  Is there a campsite near here?

# 13

## bien manger, bien boire

eating and drinking well

**In this unit you will**
- find out where to eat
- practise ordering a snack
- choose a menu and order a meal

# Before you start, revise

- saying what you want (page 62)
- the verb **prendre** (page 42)
- some, any (page 13)
- asking questions (page 39)
- likes and dislikes (page 74)

## *Bien manger* Eating well

L'art de bien vivre en France: **www.realfrance.com**

ℹ️ La cuisine en France est très variée, chaque région offrant ses produits et spécialités gastronomiques. Grâce à sa population importante d'immigrés, la France a une cuisine ethnique riche et relativement bon marché. On peut également acheter un peu partout du fast-food et **des plats à emporter** dans des McDonald's, Pizza Hut etc. Par contre, les restaurants végétariens sont rares, ainsi que les menus qui incluent des plats végétariens.

On peut très bien manger en France dans des restaurants modestes appelés **les petits restaurants du coin**. Au menu ils ont souvent des plats simples mais appétissants comme un pâté maison et **un plat garni**.

On peut aussi manger dans **une brasserie** et commander un plat unique comme **la choucroute** avec de la bière; ou encore dans **un bistrot** où on choisira entre un bifteck-frites, une excellente spécialité et **le plat du jour**; ou pour pas cher dans une **crêperie**, un bar ou un café.

Les restaurants proposent en général plusieurs **menus**, du plus cher, 'le menu gastronomique', au plus modeste, 'le menu touristique' et **la carte**.

**Le pourboire** est toujours inclus (15 %) dans l'addition. Si vous êtes satisfait, vous pouvez laisser quelques euros à la personne qui vous a servi.

| | |
|---|---|
| **le plat à emporter** | *take-away food* |
| **le petit restaurant du coin** | *local restaurant offering good but cheap food* |
| **le plat garni** | *dish with meat and vegetable or salad* |

| | |
|---|---|
| **la brasserie** | cross between a café and a restaurant |
| **la choucroute** | cabbage, bacon, sausages, potatoes |
| **le bistrot** | cheap restaurant |
| **le plat du jour** | today's special |
| **la crêperie** | pancake house |
| **le menu** | list of dishes served at a fixed price for the whole meal |
| **la carte** | list of dishes individually priced |
| **le pourboire** | tip |

## Activity 1

Without looking at the passage above, choose the correct phrase to complete the sentences below then check your answers in the **Key to the exercises** at the end of the book.

a French cuisine consists only of *regional specialities/a variety of cuisines*.

b Fast-food and take-away food *can easily/cannot be found*.

c **Les petits restaurants du coin** are usually *cheap/expensive*.

d **Un plat garni** is a dish with *meat only/meat, vegetables or noodles*.

e In a **brasserie** one can eat *pancakes/a limited range of dishes*.

f **Le plat du jour** is *'today's special'/a dish with cold food*.

g If you want a pancake you go to a *crêperie/bar*.

h If you want the cheapest menu, you choose the *menu gastronomique/le menu touristique*.

## Key words and phrases

| | |
|---|---|
| **vous désirez?** | what will you have? |
| **vous avez choisi?** | have you made a choice? |
| **qu'est-ce que vous avez ...** | what do you have ... |
| **à manger?** | to eat? |
| **à boire?** | to drink? |
| **qu'est-ce que vous avez comme boissons/snacks** | what do you have in the way of drinks/snacks |
| **il ne reste plus de ...** | there is no ... left |
| **il n'y a plus de ...** | there is no more |
| **des sandwiches au jambon/ au fromage** | ham/cheese sandwiches |

| | |
|---|---|
| une glace à la vanille | vanilla ice-cream |
| de la bière en bouteille | bottled beer |
| de la pression | draught beer |
| un café | a black coffee |
| un café crème | a white coffee (with milk not cream) |
| un thé au citron | lemon tea |
| un thé nature | tea (without milk, etc...) |
| un thé avec du lait froid | tea with cold milk |
| une orange pressée | freshly-squeezed orange |
| un jus de fruit | fruit juice |
| un jus de pomme/d'ananas/ de pamplemousse | apple/pineapple/ grapefruit juice |
| qu'est-ce que c'est le/la/les ...? | what's the ...? |
| je vais en prendre un (une) | I'll take one |
| pour commencer ... | to start with ... |
| ensuite ... | then ... |
| comme dessert ... | for dessert ... |
| le plat | dish, course |
| le plat cuisiné | ready-cooked meal |
| plats à emporter | take-away food |
| saignant/bleu | rare (lit. bleeding/blue) |
| à point | medium |
| bien cuit | well done |
| l'addition (f) | the bill |

## ▶ Dialogue 1: *Commander un snack* Ordering a snack

À la terrasse d'un café deux touristes sont prêts à commander.

*Two tourists sitting outside a café are ready to order.*

*The man asks the waiter what a **croque-monsieur** is. Listen to or read the waiter's explanations: how would you explain to someone English what a **croque-monsieur** is? What is the woman ordering? What drinks are they having?*

**Garçon** Bonjour, Messieurs-dames. Qu'est-ce que vous désirez?

**Homme** Qu'est-ce que vous avez à manger?

**Garçon** À manger, nous avons des sandwiches au jambon blanc, **rillettes**, pâté de campagne, saucisson sec, hot-dogs, omelettes, croque-monsieur ...

**Homme** Qu'est-ce que c'est un croque-monsieur?

| Garçon | Un croque-monsieur? C'est deux **tranches de pain grillé** avec jambon et fromage **au milieu**. |
| Homme | **Ça a l'air** délicieux … je vais en prendre un. |
| Garçon | Et pour vous Madame? |
| Femme | Moi, je crois que je vais prendre une omelette … qu'est-ce que vous avez comme omelettes? |
| Garçon | Omelettes au fromage, aux **champignons**, aux herbes … |
| Femme | Une omelette aux champignons. |
| Garçon | Et comme boissons, Messieurs-dames? |
| Homme | Vous avez de la bière? |
| Garçon | Oui … nous avons de la bière pression et de la Kronenbourg en bouteille. |
| Homme | Bon, une pression s'il vous plaît. |
| Garçon | Je vous sers **un demi**? |
| Homme | Oui, c'est ça. |
| Femme | Moi, je vais prendre un café crème. |
| Garçon | Bon, alors une pression, un café crème, une omelette aux champignons et un croque-monsieur. |
| Homme | Merci bien, Monsieur. |

| | |
|---|---|
| **rillettes** | *type of potted meat, usually pork, similar to pâté* |
| **tranche de pain grillé** | *slice of toasted bread* |
| **au milieu** | *in the middle* |
| **ça a l'air** | *it seems* |
| **les champignons** | *mushrooms* |
| **un demi** | *half (usually half a pint, but sometimes half a litre)* |

## Activity 2

See if you can unscramble the dialogue below, starting with the sentence in bold:

a  Je vais prendre une pression.

b  À manger nous avons des sandwiches, des croque-monsieur, des pizzas …

**c  Bonjour Monsieur, qu'est-ce que vous désirez?**

d  De la pression et de la Kronenbourg en bouteille.

e  Qu'est-ce que vous avez à manger?

f  Je vais prendre une pizza; et comme bières, qu'est-ce que vous avez?

## Activity 3

Using the menu below and dialogue in Activity 4 as a guide, act out similar situations varying the dishes and drinks. (The answers are not given in the **Key to the exercises**.)

### Salades composées

| | |
|---|---|
| Salade mixte .............................6,00 | Chef salade ...........................8,00 |
| Tomates, salade, oeuf | Tomates, pommes à l'huile, jambon, gruyère, salade, oeuf dur |
| Salade végétarienne .................6,50 | |
| Tomates, poivron, maïs, carotte concombre, salade | Salade niçoise ......................8,50 Tomates, oeuf, thon, poivrons, concombre, olives, salade, anchois |

### Buffet chaud

Croque monsieur ......................4,00
Croque madame........................4,50
Croque niçois ...........................4,80
   Croque monsieur avec tomate et anchois

### Buffet froid

Poulet froid mayonnaise.............7,50
Asseitte charcuterie ............8,00
Assiette anglaise...................8,00
Assiette de viande froide .............8,00

### Buffet chaud

Omelette nature (3 pièces) ..........4,00
Omelette jambon ......................4,80
Omelette fromage ......................4,80
Omelette savoyarde...................5,20
Omelette parmentier .................5,20

### Sandwiches

Jambon de paris ..................3,50
Paté ou rillettes ....................3,80
Camembert ou gruyère ............3,80
Saucisson sec ou à l'ail ...........3,80

### Boissons

Café express...............................2,20
Thé au citron .............................3,20
Jus de fruit ...............................3,30
Bière pression ...........................3,20
Bière bouteille ...........................3,40
Eau minérale .............................3,30
Soda.........................................3,30
Apéritif anisé .............................4,00

## Activity 4

You're hungry and decide to go to a café for a snack. Here comes the waiter ... be prepared to order:

**Garçon**  Qu'est-ce que vous désirez?
**a  Vous**  *Say that you would like a croque-monsieur.*
**Garçon**  Je suis désolé, Monsieur, mais il n'y en a plus.
**b  Vous**  *Ask him if he has any omelettes.*

**Garçon** Oui, nous avons omelettes nature, jambon et Parmentier.

**c Vous** *Ask what Parmentier is.*

**Garçon** Omelette Parmentier? C'est une omelette avec des pommes de terre.

**d Vous** *Say that you'll take the potato omelette.*

**Garçon** Bien, alors une omelette Parmentier; et à boire, Monsieur, qu'est-ce que je vous sers?

**e Vous** *Ask him what he has in the way of fruit juice* (the **s** of **jus** is not pronounced).

**Garçon** Comme jus de fruit nous avons du jus d'orange, du jus d'ananas, du jus de pamplemousse …

**f Vous** *Say that you would like a pineapple juice and the bill, please.*

# ▶ Dialogue 2: *Au restaurant* At the restaurant

*Having found a nearby restaurant on the website http://www.pariscope.fr, a tourist decides to go to 'La Poule au Pot'. Listen carefully to the recording. What menu does the customer choose? How does he want his meat? What does he want for dessert?*

| | |
|---|---|
| **Customer** | Vous avez **une table** pour une personne? |
| **Garçon** | Oui, Monsieur. Il y a une place **là-bas près de la fenêtre**. |
| **Garçon** | (*later*) Alors Monsieur, qu'est-ce que vous prenez? Nous avons un excellent plat du jour. C'est une blanquette de veau. |
| **Customer** | Qu'est-ce que c'est une blanquette de veau? |
| **Garçon** | C'est du veau en sauce blanche ... c'est très bon. |
| **Customer** | Ah non, je n'aime pas les viandes en sauce. |
| **Garçon** | Si vous préférez les **grillades, je vous conseille** le menu à 20€; pour commencer **hors d'oeuvre** et charcuterie à **volonté**, puis ensuite, **au choix**, steak au poivre ou **truite meunière**. |
| **Customer** | Très bien. Le menu à 20€ avec steak. |
| **Garçon** | Vous le voulez comment votre steak, saignant, à point ou bien cuit? |
| **Customer** | Bien cuit, s'il vous plaît. |
| **Garçon** | Et comme légumes nous avons **des petits pois, des haricots verts** et puis des frites. |
| **Customer** | Des frites ... |
| **Garçon** | Et comme boisson? Qu'est-ce que je vous sers? **Un pichet** de vin rouge? |
| **Customer** | Oui, un demi-litre de vin rouge et de l'eau minérale. |
| **Garçon** | Très bien. (*later*) **C'était bon?** |
| **Customer** | Très bon, merci. Qu'est-ce que vous avez comme desserts? |
| **Garçon** | Fromage, glace vanille, tarte aux abricots ou crème au caramel. |
| **Customer** | Je vais prendre une glace à la vanille et un express. (*later*) Monsieur, l'addition, s'il vous plaît. |

| une table | a table |
| là-bas près de la fenêtre | over there near the window |
| la grillade | grilled meat |
| je vous conseille | I advise you, I recommend to you |
| hors-d'oeuvre | starter |
| à volonté | at will, of your choice |
| au choix | as you wish |
| truite meunière | trout fried in butter |
| petits pois | peas |
| haricots verts | green beans |
| le pichet | jug, pitcher |
| c'était bon | it was good |

## Activity 5

After looking at the dialogue how would you say:

a  What's a **blanquette de veau**?
b  I don't like meat in sauce.
c  I prefer grilled meats.
d  I would like my steak well cooked.
e  In the way of vegetables, I'll have some green beans.
f  Half a litre of red wine.
g  For dessert, I'll have a cream caramel.

## Activity 6

Now it's your turn to order a meal. When you check your answers in the **Key to the exercises**, remember that there are variations to the answers given.

**Serveuse**  Bonjour, Monsieur/Madame, vous avez choisi?
**a  You**  Say that to start with you'll have a **filet de hareng**.
**Serveuse**  Je regrette, il n'y a plus de filet de hareng.
**b  You**  Say that you'll have an **avocat à la vinaigrette**.
**Serveuse**  Bien, un avocat à la vinaigrette, et ensuite …
**c  You**  Ask what is **cassoulet**.
**Serveuse**  C'est une spécialité française avec de la viande de porc et haricots blancs.
**d  You**  Say that you don't like beans. Say you'll have the **grillade du jour** with **frites**.
**Serveuse**  Vous la voulez comment, votre viande?
**e  You**  Say medium and say that you would also like a bottle of Sauvignon.

**Serveuse** (*after the starter*) Voilà. Une grillade avec frites.

**f** *You* *Ask for bread.*

**Serveuse** Encore du pain? Oui Monsieur/Madame, tout de suite.

## Activity 7

You are on holiday in 'Les Landes' with your friend and her three children. You want to take them out on Friday for a nice meal. Look at the restaurants below. Which one will you choose? Obviously, price needs to be considered plus the fact the children are boisterous. Luckily they eat any type of food!

---

BAR – TABACS - AUBERGE

## LE PLATANE

Place de la République, 40300 PEYREHORADE

TÉL. 05 57 37 66 54

Service de 12 h à 14.30 et de 19 h à 22 h

MENU du jour 14€

Dimanche menus du jour de 15€ à 24€ + CARTE

Traiteur – Cuisine régionale
et traditionnelle. Plats à emporter.
Banquets, mariages, séminaires, Groupe.

---

## L'AUBERGE AU BON COIN

**40230 SAUBRIGUES**

**TÉL. 05 58 94 71 33**

Service de 12 h à 14 h et de 19 h 30 à 22 h

MENUS: 13€ – 18€ – 23€ – 28€

CARTE: 14€ à 25€

MENU ENFANT: 8€

Fermeture: hors saison lundi soir et mardi

Cuisine traditionnelle,
spécialités régionales, dans un cadre typique
et familial au calme de la campagne landaise. Grande
capacité d'accueil, service en terrasse l'été. Grand parking.

# Mini-test

You can now test yourself on Units 11, 12 and 13.

1 How would you say:
   a Where is the nearest restaurant?
   b I'm looking for something cheaper.
   c Do you have anything else?

2 You are asked to spell your name. Choose the French equivalent:
   a Ça s'écrit comment?
   b C'est à quel nom?
   c Est-ce qu'il reste encore des chambres?

3 How would you say:
   a There are no more cheese sandwiches.
   b For dessert, I'll have a vanilla ice cream.
   c What drinks do you have?

# 14 les transports publics
## public transport

**In this unit you will**
- find out about public transport in France
- learn key expressions to make travelling by bus, taxi, train and underground easier
- find out how to ask for information

# Before you start, revise

- finding out what's available (page 13)
- asking for and understanding directions (page 50)
- expressions of time, days of the week **Key words and phrases** (page 36)
- numbers (page 224)

## Key words and phrases

| où est-ce que je peux ...? | where can I ...? |
|---|---|
| où est-ce qu'il faut ...? | where do you have to...? |
| il faut monter, descendre | you have to get on, get off |
| arriver, quitter | arrive, leave |
| changer | change |
| voyager | travel |
| composter le billet | date-stamp the ticket |
| réserver une couchette | book a sleeper |
| le billet/ticket | ticket |
| le carnet (de tickets) | set of ten tickets |
| c'est quelle direction? | which line (lit. 'direction') is it? |
| c'est direct? | is it direct? |
| le trajet, le voyage | travel, journey |
| de jour, de nuit | in the daytime, overnight |
| dans la matinée, soirée | in the morning, evening |
| le métro | the underground |
| le RER (réseau express | fast extension of the métro to |
| régional) | the suburbs of Paris |
| la banlieue | the suburbs |
| desservir | to serve |
| la station de métro | tube station |
| la correspondance | connection |
| la sortie | exit |
| le taxi | taxi |
| la station de taxis | taxi rank |
| l'autobus (m) (bus) | town bus |
| l'autocar (m) (car) | coach/long distance bus |
| la gare routière | bus station |
| l'arrêt (m) d'autobus | bus stop |
| c'est quelle ligne? | what number (bus) is it? |
| la SNCF (Société Nationale | French railways |
| des Chemins de Fer) | |
| la gare | station (train) |

| le guichet | ticket office |
| une place | a seat (also square, as in **place du Marché**) |
| un aller (simple) | single ticket |
| un aller-retour | return ticket |
| le plein tarif | full fare |
| le bureau de renseignements | information office |
| la consigne | left luggage |
| consigne automatique | left luggage lockers |
| un horaire | timetable |
| la période de pointe | peak times |
| le prochain/dernier train | the next/last train |
| en première/seconde classe | first/second class |
| dans le train | on the train |
| le quai | platform |
| la voie | track (often used for 'platform' instead of **quai**) |
| au-delà | beyond |

# *Le Métro parisien* The Paris underground

RATP: **www.ratp.fr**

Le métro parisien est très pratique et économique. Avec un seul ticket (1,30€), vous pouvez aller n'importe où (*anywhere*) dans Paris. Si vous achetez les tickets par carnet ils coûtent moins cher (dix tickets pour 9,60€).

Pour découvrir Paris et sa région d'Ile-de-France en métro, bus, RER et trains SNCF, achetez 'Paris Visite', un forfait transport (*travel pass*), valable un, deux, trois ou cinq jours consécutifs. Il permet également de bénéficier de réductions sur l'entrée de nombreux sites touristiques de la capitale.

Le métro a 14 lignes identifiables par leur numéro et leurs directions (les deux stations terminus). Pour changer d'une ligne à l'autre, suivez les panneaux oranges 'Correspondance' et le nom de la ligne que vous désirez prendre. Du métro vous pouvez passer facilement au RER. C'est un métro ultra-rapide avec cinq lignes (A, B, C, D et E) qui dessert Paris et sa banlieue. Il faut payer un supplément si vous prenez le RER, au-delà de la zone 2.

## Activity 1

Answer the following assertions with **vrai** or **faux**:

|   |   | vrai | faux |
|---|---|------|------|
| a | There is a flat rate in central Paris. | ☐ | ☐ |
| b | A set of ten tickets is more expensive than ten single tickets. | ☐ | ☐ |
| c | One can buy a tourist pass for ten days. | ☐ | ☐ |
| d | Each line is known by one name. | ☐ | ☐ |
| e | **Correspondance** is the sign to look for to change line. | ☐ | ☐ |
| f | To go on the RER you may pay more. | ☐ | ☐ |

## Activity 2

Look at the diagram below then complete the dialogue filling the blank spaces with the words in the box. The tourist is standing at the Charles de Gaulle – Étoile station.

**Touriste** Pardon Monsieur, c'est quelle **a** ........ pour la gare du Nord?

**Homme** La gare de Nord? Vous **b**........ le RER D direction Melun.

**Touriste** C'est direct?

**Homme** Non, il faut **c** ........ à Châtelet Les Halles.

**Touriste** Bon je change à Châtelet Les Halles et puis?

**Homme** Puis vous prenez le RER B ou D, directions **d** ........ ou Orry-la-Vallée et voilà vous **e** ........ à la station suivante, gare du Nord.

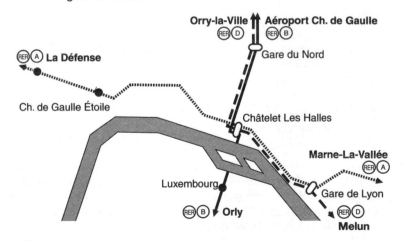

## ▶ Activity 3

An Englishman cannot understand the directions he's given to get from the **Gare de Lyon** to the **station Luxembourg**. Listen to the recording (if you haven't got it look at the diagram on page 136) and tell him in English what to do.

## *Prendre un taxi* Taking a taxi

ℹ️ In all big towns you can find a taxi in the taxi ranks (**stations de taxis**) or hail them in the streets – they can easily be identified by the light on their roof. There is an extra charge (from one to two Euros) for picking up from a station, airport, for transporting luggage, a fourth passager or an animal. The usual tip – **le pourboire** – is 10 %.

## ▶ Dialogue 1: *La station de taxis* The taxi rank

*Listen carefully to the recordings, or read below, then answer the following questions:*

*The tourist doesn't get any information from the first passer-by: why? How far is the taxi rank? At the crossroads does he have to go right or straight on?*

**Touriste**  Pardon, Monsieur, où est la station de taxis la plus proche?

**Homme**  Je ne sais pas, je ne suis pas d'ici ...
(*Later ...*)

**Touriste**  S'il vous plaît, Madame, savez-vous où il y a une station de taxis?

**Femme**  Mais oui, c'est très simple, vous en avez une, à 500 mètres, à côté de la gare du Nord.

**Touriste**  La gare du Nord, c'est où exactement?

**Femme**  Bon, il faut d'abord monter le boulevard Magenta. Au carrefour, vous allez continuer tout droit et prendre le boulevard Denain et à droite de la gare du Nord vous allez trouver la station de taxis.

## Activity 4

Would you be able to find the taxi rank? Choose the correct word:

**a Il faut monter** means
   i turn  ii go up  iii cross

**b Un carrefour** is
   i crossroads  ii traffics light  iii sign post

**c Vous continuez tout droit** means
   i turn left  ii turn right  iii carry straight on

# *Voyager en autobus* Travelling by bus

> Information on Eurolines: **www.eurolines.fr**
> Gare routière internationale de Paris: 01 49 72 51 51

**i** In Paris, the same tickets are used on the metro and on the bus. They can be purchased at metro stations and in some tobacconists (look for the **Tabac** sign). You will find a bus route map and details at each bus stop. One ticket only is necessary unless you use several different buses.

# ▶ Dialogue 2: *À la gare routière* At the bus station

| | |
|---|---|
| **Touriste** | Pardon, Monsieur, c'est quelle ligne pour aller au musée d'Orsay? |
| **Homme** | La ligne 49 … |
| **Touriste** | C'est direct? |
| **Homme** | Non, il faut changer; vous descendez aux Invalides puis vous pouvez prendre la ligne 63 ou bien vous y allez à pied. |
| **Touriste** | C'est loin à pied? |
| **Homme** | Des Invalides? Non, **il vous faudra** une quinzaine de minutes. |
| **Touriste** | Le bus part à quelle heure? |
| **Homme** | Dans dix minutes. |
| **Touriste** | Et … où est-ce que je peux acheter un ticket? |

| Homme | Au guichet là-bas ... |
|---|---|
| Touriste | (*later*) Je voudrais acheter un ticket aller-retour pour les Invalides. |
| Femme | Il n'y a pas de tickets aller-retour. Achetez deux tickets ou bien alors un carnet, c'est plus pratique et moins cher. |
| Touriste | Un carnet, qu'est-ce que c'est? |
| Femme | C'est dix tickets pour le prix de sept. |
| Touriste | Très bien. Je vais prendre un carnet. |

---

**il vous faudra ...**    *it will take you ...*

---

# ▶ Dialogue 3: *Être dans le bon autobus* On the right bus

| Touriste | Ce bus va bien aux Invalides? |
|---|---|
| Chauffeur | Oui, c'est bien ça. |
| Touriste | Vous pouvez me dire où il faut descendre? |
| Chauffeur | Oui, bien sûr mais c'est très facile, c'est l'arrêt où il y a un grand monument avec un dôme. |
| Touriste | Euh ... oui mais je ne connais pas Paris. |

## Activity 5

How would you say:

a  What bus number goes to the musée d'Orsay?
b  Is it direct?
c  Is it far on foot?
d  At what time does the bus leave?
e  Where can I buy a ticket?
f  I would like to buy a return ticket to les Invalides.
g  I'll take a set of tickets.

# *La SNCF* French railways

**i** In France, tickets must be stamped by each passenger at the point of departure using one of the **composteurs** (machine in which you have to insert your ticket). You will be fined if you board a train without having done so.

**www.sncf.fr**
01 53 90 20 20 for suburban services
**www.voyages-sncf.com**

When travelling on TGV (**train grande vitesse**) or Eurostar, you need to reserve a seat; when travelling on the other SNCF lines you are advised to do so, particularly at the beginning and the end of school holidays.

# ▶ Dialogue 4: *Au bureau de renseignements* At the information office

*We are in the information office in la Gare de Lyon. A man inquires about trains. Listen to the recording or read the dialogue. Try to answer the following questions: Where does the man want to go? Which train does he want to catch? Does he need to reserve his seat? How much is his ticket? Can he eat on the train?*

**Homme**    Bonjour, Madame, je voudrais un aller pour Marseille.

**Hôtesse**   Marseille … bon. Vous voyagez quel jour?

**Homme**    Le 10 juin … un samedi.

**Hôtesse**   A quelle heure voulez-vous quitter Paris?

**Homme**    Dans la matinée.

**Hôtesse**   Bon, vous avez quatre TGV: le premier est à 10.48, le second à 11.06, le troisième à 12.06 …

**Homme**    **Celui de** 11.06 **me convient** très bien.

**Hôtesse**   Il quitte Paris gare de Lyon à 11.06 et arrive à Marseille à 15.24. La réservation est obligatoire.

**Homme**    D'accord … bon alors … **il met un peu plus de** quatre heures?

**Hôtesse**   Oui, c'est bien ça.

**Homme**    C'est combien l'aller simple?

**Hôtesse**   Vous avez une réduction?

**Homme**    Non, je n'ai plus de jeunes enfants, je ne suis pas **assez vieux** pour avoir une carte senior… et je ne suis pas militaire!

**Hôtesse**   OK … alors en 1ère ou en 2ème classe?

**Homme**    Quelle est la différence?

| Hôtesse | Alors en première classe, le billet simple plein tarif coûte 94€; en seconde classe euh ... 69€, la réservation **étant incluse** dans le prix. |
| --- | --- |
| Homme | Bon, je vais voyager en seconde classe. On peut manger dans le train? |
| Hôtesse | Oui, bien sûr... vous avez une voiture-bar où vous pouvez acheter des sandwiches, des salades ou des **plats cuisinés** ainsi que des boissons chaudes et fraîches. |
| Homme | Bon, alors pour la réservation ... |
| Hôtesse | Alors ... place fumeur ou non fumeur ... |
| Homme | Non fumeur et près du couloir. |

| | |
| --- | --- |
| **celui de ... me convient** | *the one at ... suits me* |
| **il met un peu plus de ...** | *it takes a bit more than ...* |
| **assez vieux** | *old enough* |
| **étant incluse** | *being included* |
| **plats cuisinés** | *hot food* |

## Activity 6

| Choisissez votre horaire (heures locales) | | | | | |
| --- | --- | --- | --- | --- | --- |
| ALLER | départ | | arrivée | type de train | niveau de prix |
| **Choix 1** *(4h26mn)* | MARSEILLE ST CHARLES | 09:04 | PARIS GARE DE LYON 13:30 | TGV Réservation obligatoire | * |
| **Choix 2** *(4h28mn)* | MARSEILLE ST CHARLES | 11:12 | PARIS GARE DE LYON 15:40 | TGV Réservation obligatoire | * |
| **Choix 3** *(8h15mn)* | MARSEILLE ST CHARLES | 11:30 | PARIS BERCY 19:45 | Auto train Réservation recommandée | – |
| **Choix 4** *(10h54mn)* | MARSEILLE ST CHARLES | 12:09 | PARIS GARE DE LYON 23:03 | TGV Réservation recommandée | – |
| **Choix 5** *(4h23mn)* | MARSEILLE ST CHARLES | 12:35 | PARIS GARE DE LYON 16:58 | TGV Réservation obligatoire | * |

*Signale un TGV circulant en période de pointe.

Source: SNCF 2000

Before taking the part of the traveller in this conversation, look at the Marseille–Paris timetable accessible on the SNCF website. How many TGVs are leaving Marseille in the morning?

| a **Vous** | *Ask for a return to Paris.* |
| --- | --- |
| **Employé** | Oui, un aller-retour. Vous voulez partir quel jour? |
| b **Vous** | *Say on the 24th June, in the morning, around 9 a.m.* |
| **Employé** | Alors vous avez un train à 9.04 qui arrive à 12.30 et un autre à 11.12 qui... |

| | |
|---|---|
| c **Vous** | *Say that you will take the first one at 9.04. Ask how much the ticket in second class is.* |
| **Employé** | Vous avez des réductions? |
| d **Vous** | *Say 'no'.* |
| **Employé** | Alors un aller-retour, Marseille-Paris, en seconde classe, tarif plein … 138€. |
| e **Vous** | *Find out if you need to reserve your seat.* |
| **Employé** | Oui, et la réservation est incluse dans le prix. |

# Mini-test

Test yourself to find out how much you can remember from Units 13 and 14.

How would you say:

1 I would like a cheese sandwich?
2 What do you have to drink?
3 I would like a set of ten tickets?
4 At what time does the next train to Paris leave?

# 15

## faire du tourisme

### tourisme

sightseeing

**In this unit you will**

- learn how to ask for a town map
- find out about visiting interesting places
- practise buying admission tickets
- find out about museums in France
- book an excursion

# Before you start, revise

- saying what you want (page 62)
- asking and understanding directions (page 50)
- asking what you can do (page 39)
- expressions of time, days of the week **Key words and phrases** (page 36)

## Key words and phrases

| | |
|---|---|
| le plan de la ville | *town map* |
| les environs | *surroundings* |
| qu'est-ce qu'il y a à faire? | *what is there to do?* |
| qu'est-ce qu'il y a à voir? | *what is there to see?* |
| une visite guidée | *guided tour* |
| les jours fériés/les jours de fête | *public holidays* |
| l'entrée | *way in, admission charge* |
| en pleine saison | *in high season* |
| le tarif réduit, plein tarif | *reduced rate, full rate* |
| accès (m) gratuit | *free entry* |
| nocturne | *late-night opening* |
| hors saison | *out of season* |
| le musée | *museum* |
| faire une excursion | *to go on an excursion* |
| pique-niquer | *to picnic* |
| une agence de voyages | *travel agency* |

## *Se renseigner sur les choses à voir*
## Getting information on things to see

- Fédération Nationale des Offices de Tourisme et Syndicats d'Initiative: **www.tourisme.fr**
- Office de Tourisme à Paris: **www.paris-touristoffice.com**
- Visites guidées en autocar ou en minibus à Paris: **www.cityrama.com, www.touringscope.com**
- Croisières sur la Seine: **www.vedettesdeparis.com**
- Croisières sur les canaux: **www.pariscanal.com**
- D'autres sites utiles:
  **www.paris.org**
  **www.maison-de-la-france.fr**
  **www.guideweb.com** (sur les régions françaises)

www.realfrance.com (informations sur l'art de vivre, l'art de la table, l'art et la culture et l'art de voyager)
www.skifrance.fr (informations sur les stations de ski, etc.)

**i** Dès votre arrivée dans une ville ou une région, rendez-vous à l'office de tourisme le plus proche pour demander un plan ainsi que des brochures sur la ville et ses environs. Son personnel multilingue répondra à toutes vos questions sur les hébergements, visites, musées, loisirs, manifestations culturelles, circuits touristiques ...

# ▶ Dialogue 1: *À l'office du tourisme* At the tourist office

*Listen to the recording or read the dialogue below. Can you name at least three things the tourist could see or do?*

**Touriste**  Bonjour, Madame, je voudrais un plan de la ville, s'il vous plaît.

**Hôtesse**  Oui, voilà.

**Touriste**  Nous ne sommes pas d'ici. Qu'est-ce qu'il y a à voir à Orléans?

**Hôtesse**  Il y a beaucoup de monuments historiques, surtout dans la vieille ville, comme la maison de Jeanne d'Arc, au numéro 52 sur le plan, à côté de la cathédrale Sainte-Croix; et puis il y a une belle promenade à faire le long de la Loire. Du pont George V, vous avez une vue magnifique sur la Loire.

**Touriste**  Et qu'est-ce qu'il y a à faire pour les enfants?

**Hôtesse**  Près d'ici, il y a une piscine couverte ou même le Musée des sciences naturelles qui se trouve rue Emile Zola. Un peu plus loin, vous avez le Parc Floral.

**Touriste**  Et pour aller au Parc Floral ... il y a un bus?

**Hôtesse**  Oui, vous avez un autobus toutes les 30 minutes. Il part du centre ville, place du Martroi.

## Activity 1

**a**  How would you ask for a town map?
**b**  Ask what there is to see.
**c**  Ask what there is to do for the children.
**d**  Ask if there is an indoor swimming pool.
**e**  Ask if there is a bus to go to the *Parc Floral*.

## Activity 2

The Wilsons want to visit the *Parc Floral*, a 35 hectare designed landscape garden near Orléans, on their way to the South of France. Read the brochure below and answer the questions.

a Would the visit be enjoyable for their seven-year-old boy?

b Can they eat there?

c They intend to visit the park in the summer months. What will they be able to see besides the gardens?

---

- PETIT TRAIN
- PARC ANIMALIER
- AIRE DE JEUX
- GOLF MINIATURE
- BOUTIQUES
- AIRE DE PIQUE-NIQUE

- ANIMATIONS
  PÉDAGOGIQUES
- VISITES GUIDÉES
  (sur réservation) :
  15 personnes
  minimum

- JARDIN
  DE LA SOURCE

### LES RENDEZ-VOUS
# 2000

**TOUT LE MOIS D'AVRIL**
Renaissance du sous-bois !
Floraison exceptionnelle de 200 000 tulipes,
narcisses, jacinthes, muscaris…

**DIMANCHE 23 AVRIL**
"A la recherche des œufs de Pâques"

**DE MI MAI À DÉBUT JUIN**
Floraison de la Collection Nationale d'iris
(900 variétés), rassemblée dans un jardin
contemporain

**SAMEDI 20 ET DIMANCHE 21 MAI**
Fête de l'iris - Conseils, vente

**DIMANCHE 18 JUIN**
La Saint-Fiacre et les Peintres au Jardin

**SAMEDI 9 ET DIMANCHE 10 SEPTEMBRE**
Journées de découverte du nouveau potager
Conseils, vente

**DIMANCHE 17 SEPTEMBRE**
Concert par la Musique Municipale d'Orléans

**DU 28 OCTOBRE AU 12 NOVEMBRE**
31$^e$ Salon du Chrysanthème

**DU 1$^{er}$ AVRIL AU 12 NOVEMBRE**
La serre aux papillons - Découverte du monde
coloré des papillons exotiques dans un jardin
tropical de 250 m$^2$.
Exposition : l'univers fascinant des couleurs
chez les insectes. Insectes en 3D

# 02 38 49 30 00
## www.parcfloral-lasource.fr

**PARC FLORAL DE LA *source*, ORLÉANS**
DÉPARTEMENT DU LOIRET, VILLE D'ORLÉANS
45072 Orléans cedex 2 - Fax 02 38 49 30 19

# ▶ Dialogue 2: *On visite* Let's visit

*Mrs Wilson phones the Parc Floral to find out about opening hours, prices, etc. Listen to the recording or read the dialogue twice and answer the following question: How much would the family pay to visit the park and the butterfly glasshouse?*

**Touriste** À quelle heure ouvre le parc?

**Hôtesse** À partir du 1er avril, il est ouvert tous les jours de 9h à 18h.

**Touriste** Ah … merci. C'est combien l'entrée?

**Hôtesse** Alors pour le parc seul, c'est 3,25€. Pour le parc et la serre, c'est 5,80€. C'est pour combien de personnes?

**Touriste** Trois, deux adultes et un enfant de sept ans.

**Hôtesse** Pour l'enfant c'est 3€ pour le parc et la serre.

**Touriste** Ah bon. Et le parc est facile à trouver … en voiture?

**Hôtesse** Oui, très. Si vous prenez la A71, c'est sortie Orléans – la Source.

**Touriste** Ah bon, merci beaucoup madame …

## Activity 3

Now it is your turn to buy some tickets for the park. You are accompanied by your daughter, who is 12. She wants to go on the **petit train** and play **mini golf**.

**a** *You* *Ask how much the admission charge is.*

**Hôtesse** L'entrée coûte 3,25€ par personne, 5,80€ avec la serre.

**b** *You* *Ask what the 'serre' is.*

**Hôtesse** C'est pour l'exposition des papillons. Votre fille a quel âge?

**c** *You* *Say her age. Ask if you need to pay for the 'petit train' and the mini golf.*

**Hôtesse** Oui, c'est 1€ pour elle et 1,20€ pour vous. Le golf miniature est gratuit.

**d** *You* *Ask if you can have a picnic.*

**Hôtesse** Oui, bien sûr. Je vais vous montrer sur le plan.

**e** *You* *Thank her and ask what time the park closes.*

**Hôtesse** Nous fermons à 18 heures.

# *Les musées* Museums

ℹ️ Les musées et monuments sont généralement ouverts tous les jours, sauf le lundi ou le mardi, de 10 à 12h et de 14 à 18h en été. Ces horaires peuvent varier. La plupart sont fermés les jours fériés.

L'entrée est gratuite pour les enfants de moins de 18 ans. Les étudiants ont droit à une réduction et quelquefois l'entrée est gratuite un jour par semaine.

## Carte musées–monuments

> Musées et monuments en Ile-de-France: **www.intermusees.com**
> Musées et monuments en France: **www.monuments-france.fr**

Valable un, trois ou cinq jours, la carte musées-monuments permet de visiter librement et sans attente 70 musées et monuments de Paris et d'Île-de-France. Elle est en vente dans les musées et monuments, principales stations de métro, office de tourisme de Paris, magasins FNAC. Le forfait pour un jour est de 12,21€, pour trois jours consécutifs: 24,50€ et cinq jours consécutifs: 36,65€.

## Activity 4

**A**

> **Art Moderne (Musée National d')**
> *Centre Georges-Pompidou*
> Place Beaubourg – 75004 Paris
> Tél. 01 44 78 12 33          Métro: Hôtel-de-ville, Rambuteau
> www.cnac.gp.fr               RER A: Châtelet-Les Halles
>
> *Ouvert tous les jours de 11h à 21h sauf mardi (avec possibilité de nocturnes pour les expositions). Plein tarif: 10€ – Tarif réduit: 8€.*
>
> *Ce billet est valable le jour même pour toutes les expositions en cours, le Musée et l'Atelier Brancusi. Accès gratuit le 1er dimanche de chaque mois.*
>
> Collection d'oeuvres d'artistes modernes et d'artistes contemporains, sans oublier les architectes, les designers, les photographes ainsi que les cinéastes.

**B**

> **Cité des Sciences et de l'Industrie – la Villette**
> *Centre Parc de la Villette*
> 30, avenue Corentin-Cariou – 75019 Paris
> Tél. 01 40 05 80 00          Métro: Porte-de-la-Villette
> www.cite-sciences.fr
>
> *De 10h à 18h. Le dimanche de 10h à 19h. Fermé le lundi. Plein tarif: 7,60€. Cité des enfants: 5€. Planétarium: 2,50€. Tarif réduit : 5,50€.*
>
> Située dans le parc de la Villette, la cité présente un panorama complet des sciences et techniques à travers des expositions, des spectacles, des maquettes, des conférences et des jeux interactifs.

C

**Louvre (Musée du)**
*Entrée principale par la Pyramide*
Cour napoléon – 75001 Paris
Tél. 01 40 20 51 51          Métro: Palais-Royal-Musée-du-Louvre
www.louvre.fr

*Ouvert tous les jours de 9h à 18h, sauf le mardi et certains jours fériés. Nocturnes le lundi et le mercredi jusqu'à 21h45.*

*Plein tarif : 7,5€ – Tarif réduit : 5€. Tarif réduit appliqué à tous à partir de 15h ainsi que le dimanche. Gratuité appliquée aux moins de 18 ans et le 1er dimanche de chaque mois.*

Le Musée du Louvre, ancienne demeure des rois de France, et l'un des plus grands musées du monde.

**Picasso (Musée National)**
*Hôtel Salé*
5, rue de Thorigny – 75003 Paris
Tél. 01 42 71 25 21          Métro: Saint-Paul ; RER: Châtelet-Les Halles
www.paris.org/Musées/Picasso

*Été: 9h30–18h – Hiver: 9h30–17h30.*
*Nocturne le jeudi jusqu'à 20h.*
*Plein tarif: 5€. Tarif réduit et le dimanche pour tous: 4€.*
*Fermé le mardi, le 1er janvier et le 25 décembre.*

Installé dans l'Hôtel Salé (XVIIe siècle), le musée rassemble une importante collection des oeuvres de l'artiste.

a  If you were in Paris on a Tuesday, what could you visit?
b  If you did not have much money, which day would you choose to visit the attractions above?
c  What could you visit late in the evening and when?
d  Which museum would most interest a child?

# *Faire une excursion* Going on an excursion

## Activity 5

You're interested in French wines, so you've decided to go with your partner on a coach excursion following **la route des vins de Bourgogne.** Look at the information and answer the questions:

a  At what time should you be at the bus stop in the morning?
b  How long do you stop at Vezelay?

c Name at least two things you could do from lunchtime until
   4 p.m.
d How much is the excursion for two people?

## LA ROUTE DES VINS DE BOURGOGNE

**1 JOUR**

13 mai
3/17 juin
22 juillet
20 oct
11 nov

Aller/retour....79,50€

**Rendez-vous 7h15.
Départ 7h30.**

Arrivée à Vezelay vers 10h.
Arrêt d'une heure pour visiter
la basilique Sainte-Madeleine.
Continuation vers Beaune. Arrêt
pour déjeuner et temps libre

pour visiter les Hospices et
le Musée du vin. Visite d'une
cave avec dégustation.

Départ à 16h par la route des vins.
(Nuits-Saint-Georges, Gevrey-
Chambertin).
Retour à Paris vers 23h.

## Activity 6

You and your friend decide to book the trip to Beaune. Speak
for both of you.

**a You**      *Say you would like to go on the excursion of **la route des
vins de Bourgogne.***

**Employé**   Vous voulez réserver des places pour quel jour?

**b You**      *Say you'd like two places for the 22nd July.*

**Employé**   Le 22 juillet? Bon... ça va, il y a de la place ... ça fait
159€.

**c You**      *Ask if the coach leaves from here.*

**Employé**   Non, le car part de la place Denfert-Rochereau, devant le
café de Belfort.

**d You**      *Ask him to repeat.*

**Employé**   Oui, place Denfert-Rochereau devant le café de Belfort;
mais je vais vous donner tous ces renseignements par
écrit.

**e You**      *Thank him; ask what time the coach leaves.*

**Employé**   Le car part à 7h.30 mais il faut être là à 7h.15.

**f You**      *Ask if you can buy some wine in the wine cellar.*

**Employé**   Oui, vous pouvez déguster et acheter des vins de
Bourgogne à un prix spécial.

## ▶ Activity 7

Listen to Michel discussing the possibility of going on a coach
excursion to Versailles and Trianon with his friend Agnès. If you
haven't got the recording, read the tour description. Then fill in
the grid with the relevant information. You will need to listen to
the recording to be able to answer all the questions.

*Versailles et Trianon*
*(Journée)*
*Le château, son parc, l'Orangerie* **61€**

**Guide-interprète officiel**
**Jeudi et Dimanche.**
**Départ: À 9h30**
**Retour à Paris: vers 16h30**
**Réservation obligatoire**

Cette excursion inclut: Le matin, une visite guidée des Grands Appartements du château (Galerie des Glaces, l'Appartement de la Reine).

À midi, temps libre pour déjeuner et visiter les Jardins à la Française.

L'après-midi, visite guidée du Grand Trianon et du Hameau de la Rcinc Marie-Antoinette: un délicieux petit village aux toits de chaume et au style normand construit pour le divertissement de la Reine.

---

**Versailles et Trianon**
**Le château, son parc, l'Orangerie**

**a** Jour du départ _____
**b** Heure du départ de Paris _____
**c** Durée du tour _____
**d** Prix du tour _____
**e** Programme de la visite _____

## Mini-test

How would you ask:

1 for a town map?
2 if the museum closes between 12.00 and 14.00?
3 if there is a guided tour?

# sortir

going out

**In this unit you will**
- practise finding out what's on
- book tickets for a concert
- find out where you can play tennis and other sports

## Before you start, revise

- finding out what's on and where (page 144)
- saying what you want (page 62)
- asking what you can do (page 39)
- talking about your likes and dislikes (page 74)
- expressions of time, days of the week **Key words and phrases** (page 36)

## Key words and phrases

| | |
|---|---|
| qu'est-ce qu'il y a comme ...? | *what sort of ... is/are there?* |
| qu'est-ce qu'on peut faire? | *what can I/we/one do?* |
| un spectacle | *a show* |
| une soirée | *evening entertainment, party* |
| un dîner-dansant | *dinner dance* |
| l'ambiance (f) | *atmosphere* |
| la salle | *room, hall, auditorium* |
| une boîte (de nuit) | *nightclub* |
| un piano-bar | *all night restaurant with small band* |
| louer | *to book, to hire* |
| la location | *hiring* |
| le prêt | *lending* |
| le bureau de location | *booking office* |
| la place | *seat* |
| une séance | *performance, film showing* |
| entrée (f) libre | *free admission* |
| il/elle doit payer? | *he/she must pay?* |
| c'est combien l'heure? | *how much is it an hour?* |
| c'est combien la journée? | *how much is it a day?* |
| une carte d'abonnement | *season ticket* |
| un court de tennis | *tennis court* |
| un cours particulier | *private lesson* |
| l'inscription (f) | *enrolment* |
| faire une promenade | *to go for a walk* |
| faire une randonnée | *to go for a walk/hike* |
| faire du vélo | *to go cycling* |
| le jeu de société | *board game* |

# *Où aller?* Where to go?

**i** Pour connaître le programme des spectacles, adressez-vous à l'office du tourisme – qui vous réservera des places, si vous le leur demandez. Si vous êtes à Paris, achetez un journal spécialisé comme *Pariscope* ou *l'Officiel des Spectacles* ou alors consulter sur l'Internet le site **www.pariscope.fr**

# ▶ Dialogue 1: *Sortir le soir* Going out in the evening

**Touriste**  Je passe quelques jours dans la région. Qu'est-ce qu'on peut faire ici le soir?

**Hôtesse**  Il y a beaucoup de choses à faire mais ça dépend, qu'est-ce que vous aimez? Le jazz? La danse?

**Touriste**  Oui, nous aimons danser mais surtout … bien manger.

**Hôtesse**  Eh bien pourquoi n'allez-vous pas à un dîner-dansant ou dans un restaurant piano-bar?

**Touriste**  Un restaurant piano-bar, qu'est-ce que c'est?

**Hôtesse**  C'est un restaurant où il y a de la musique avec orchestre. En général, il y a une très bonne ambiance et ça reste ouvert toute la nuit. Mais … (*pause*) si vous aimez danser, vous avez le restaurant 'Raspoutine' tout près d'ici qui organise des soirées dansantes avec repas et orchestre tzigane.

**Touriste**  C'est combien pour la soirée dansante?

**Hôtesse**  C'est 100€ par personne, tout compris, avec spectacle.

**Touriste**  Je peux acheter les billets ici?

**Hôtesse**  Non, il faut aller au restaurant qui se trouve au bout du boulevard Victor Hugo; mais … attendez un instant, je vais vous chercher le programme des spectacles de la semaine avec la liste des restaurants et des bars.

## Activity 1

Without looking back at the text say if the following assertions are **vrai** or **faux** and correct the false answers:

|   |   | vrai | faux |
|---|---|------|------|
| a | The tourist wants to know what's on in the daytime. | ☐ | ☐ |
| b | They like going to concerts. | ☐ | ☐ |
| c | A piano-bar is a place that is open only at lunchtime. | ☐ | ☐ |
| d | At 'Raspoutine' you can eat and dance. | ☐ | ☐ |
| e | The price for everything including the meal is 100€ per person. | ☐ | ☐ |
| f | The hostess gives the tourist the programme of the week. | ☐ | ☐ |

## Activity 2

Here are the kinds of night attractions described in a brochure that you can find at the tourist office. Read what is on at each night-spot and say who would enjoy which one most:

a A single lady who likes disco dancing – particularly older tunes – and would love to meet a male friend.

b A couple who like playing bowls with their friends on Sundays.

c A single person who likes betting and socializing on a regular basis.

d A group of students who enjoy Latin music and dancing.

e A man who enjoys tasting different types of beer, has a sweet tooth and likes music.

---

### ACTIVITÉS NOCTURNES

A **Sax y Rock Café**
**Bar glacier**          Tel. 05 58 56 21 82
5, avenue Milliès Lacroix
Spécialités : bières du monde, glaces et pâtisseries, animations musicales.
**Ouvert tous les jours de 8 h à 2 h.**

B **Havana Café**
**Bar latino américain**          Tel. 05 58 74 09 92
19, rue Georges Chaulet
Spécialités : cubaines. Ambiance salsa. Soirées concerts.
Possibilité de location d'une salle pour soirée privée.
**Ouvert du mardi au dimanche à partir de 18 h.**

C  **Casino de Dax**          Tel. 05 58 56 86 86
Avenue Milliès Lacroix
Roulette, Black-jack, animations (spectacles, Calas),
arts et culture, restaurant, bar.
**Ouvert tous les jours à partir de 15 h.**


D  **César Palace**
**Casino**                  Tel. 05 58 91 52 72
Lac de Christus,
40990 Saint-Paul-lès-Dax - 3 km Ouest
**Boule le dimanche de 16 h à 19 h et tous les soirs
de 22 h à 4 h. Machines à sous de 12 h à 4 h.**


E  **Club rétro**
**Le Richelieu – Club**     Tel. 05 58 90 20 53
                            ou 05 58 58 49 49
Rue Sainte-Eutrope
Pour danser sur les souvenirs du temps passé.
Entrée + consommation : 8€. Samedi : 9,50€
(autres consommations : 6€).
**Ouvert du mercredi au dimanche à partir de 21 h 30.
Le mercredi entrée gratuite pour tous jusqu'à minuit.
Le jeudi entrée gratuite pour les dames jusqu'à minuit.**


## ▶ Activity 3

Listen to Michel booking a table by phone at the 'Burro Blanco'
restaurant. Can you answer the following questions? You will
need to listen to the recording to be able to answer all the
questions (**dîner aux chandelles** = *dinner by candlelight*).

### Espagnoles

**BURRO BLANCO. 79, rue Cardinale Lemoine
(5e) 01 43 25 72 53.**
Tlj jsq 5h du mat. F. Lun. A la Contrescarpe, véritable
flamenco avec chanteurs, guitaristes et danseurs.
Tapas. Menus 40€ à 50€. Carte.

**GRENIER DE TRIANA, 7, rue Mouffetard (5e)
01 43 57 97 33. Tls jsq 4h du mat.**
La meilleure ambiance espagnole de Paris. Chants,
guitare, paëlla, zarzuella. Menus 30€ à 60€ + Carte.
Groupes.

a Which day is the restaurant shut?
b What special occasion is Michel celebrating?
c What does he ask for?
d What type of cooking is served?
e At what time does the show finish?
f What is included in the price?

## ▶ Dialogue 2: *Réserver une place* Booking a ticket

**Jeune fille**   Pardon Monsieur, je voudrais des places pour le récital de guitare, samedi prochain.

**Employé**   Je regrette, samedi c'est complet mais il reste encore des places pour jeudi et vendredi.

**Jeune fille**   Bon, eh bien je vais prendre deux places pour jeudi. Ça finit à quelle heure le concert?

**Employé**   Le concert commence à 19h.45 donc je pense qu'il finira vers 22h.

**Jeune fille**   Bon, ça va, ce n'est pas trop tard. C'est combien la place, j'ai une carte étudiante?

**Employé**   Alors avec une carte étudiante, c'est tarif réduit à 20,60€.

**Jeune fille**   Ma soeur a 15 ans. Elle doit payer?

**Employé**   C'est entrée libre jusqu'à 16 ans.

## Activity 4

How do you say:

a I would like some seats for next Sunday.
b At what time does the concert finish?
c How much is it for a ticket?
d It is reduced rate.
e Does my sister have to pay?

## Activity 5

Using the Internet may be a useful way to find out what's on in the cinemas but the information can be a little confusing. Look at the example overleaf and try to work out the address of the cinema, who is entitled to a reduced rate, and on which days? If you find it puzzling, look at the upside-down clues on page 158, then check with the **Key to the exercises.**

## Cinéma Gaumont Opéra Impérial

**29, bd des Italiens (2ème arr.)**
**Métro/accès: Opéra**
**Tél: 08.36.68.75.55**
**Place 8,20€**
Tarif réduit: 6,70€ étud., CV, fam. nombr., mil., −18, du
lun. au ven. 18h., sf. fêtes et veilles de fête
**Carte 5 places: 24,44€**

## ▶ Dialogue 3: *Réserver un court de tennis* Booking a tennis court

Une touriste veut jouer au tennis. Elle se renseigne à l'office du tourisme.

*A tourist wants to play tennis. She inquires at the tourist office. She asks five questions; try to note at least three of them.*

| | |
|---|---|
| **Touriste** | Où est-ce qu'on peut jouer au tennis? |
| **Hôtesse** | Vous avez à Anglet le Club de Chiberta avec 15 courts. |
| **Touriste** | Ah très bien, et où est-ce qu'on réserve les courts? |
| **Hôtesse** | Vous réservez les courts au club. |
| **Touriste** | C'est combien l'heure? |
| **Hôtesse** | Je ne sais pas. Il faut vous renseigner là-bas mais si vous jouez souvent, vous pouvez certainement prendre une carte d'abonnement. |
| **Touriste** | Je n'ai pas ma raquette de tennis avec moi. On peut louer une raquette au club? |
| **Hôtesse** | Je pense que oui. |
| **Touriste** | Vous pouvez me donner l'adresse du club, s'il vous plaît? |
| **Hôtesse** | Mais oui, la voilà. |

**veille de fêtes**  *the day before public holidays*

**et veilles de fête**
29, boulevard des Italiens in the 2nd **arrondissement**
Tarif réduit: 6,70€ étudiants, Carte Vermeille (for OAPs), famille
nombreuse, militaires, −18, du lundi au vendredi 18h, sauf fêtes

## Activity 6

How would you ask:

a Where can I play tennis?
b Where do I book the court?
c How much is it for one hour?
d Can one hire a racket?
e Can you give me the address of the club?

## Activity 7

You are working at the **office du tourisme** in Vittel. An English family comes in. The members are all very eager to join in the various activities organized by the town (see below). Can you answer their questions?

---

● **ACTIVITÉS SPORTIVES ET DE LOISIRS avec JEAN-LOUIS et ANNE**

**Jogging**: dans le parc en petites foulées sur un rythme progressif.
**Gymnastique**: en salle, assouplissement et tonification musculaire.
**Tir à l'arc**: initiation et perfectionnement de la maîtrise du tir.
**Promenades et randonnées (pédestre, vélo)**: parcourir la campagne et les bois environnants.
**Self défense**: initiation, découverte des gestes d'auto-défense.
**Volley et sports collectifs**, ✎
**Gym, danse et stretching.**
**Promenade VTT**: initiation. ✎ ✳

● **ACTIVITÉS TENNIS et GOLF avec BRUNO**

Usage des cours et du practice, du putting green. Initiation golf et tennis en groupe. ✎

Cours particuliers. ✎ ✳

● **L'OFFICE DU TOURISME EST A VOTRE DISPOSITION POUR**
Ses locations ou prêts de vélos, matériels de golf ✳, de tennis de table, jeux de société;
Son coin lecture (journaux, hebdomadaires).

✳ Activité avec participation financière.

✎ Activité avec inscription.

a The woman is very keen on playing tennis:
   i  Can she have private classes?
   ii Can she hire a tennis racket?

b The husband would like to go for a bicycle ride:
   i  Can he hire a bicycle?
   ii Does he need to enrol if he goes on an organized trip?

c Her youngest son would like to try out mountain biking
   (**VTT** – **vélo tous terrains**).
   i  Is it free?
   ii Does he need to enrol?

d Her daughter is very keen on doing archery. They have been
   told that the town runs archery classes:
   i  Is it true?
   ii Does she have to pay?

e If it rains what can they do indoors?
   i  ......................................................................................
   ii .....................................................................................

# Mini-test on Units 14, 15 and 16

1 If you saw the following signs in a French station, would
  you know what they meant?
  a composter
  b sortie
  c correspondance
  d consigne
  e quai
  f guichet

2 Can you ask for:
  a a book of ten tickets
  b a return ticket
  c a timetable
  d a bus stop
  e the information office
  f a single ticket?

Complete the three following sentences by choosing the ending **a, b,** or **c.**

3 Si vous voulez faire un pique-nique vous cherchez le panneau (*sign*)

   **a** sortie.
   **b** restaurant.
   **c** aire de pique-nique.

4 Pour faire une excursion vous allez
   **a** au musée.
   **b** à la piscine couverte.
   **c** à l'agence de voyages ou à l'office du tourisme.

5 L'entrée dans les parcs et les monuments historiques est souvent plus chère
   **a** en pleine saison.
   **b** hors saison.
   **c** les jours fériés.

6 Fill in the blanks:
   **a** (au cinéma) Je voudrais une p..... pour la séance de 17h30.
   **b** Le lundi, c'est t..... réduit pour les étudiants.
   **c** J'adore danser; je voudrais aller dans une b..... d..... n.....
   **d** Il y a une très bonne a..... dans ce piano-bar.
   **e** Demandez le programme des s..... à l'office du tourisme.

# bonne route
## safe journey

**In this unit you will**
- learn useful information for travelling on French roads
- learn some French road signs
- practise asking directions
- buy some petrol and get your tyre pressures checked
- find out what to do in case of breakdown
- learn some essential words for describing what's wrong with your car

## Before you start, revise

- asking the way and understanding directions (page 50)
- asking for assistance (page 83)
- understanding what you need to do (page 84)
- numbers (page 224)

## *Les routes françaises* French roads

Pour avoir des informations sur la circulation, les itinéraires conseillés et la météo, consultez les sites suivants:

- Les autoroutes françaises:**www.autoroutes.fr**
  01 47 05 90 01
- Bison Futé: **www.bison-fute.equipement.gouv.fr**
- Chaîne d'hôtels bon marché:
  Hôtel Formule 1:   **www.hotelformule1.com**

**i** Le réseau routier français est l'un des plus denses du monde; il est donc facile de visiter le pays en prenant les autoroutes qui sont payantes ou les petites routes 'de campagne'. Comme dans la plupart des pays, la circulation se fait à droite. N'oubliez pas, avant de partir, de vous munir de la carte verte d'assurance internationale.

Par temps sec, la vitesse est limitée à 50 km/h en agglomération, 90 km/h sur route nationale (N) ou départementale (D), 110 km/h sur route à deux voies séparées et à 130 km/h sur autoroute (A). Par temps de pluie, la vitesse maximale est abaissée à 110 km/h sur autoroute et 100 km/h sur route à deux voies séparées.

Pour éviter les bouchons (longues files de voitures bloquées) consultez avant votre départ les sites d'Internet (voir ci-dessus) et suivez les itinéraires bis et les conseils de Bison Futé (*a 'clever Red Indian' character*).

**Les itinéraires bis:**          **Bison Futé:**

## Activity 1

To see how well you've understood the passage above, try to answer the following questions (see **Key words and phrases** on page 166).

a  Do you need to pay a toll on motorways?
b  Does the speed limit change according to dry and wet conditions?
c  What does N stand for on a French road map?
d  What is an **itinéraire bis**?

## Activity 2

When travelling in France, it is best to avoid the weekends of the busy months in the summer. Study the 'Calendrier du traffic routier' prepared by Bison Futé (page 165) and answer the questions:

a  Quels sont les mois où la circulation est moins dense?
b  Quel est le week-end en juillet où il y a le plus de monde sur les routes?
c  Quels sont les deux week-ends en août où les Français retournent chez eux?

# Calendrier du traffic routier 2003. Prévisions de difficultés

**LÉGENDE**

- ☐ Circulation habituelle
- ▨ Circulation dense
- ▩ Circulation difficile
- ▪ Circulation exceptionnelle

**Situation générale en France**

DÉPART Sens départ vers les lieux de vacances.

RETOUR Sens retour depuis les lieux de vacances.

| MAI | DÉPART | RETOUR | JUIN | DÉPART | RETOUR | JUILLET | DÉPART | RETOUR | AOÛT | DÉPART | RETOUR |
|---|---|---|---|---|---|---|---|---|---|---|---|
| 1 J | Fête du Travail | | 1 D | | ▩ | 1 M | | | 1 V | ▩ | ▨ |
| 2 V | | | 2 L | | | 2 M | | | 2 S | ▪ | ▩ |
| 3 S | | | 3 M | | | 3 J | | | 3 D | ▨ | |
| 4 D | | ▩ | 4 M | | | 4 V | | | 4 L | | |
| 5 L | | | 5 J | | | 5 S | ▨ | | 5 M | | |
| 6 M | | | 6 V | | ▩ | 6 D | | | 6 M | | |
| 7 M | ▨ | | 7 S | | ▨ | 7 L | | | 7 J | | |
| 8 J | Victoire 1945 | | 8 D | Pentecôte | | 8 M | | | 8 V | ▨ | |
| 9 V | | | 9 L | | ▩ | 9 M | | | 9 S | ▨ | |
| 10 S | | | 10 M | | | 10 J | | | 10 D | | |
| 11 D | | ▩ | 11 M | | | 11 V | ▩ | | 11 L | | |
| 12 L | | | 12 J | | | 12 S | | ▨ | 12 M | | |
| 13 M | | | 13 V | | | 13 D | | | 13 M | | |
| 14 M | | | 14 S | | | 14 L | Fête Nationale | | 14 J | | |
| 15 J | | | 15 D | | | 15 M | | | 15 V | Assomption | |
| 16 V | | | 16 L | | | 16 M | | | 16 S | ▩ | |
| 17 S | | | 17 M | | | 17 J | | | 17 D | | |
| 18 D | | | 18 M | | | 18 V | | | 18 L | | |
| 19 L | | | 19 J | | | 19 S | ▨ | ▨ | 19 M | | |
| 20 M | | | 20 V | | | 20 D | | | 20 M | | |
| 21 M | | | 21 S | | | 21 L | | | 21 J | | |
| 22 J | | | 22 D | | | 22 M | | | 22 V | | ▨ |
| 23 V | | | 23 L | | | 23 M | | | 23 S | | ▩ |
| 24 S | | | 24 M | | | 24 J | | | 24 D | | |
| 25 D | | | 25 M | | | 25 V | | ▨ | 25 L | | |
| 26 L | | | 26 J | | | 26 S | | ▨ | 26 M | | |
| 27 M | | | 27 V | ▨ | | 27 D | | | 27 M | | |
| 28 M | ▪ | | 28 S | ▨ | | 28 L | | | 28 J | | |
| 29 J | Ascension | | 29 D | | | 29 M | | | 29 V | | ▨ |
| 30 V | | | 30 L | | | 30 M | | | 30 S | | ▪ |
| 31 S | | | | | | 31 J | | | 31 D | | ▨ |

# Key words and phrases

| | |
|---|---|
| **Quelles sont les directions pour...?** | *How do you get to ... ? (lit. what are the directions to...?)* |
| **l'autoroute (f)** | *motorway* |
| **la rocade** | *ring road, bypass* |
| **la sortie** | *exit* |
| **la (route) nationale (N)** | *similar to an 'A' road in Britain* |
| **à péage** | *toll payable* |
| **une aire de repos** | *service area* |
| **suivez le panneau** | *follow the sign* |
| **c'est indiqué** | *it is signposted* |
| **le carrefour** | *the crossroads* |
| **les feux (m.pl.) rouges** | *traffic lights (often shortened to **les feux**)* |
| **une station-service** | *petrol station* |
| **où peut-on se garer?** | *where can I park?* |
| **le parking** | *car park* |
| **défense de stationner** | *no parking* |
| **le parcmètre** | *parking meter* |
| **je suis en panne** | *I've broken down* |
| **le service de dépannage** | *breakdown service* |
| **le moteur ne marche pas** | *the engine does not work* |
| **vérifier la pression des pneus** | *to check the tyre pressure* |
| **le gonflage des pneus est gratuit** | *pumping up the tyres is free* |
| **faire le plein** | *filling up the car with petrol* |
| **je vous en remets?** | *shall I top it up for you?* |
| **l'essence** | *petrol* |
| **le sans plomb** | *lead-free (petrol)* |
| **le gazole** | *diesel* |
| **l'huile (f)** | *the oil* |
| **réparer** | *to repair* |
| **la carte** | *map* |
| **la route à deux voies séparées** | *dual carriageway* |
| **une agglomération** | *built-up area* |
| **la (route) départementale (D)** | *equivalent to a 'B' road in the UK* |
| **le jour férié** | *bank holiday* |
| **le bouchon** | *bottleneck, traffic jam* |
| **la plupart de** | *most of* |
| **le pompiste** | *petrol pump attendant* |

**i** When driving in France, remember that at junctions you normally give way to traffic from the right (**priorité à droite**). But you always have right of way on a priority road marked with a yellow-on-white sign.

# ▶ Dialogue 1: *Les directions pour ...?* The way to ...?

*You may want to look at the road map of **Bordeaux et son Agglomération** on page 169 before listening to the recording.*

*In this telephone conversation a tourist is calling the manager of the Bordeaux Aéroport Hôtel to enquire about accommodation and directions. Listen to the beginning of the conversation.*

**Gérant**  Allô, Bordeaux Aéroport, j'écoute.

**Touriste**  Bonjour, Monsieur. Voilà, j'ai l'intention de m'arrêter dans votre hôtel dans deux semaines et je voudrais connaître les directions pour y arriver.

**Gérant**  Vous viendrez d'où?

**Touriste**  De Bayonne, donc j'arriverai **soit** par la A63 **soit** la N10.

**Gérant**  **Il vaudrait mieux** prendre la A63 car la N10 **ne débouche pas sur** la rocade.

**Touriste**  La rocade?

**Gérant**  Oui... c'est l'autoroute qui **contourne** Bordeaux. Alors c'est très simple. **Une fois sur** la rocade il faut prendre direction aéroport Mérignac puis la sortie 11.

**Touriste**  Bon, **j'ai compris**. Et après?

**Gérant**  Après? L'hôtel est très bien indiqué. Suivez les panneaux. Il est dans le grand centre hôtelier de l'aéroport entre Novotel et Mercure.

**Touriste**  Pour avoir une chambre, que faut-il faire?

**Gérant**  Soit vous nous téléphonez quelques jours à l'avance en nous laissant le numéro de votre carte de crédit, soit vous arrivez le jour même – il y a quelqu'un à la réception à partir de 17 heures – et **vous nous laissez** alors juste votre nom.

**Touriste**  Et si j'arrive tard?

**Gérant**  Si vous arrivez au-delà des heures de la réception, donc après 22 heures, vous devez insérer dans le distributeur votre carte bancaire. La carte sera débitée du **montant** de la chambre et vous obtiendrez le numéro de votre chambre.

**Touriste**  Ah bon... ça a l'air très simple... Et c'est combien?

| Gérant | 23,63€ la nuit. Le petit-déjeuner est extra: 3,35€. |
| Touriste | Et où peut-on se garer? |
| Gérant | Nous avons un parking fermé. |

| | |
|---|---|
| **soit … soit** | *either … or* |
| **il vaudrait mieux** | *it would be better* |
| **ne débouche pas sur** | *does not merge with* |
| **contourner** | *to go round* |
| **une fois sur** | *once on* |
| **j'ai compris** | *I have understood* |
| **vous nous laissez** | *you give us (you leave to us)* |
| **le montant** | *the amount* |

## Activity 3

Have you understood the conversation between the manager and the tourist? Read the directions below and put them in the right sequence.

a Une fois sorti de la rocade, suivez les panneaux
b puis la sortie 11
c Quand vous arrivez sur la rocade,
d il faut prendre la direction aéroport Mérignac
e Il vaudrait mieux prendre la A63

## Activity 4

Looking at the **Formule 1** brochure on the next page, you decide that Est-Artigues is the most conveniently placed hotel in the area around Bordeaux for your journey from Bayonne to Paris. You phone the **gérante** asking her for the directions. Fill in your part.

**a** *You*     *Tell her that you would like to stay one night in the hotel. Ask her politely how to get to Est-Artigues.*

**Gérante**   Vous arrivez d'où?

**b** *You*     *From Bayonne.*

**Gérante**   De Bayonne? Alors c'est très simple. La A63 vous mène directement sur la Rocade. Prenez la direction est vers Paris, puis sortie 26 … Aux …

**c** *You*     *Can you repeat, please?*

**Gérante**   Oui, alors vous allez prendre la rocade direction est, Paris–Libourne, sortie 26. Une fois sorti, prenez à droite aux feux, sortie CourtePaille, et nous sommes à 500 mètres de là.

**d** *You*     *Repeat her instructions from exit 26.*

| **Gérante** | Voilà, l'hôtel est indiqué. Suivez les panneaux. |
|---|---|
| **e *You*** | *Is there a restaurant?* |
| **Gérante** | Oui, nous avons un restaurant sur place. |
| **f *You*** | *Ask at what time you can arrive.* |
| **Gérante** | Il y a quelqu'un à la réception à partir de 17 heures jusqu'à 22 heures. |

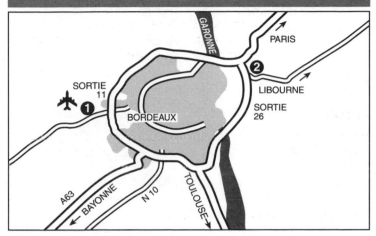

## *Stationnement* Parking

**i** Le stationnement dans la plupart des villes est payant, sous forme d'horodateurs. Le tarif horaire varie en moyenne entre un et deux euros.

## Activity 5

If you don't want to get fined or have your car towed away when in France, make sure that you understand what you are supposed to do or not do. In the next activity match the words in the left column with the words on the right:

| a | défense de stationner | i | parking ticket machine |
|---|---|---|---|
| b | une amende/contravention | ii | parking meter |
| c | une zone piétonne | iii | free parking |
| d | la fourrière | iv | pedestrian precinct |
| e | parking gratuit | v | parking forbidden |
| f | un horodateur | vi | fine |
| g | un parcmètre | vii | pound |

## Activity 6

Here are the kind of instructions which are displayed on **horodateurs** or **distributeurs** in France. Read them, then answer the questions with true or false. Correct the false ones:

- Stationnement payant: tous les jours de 9h à 13h et de 14h à 19h sauf dimanches et jours fériés

- Stationnement (de moyenne et longue durée): 8h maximum

- Tarifs horaires
  | | |
  |---|---|
  | 30 m = 0,5€ | 3h = 4€ |
  | 1h = 1€ | 4h = 5€ |
  | 1h30 = 2€ | 8h = 8€ |
  | 2h = 2,5€ | |

- Sommes autorisées 0,50€, 1€, 2€

- Cet appareil ne rend pas la monnaie

- Droit de stationnement exclusif de toute garantie

- En cas de panne, utiliser l'appareil voisin. Merci

a Parking is free after six o'clock and at weekends.
b You can park your car for short or longer periods.
c All coins are allowed.
d Change is given.
e **Droit de Stationnement exclusif de toute garantie** means that the car is parked at the owner's own responsibility.
f If the parking ticket machine is out of order, you are advised to use a nearby machine.

## *Le code français de la route* The French highway code

### Activity 7

See how good a driver you are! Match the following signs with the right definition then check your answers in the **Key to the exercises** giving yourself three points for each correct answer.

- Si vous avez 15 points ou plus, vous êtes un **bon conducteur/ une bonne conductrice.**
- Si vous avez 9 points ou plus, il faut réviser le code français.

- Si vous avez moins de 9 points, vous êtes un conducteur dangereux/une conductrice dangereuse: **un chauffard!** Apprenez le code!

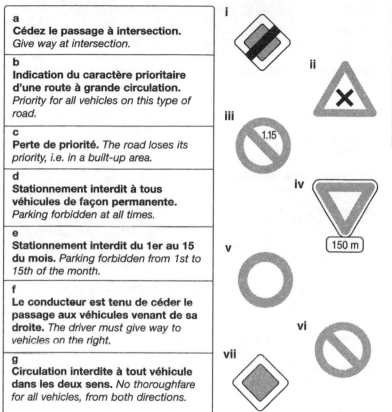

**a**
**Cédez le passage à intersection.**
*Give way at intersection.*

**b**
**Indication du caractère prioritaire d'une route à grande circulation.**
*Priority for all vehicles on this type of road.*

**c**
**Perte de priorité.** *The road loses its priority, i.e. in a built-up area.*

**d**
**Stationnement interdit à tous véhicules de façon permanente.**
*Parking forbidden at all times.*

**e**
**Stationnement interdit du 1er au 15 du mois.** *Parking forbidden from 1st to 15th of the month.*

**f**
**Le conducteur est tenu de céder le passage aux véhicules venant de sa droite.** *The driver must give way to vehicles on the right.*

**g**
**Circulation interdite à tout véhicule dans les deux sens.** *No thoroughfare for all vehicles, from both directions.*

# *Faire le plein* Filling up with petrol

**i** When travelling through France you'll probably buy **l'essence** or **le carburant** at a self-service station. If you don't and are faced with an attendant, **pompiste**, ask for **le plein**, to have the tank filled up or buy so many Euros' worth, say 50 € or 60 € . There is usually a choice between **l'octane 95 sans plomb** (lead-free petrol with an octane rating of 95), **l'octane 98 sans plomb** (super-plus lead-free petrol) and **le gazole**.

# ▶ Dialogue 2

| | |
|---|---|
| **Pompiste** | Bonjour, Monsieur, qu'est-ce que vous voulez? Du sans plomb? |
| **Client** | Je prends du sans plomb 95. |
| **Pompiste** | Je vous fais le plein? |
| **Client** | Non, seulement pour 46€ … et vous pouvez vérifier l'huile? |
| **Pompiste** | Oui, bien sûr … votre niveau d'huile est un peu bas, je vous en remets un peu? |
| **Client** | Oui, un litre alors. |
| **Pompiste** | Et pour la pression des pneus, vous voulez que je regarde? Le gonflage des pneus est gratuit. |
| **Client** | Bon, d'accord. |
| | (*after a while*) |
| **Pompiste** | Voilà, ça fait 53,50€ avec l'huile. |

## Activity 8

Most of the dialogue above is based on two key structures:

| | | |
|---|---|---|
| vous pouvez …? | *can you …?* | to ask for help |
| vous voulez …? | *do you want …?* | to offer something |

Read the questions below; can you guess who's asking them? The client or the **pompiste**? Put a tick in the correct column.

| | Client | Pompiste |
|---|---|---|
| a Vous voulez le plein? | ............. | ............. |
| b Vous pouvez regarder le niveau d'eau? | ............. | ............. |
| c Vous voulez du super? | ............. | ............. |
| d Vous pouvez me faire le plein? | ............. | ............. |
| e Vous pouvez vérifier la pression des pneus? | ............. | ............. |
| f Vous voulez 1 litre d'huile? | ............. | ............. |

## Activity 9

Now it's your turn: you need some unleaded petrol and want to have your oil checked.

| | | |
|---|---|---|
| a | ***You*** | *Say hello. Ask for unleaded petrol.* |
| | **Pompiste** | Vous voulez le plein? |
| b | ***You*** | *Say no. 38€'s worth.* |
| | **Pompiste** | C'est tout? |
| c | ***You*** | *Ask if he can check the oil.* |

| Pompiste | Oui, effectivement, vous avez besoin d'huile. Vous en voulez combien? |
|---|---|
| **d** *You* | *Say one litre.* |
| Pompiste | Un litre, bon très bien. Vous voulez que je vérifie la pression des pneus? Le gonflage est gratuit. |
| **e** *You* | *Say no thank you; it's OK (**ça va**).* |
| Pompiste | Ça fait 45€. Vous payez à la caisse. |

# *En panne* Breaking down

**i** In case of accidents and thefts (**accidents et vols**) phone the police. In case of breakdowns look in the yellow pages (**annuaire professions**) under **dépannage** or call the police.

If you break down on the motorway, go to the nearest telephone. All you need to do is press the emergency button, release it and wait for the operator to connect you.

# ▶ Dialogue 3

Une femme est tombée en panne sur l'autoroute. Elle appelle le service de dépannage.

*A woman has broken down on the motorway. She rings the breakdown service.*

*Listen to the recording or read the dialogue and try to answer the following questions: On which motorway has the woman broken down? Where is she going? How long is it going to take the garagiste to get there?*

| Femme | Allô, le service de dépannage? |
|---|---|
| Garagiste | Ici, Dépannage Ultra-rapide, j'écoute. |
| Femme | Voilà, je suis en panne; je ne comprends pas, le moteur ne marche plus. Vous pouvez m'aider? |
| Garagiste | Où êtes-vous, Madame? |
| Femme | Je suis sur l'autoroute A26, entre Reims et St. Quentin. |
| Garagiste | Et dans quelle direction allez-vous? |
| Femme | Vers Calais. |
| Garagiste | Elle est comment votre voiture? |
| Femme | C'est une Peugeot 406 LX blanche. |
| Garagiste | Bon, j'arrive dans une demi-heure. |

## Activity 10

Let's hope you won't be so unlucky! But to be prepared for all emergencies practise the following situation: look at the map below; you've broken down with your English Ford and you've just got through to the breakdown service. Fill in your part:

**Homme** Allô, service de dépannage.

**a You** *Ask if they can help you – say you've broken down.*

**Homme** Quel est le problème?

**b You** *Say that you don't know; the engine is not working.*

**Homme** Où êtes-vous?

**c You** *Say you are on the motorway A10 between Orléans and Blois.*

**Homme** Où allez-vous?

**d You** *Say which direction you're going in (towards Tours).*

**Homme** Qu'est-ce que vous avez comme voiture?

**e You** *Say that it's an English car: a blue Ford Mondeo. Ask him when he's arriving.*

**Homme** D'ici une heure (*within an hour*).

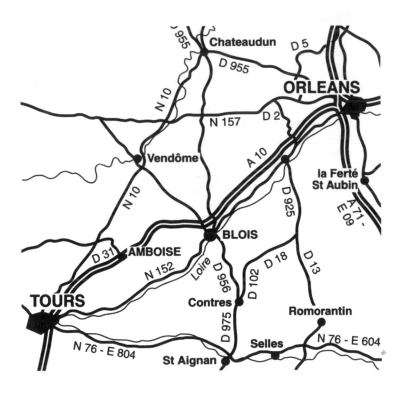

# ▶ Activity 11

Nothing seems to work in Michel's car. Study the illustrations and explanations below describing what's wrong with his car.

Now listen to him explaining his trouble to the mechanic (**mécanicien**). What he says is not in the same order as below. Fill in the boxes with **A, B, C, D, E, F, G, H** to show the order in which you hear it. (Check your answer at the back of the book.)

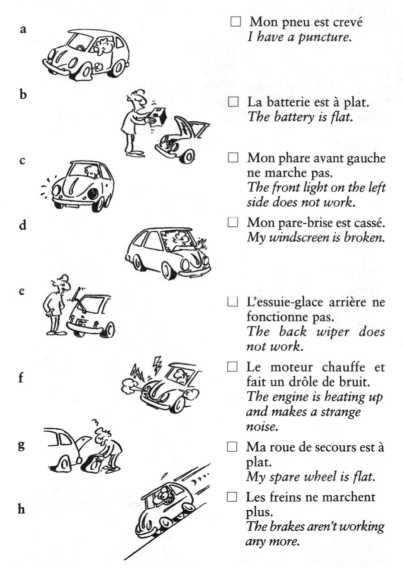

a

☐ Mon pneu est crevé
*I have a puncture.*

b

☐ La batterie est à plat.
*The battery is flat.*

c

☐ Mon phare avant gauche ne marche pas.
*The front light on the left side does not work.*

d

☐ Mon pare-brise est cassé.
*My windscreen is broken.*

e

☐ L'essuie-glace arrière ne fonctionne pas.
*The back wiper does not work.*

f

☐ Le moteur chauffe et fait un drôle de bruit.
*The engine is heating up and makes a strange noise.*

g

☐ Ma roue de secours est à plat.
*My spare wheel is flat.*

h

☐ Les freins ne marchent plus.
*The brakes aren't working any more.*

**18**

**l'argent**

money

**In this unit you will**
- find out how to ask for change
- familiarize yourself with French coins and notes
- practise changing traveller's cheques
- learn to say that there is an error in a bill

# Before you start, revise

- saying what you want (page 62)
- asking for help (page 83)
- expressions of time, days of the week **Key words and phrases** (page 36)
- numbers (page 224)

## *Pièces et billets de banque en euros*
## Euro coins and banknotes

**i** En région parisienne, les banques sont principalement ouvertes du lundi au vendredi de 10 à 17h. En province, elles ouvrent du mardi au samedi et ferment entre 13 et 15h.

Le premier janvier 2002 les euros ont remplacé les francs. Il y a 8 pièces: la face avec la valeur en euro est commune à tous les pays; la face portant un symbole national est propre à chaque pays pour identifier clairement le pays émetteur.

Il y a 7 billets: 5, 10, 20, 50, 100, 200 et 500 euros.

## Activity 1

**a** Do banks shut over lunchtime in France?
**b** Are euro coins the same throughout the EU?
**c** In what ways do they differ?

# Key words and phrases

If you have not got the recording, check the pronunciation of the words preceded by an * in the **Pronunciation tips** opposite.

| | |
|---|---|
| * une pièce | coin |
| * un billet | banknote |
| * un franc | franc (old currency) |
| * un euro | a euro |
| * la monnaie | small change |
| * l'argent (m) | money |
| la livre (sterling) | (English) pound |
| le dollar | dollar |
| * le cours du change | exchange rate |
| * le traveller | traveller's cheque |
| (or chèque de voyage) | |
| en bas | at the bottom |
| un stylo | a pen |
| une pièce d'identité | means of identification |
| un changeur de monnaie | coin changing machine |
| une télécarte | telephone card |
| la carte bleue | the French banker's card |
| une carte bancaire | banker's card |
| la note | hotel bill |
| l'addition (f) | bill (drinks, snacks) |
| régler | to settle (bill) |
| une erreur | a mistake |
| un distributeur automatique | a cashpoint machine |

## For you to say

| | |
|---|---|
| vous pouvez changer ... euros? | can you change... euros? |
| vous avez de la monnaie svp? | do you have any change please? |
| il me faut des pièces de 1€ | I need 1€ coins |
| changer de l'argent | change some money |
| la livre est à combien? | what's the rate of exchange for the pound? |
| vous acceptez les cartes de crédit? | do you accept credit cards? |

## Worth knowing

| | |
|---|---|
| faites (faire) l'appoint | put in the exact money |
| l'appareil ne rend pas l'argent | no change given |

# ℹ Pronunciation tips

You do not need to know many words when changing money but they need to be pronounced correctly; here is an opportunity to practise saying them:

**pièce** pee–esse
**billet** bee–yeah
**franc** remember not to pronounce the **c**
**euro** ir (as in *sir*) – ro
**monnaie** mo–nay
**argent** make sure the r is pronounced otherwise it could sound like **agent** (**de police**): *policeman*
**cours** don't pronounce the **s**
**traveller** as in English but with a French **r**

And now re-read the **Key words and phrases**, checking your pronunciation.

## *Faire de la monnaie* Getting small change

### Activity 2

Try to answer the following, using the phrases in the box on page 178.

**a** How would you ask: Can you change 10€ please?
**b** How would you say: I need 1€ coins?
**c** What does **la machine ne rend pas l'argent** mean?

(Check your answers in the **Key to the exercises**.)

### Activity 3

Read the conversation that takes place between a passer-by and a motorist, who needs some small change for the pay-and-display machine. Then do the activity.

**Femme** Pardon, Madame, vous pouvez changer mon billet de 5€, s'il vous plaît?
**Passante** Je ne sais pas, mais je vais regarder. Qu'est-ce qu'il vous faut?
**Femme** C'est pour l'horodateur. Il me faut cinq pièces de 1€, ou alors une pièce de 1€ et deux pièces de 2€.
**Passante** La machine ne rend pas la monnaie?

| Femme | Non, et elle **n'**accepte **que** des pièces de 50 centimes, 1€ et 2€. |
|---|---|
| Passante | Et nous n'avez pas de carte bancaire? |
| Femme | Euh, non, je n'en ai pas. |
| Passante | Eh, bien, **vous avez de la chance!** J'ai quatre pièces de 1€ et deux pièces de 0.50 centimes. **Ça vous va?** |
| Femme | Merci beaucoup, Madame. |

| | |
|---|---|
| **ne ... que** | *only* |
| **vous avez de la chance** | *you're lucky, you're in luck* |
| **ça vous va?** | *is that OK (for you)?* |

Find the French for the following phrases:

a Don't you have a bank card?
b I need five coins of 1€
c it only accepts ...
d Can you change ...?
e I haven't got any (card)
f I don't know
g Is that OK?
h you're lucky
i I am going to see

## Activity 4

You want to make a phone call but only have a 5€ note on you. Fill in your part of the dialogue.

| a *You* | *Stop a man in the street. Ask him if he has any small change for the telephone.* |
|---|---|
| Passant | Qu'est-ce qu'il vous faut? |
| b *You* | *Say: I've only got a 5€ note and I need 1€ coins.* |
| Passant | Je suis désolé mais je n'ai pas de monnaie. Pourquoi n'achetez-vous pas une télécarte? |
| c *You* | *Ask: a 'télécarte'? What is it?* |
| Passant | Une carte pour téléphoner. Toutes les cabines téléphoniques marchent avec des télécartes. |
| d *You* | *Ask: where can I buy a phone card?* |
| Passant | Dans les tabacs, les postes, les gares de métro ... un peu partout. |

## *Changer de l'argent* Changing money

**i** On trouve de très nombreux bureaux de change dans les grandes villes (les gares, les aéroports, les grandes agences de banque, les points de change) ainsi qu'au bureau central de l'office du tourisme à Paris. Avec une carte bancaire internationale: Visa, Mastercard, Eurocard, vous pourrez retirer de l'argent dans la plupart des distributeurs automatiques de billets (DAB).

## ▶ Dialogue 1

Un étranger change des travellers dans une banque.

*A foreigner is in a bank changing traveller's cheques.*

*Listen to the recording or read below and find out: How many pounds does he want to change? What does he need before signing his traveller's cheques?*

| | |
|---|---|
| **Étranger** | Je voudrais changer des travellers, s'il vous plaît. |
| **Employée** | Oui, très bien. Vous avez une pièce d'identité? |
| **Étranger** | Oui, voici mon passeport. |
| **Employée** | Bon, qu'est-ce que vous voulez? |
| **Étranger** | Je voudrais changer 150 livres sterling en euros. |
| **Employée** | D'accord, alors vous allez signer en bas des travellers. |
| **Étranger** | Euh … vous avez quelque chose pour écrire s'il vous plaît? |
| **Employée** | Un instant … voici un stylo. |
| **Étranger** | La livre est à combien aujourd'hui? |
| **Employée** | Aujourd'hui le cours de la livre est à 1,65 €. |
| **Étranger** | Il y a une commission à payer? |
| **Employée** | Non, pas pour les travellers. |

## Activity 5

Without looking at the text above, fill in the missing words.

a  Je voudrais ……… des travellers.
b  Vous avez une ……… d'identité?
c  Vous allez ……… en bas des travellers.
d  Vous avez quelque chose pour ………?
e  La livre est à ……… aujourd'hui?
f  Il y a une commission à ………?

## Activity 6

Take part in this conversation in **le bureau de change** at the **Gare du Nord** in Paris.

**a** *You*     *Say that you would like to change some dollars.*
**Employé**   Des dollars américains, canadiens, australiens?
**b** *You*     *Say American dollars.*
**Employé**   Oui; vous voulez changer des billets ou des travellers?
**c** *You*     *Say bank notes.*
**Employé**   Combien voulez-vous changer?
**d** *You*     *Say 200 dollars. Ask the exchange rate.*
**Employé**   Le dollar est à 1,11 € aujourd'hui.
**e** *You*     *Ask if they are open on Sundays.*
**Employé**   Oui, tous les jours de 7h à 21h.30. ...(*later*) Voici votre argent!

# *Une erreur dans la note* An error in the bill

## ℹ *Pour régler la note* Paying your hotel bill

- It's a good idea to ask for the bill in advance in order to check it.
- You ask for **la note** to pay for your hotel bill and for **l'addition** to pay for food and drink.
- Remember to check the price of hotel rooms which, by law, should be displayed at the reception and in each room.
- Extras (telephone, mini-bar, etc.) should be charged separately.
- TTC (toutes taxes comprises) means inclusive of tax.
- TVA (taxe à la valeur ajoutée) means 'VAT'.

## ▶ Activity 7

It is essential for you to be confident in using and understanding numbers, particularly when paying bills! You can revise them at the back of the book, where they are all listed.

Here is some extra practice to help you cope with French prices. Listen to Michel and write down the prices you hear.

**a** .......         **f** .......
**b** .......         **g** .......
**c** .......         **h** .......
**d** .......         **i** .......
**e** .......

# ▶ Dialogue 2

## Une erreur dans la note

*A client is about to leave the hotel. Having asked for the bill, he spots a mistake. Listen to the recording, or read the dialogue below, and say what mistake was made.*

| | |
|---|---|
| **Client** | Je voudrais régler ma note, s'il vous plaît. |
| **Réceptionniste** | Bien, vous partez aujourd'hui? |
| **Client** | Oui, après le petit-déjeuner. |
| **Réceptionniste** | Bon, c'est pour quelle chambre? |
| **Client** | Chambre quatorze. Vous acceptez les cartes de crédit? |
| **Réceptionniste** | Oui, bien sûr. Alors un instant ... nous allons vérifier. Si vous voulez bien, repassez après votre petit-déjeuner? *(after breakfast)* |
| **Client** | Pardon, Madame, il y a une erreur. Qu'est-ce que c'est 'mini-bar dix euros'? |
| **Réceptionniste** | Ce sont les boissons du mini-bar **que vous avez consommées** dans votre chambre. |
| **Client** | Mais **je n'ai rien pris** du mini-bar. |
| **Réceptionniste** | Vraiment? Bon, eh bien c'est sans doute une erreur de notre part...! **Nous avons dû nous tromper** de chambre. Je m'excuse Monsieur. Donc ça fait 94€ moins 10€ pour la boisson... euh 84€. |
| **Client** | C'est avec service et taxes? |
| **Réceptionniste** | Oui, taxe de séjour et service sont compris. |

| | |
|---|---|
| **que vous avez consommées** | *that you've drunk* |
| **je n'ai rien pris** | *I haven't taken anything* |
| **nous avons dû nous tromper de chambre** | *we must have mistaken the room* |

## Activity 8

Have you understood the dialogue well enough to answer the following questions?

a  When does the client intend to leave the hotel?
b  What was the number of his room?
c  Was the bill correct?
d  What does the amount of 10€ correspond to?
e  Is the bill inclusive of tax and service?

# Mini-test on Units 17 and 18

How would you ask/say:

1  Is there a car park near here?
2  I need four 1€ coins for the parking meter.
3  Can you help me please? I've broken down.
4  I need 1 litre of oil.
5  Have you any small change?
6  Do you accept credit cards?
7  I would like to settle my bill.
8  Can you check the tyre pressure?
9  Can you fill up my car with petrol?
10  I would like to change £150 into euros.

# 19

## savoir faire face
troubleshooting

**In this unit you will**
- find out how to ask for medicine at the chemist's
- familiarize yourself with the French health system
- practise making an appointment with the doctor/dentist
- find out about the telephone in France
- learn some key expressions to describe your problems

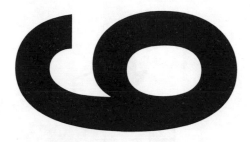

# Before you start, revise

- saying what you want (page 62)
- how to describe things (page 63)
- how to spell in French (page 118)
- how to say my, your, his, etc. (page 38)
- expressions of time, days of the week **Key words and phrases** (page 36)
- numbers (page 224)

Sign for a French chemist's

## *La pharmacie en France* The chemist's in France

**i** The French chemist's is easily recognizable, with its green neon cross sign outside. For minor ailments you'll find that the trained pharmacist, **pharmacien(-ne)** is usually happy to give you advice. You will not be able to buy medicines (even aspirin!) anywhere except at the **pharmacie**.

Many chemist's display in their windows the address of the nearest pharmacy which stays open late. In Paris, the following chemist's stay open all night:

- Pharmacie Dhéry (24h) inside the shopping arcade at 84, avenue des Champs-Elysées (8e), tél: 01 45 62 02 41

- Pharmacie Européenne de la Place de Clichy (24h), 6 place de Clichy (17e), tél: 01 48 74 65 18

# Key words and phrases

## *For you to say*

| | |
|---|---|
| **la pharmacie** | *chemist's* |
| **le pharmacien, la pharmacienne** | *chemist* |
| **chez le médecin** | *at the doctor's* |
| **chez le dentiste** | *at the dentist's* |
| **le cabinet médical/dentaire** | *doctor's/dentist's surgery* |
| **prendre rendez-vous** | *to make an appointment* |
| **souffrir** | *to suffer, be in pain, feel ill* |
| **depuis quand** | *since when* |
| **je voudrais quelque chose pour...** | *I would like something for …* |
| **\* la piqûre d'insectes** | *insect bite* |
| **le mal de gorge** | *sore throat* |
| **le mal de dents** | *toothache* |
| **le mal de tête** | *headache* |
| **j'ai mal à la gorge** | *I've got a sore throat* |
| **j'ai mal aux dents** | *I've got toothache* |
| **j'ai mal à la tête** | *I've got a headache* |
| **j'ai mal au ventre** | *I've got stomachache* |
| **il a de la fièvre** | *he's got a temperature* |
| **le dentifrice** | *toothpaste* |
| **le shampooing** | *shampoo* |
| **contre** | *against* |
| **j'ai perdu (il a perdu)...** | *I've lost (he's lost)* |
| **j'ai laissé (il a laissé)...** | *I've left (he's left)* |
| **... est cassé(e)** | *… is broken* |
| **... sont cassés(ées)** | *… are broken* |
| **on a volé** | *… was stolen* |
| **le sac à main** | *handbag* |
| **le portefeuille** | *wallet* |
| **le porte-monnaie** | *purse* |
| **les lunettes** | *glasses* |

## *For you to understand*

| | |
|---|---|
| **un médicament** | *medicine* |
| **une crème** | *cream* |
| **une huile** | *oil* |
| **une aspirine effervescente** | *soluble aspirin* |
| **en comprimés** | *in tablet form* |
| **je vous conseille** | *I advise you, I recommend to you* |

\* **piqûre** is pronounced 'pic-oore' (with French **u**)

# ▶ Dialogue 1: À *la pharmacie* At the chemist's

*Listen to the recording or read below: What's wrong with the customer's husband? Has he got a temperature? Name at least three items the customer buys.*

| | |
|---|---|
| **Pharmacien** | Bonjour, Madame. Vous désirez? |
| **Cliente** | Vous avez quelque chose pour le mal de gorge? |
| **Pharmacien** | C'est pour vous, Madame? |
| **Cliente** | Non, c'est pour mon mari. |
| **Pharmacien** | Il a de la fièvre? |
| **Cliente** | Non, mais il a aussi mal à la tête. |
| **Pharmacien** | Bon, pour le mal de gorge je vous donne des pastilles. Il en prend une quand il a mal. Pour le mal de tête, je vous donne de l'aspirine effervescente, deux comprimés toutes les quatre heures. Il n'est pas allergique à l'aspirine? |
| **Cliente** | Non, non … merci. Je voudrais aussi du dentifrice et quelque chose contre le soleil. |
| **Pharmacien** | Vous préférez une crème ou une huile? |
| **Cliente** | Une crème. |
| **Pharmacien** | Alors voilà du dentifrice fluoré et une crème pour le soleil; c'est tout? |
| **Cliente** | Oui, merci. |
| **Pharmacien** | Bon, eh bien ça fait 38,15€. |

## Activity 1

Read the dialogue again and choose the right answers for the patient's medical record card below. (Check your answers in the Key to the exercises.)

| a Patient complains of | | b Temperature | |
|---|---|---|---|
| i stomachache | ☐ | | |
| ii headache | ☐ | Yes ☐ | |
| iii toothache | ☐ | | |
| iv sore throat | ☐ | No ☐ | |

| c Treatment | | d To be taken |
|---|---|---|
| i antibiotics | ☐ | .................... |
| ii suppositories | ☐ | .................... |
| iii aspirin | ☐ | .................... |
| iv pastilles | ☐ | .................... |

## Activity 2

Now it's your turn to go to the chemist's to get some medicine for your daughter, who has toothache.

**Pharmacienne** Bonjour, Monsieur/Madame. Vous désirez?
**a You** *Say: my daughter has toothache.*
**Pharmacienne** Elle a de la fièvre?
**b You** *Say: yes, a little.*
**Pharmacienne** Depuis quand souffre-t-elle?
**c You** *Say: since yesterday.*
**Pharmacienne** Bon, je vais vous donner de l'aspirine vitaminée et si ça continue dans un jour ou deux il faudra aller chez le dentiste.
**d You** *Thank her. Ask for something for insect bites.*
**Pharmacienne** Pour les piqûres d'insectes? Certainement. Je vous conseille cette crème anti-démangeaisons … elle est très bonne …
**e You** *You didn't get everything she said but you understood that she was recommending the cream. Say: I'll take it and ask to pay.*

## *Le service médical* Medical treatment

**i** EU residents are covered for emergency medical treatment throughout the European Union. US visitors with private health insurance are also covered for a limited period. Canadians with a valid **Assurance-maladie du Québec** card can receive reimbursement in some cases. Australian Medicare provides absolutely no coverage in France. However any foreigner who is sick can receive treatment in the casualty ward of any public hospital. In emergencies phone:

**SAMU**/*24 hour ambulance*: 15 or 01 45 67 50 50
**SOS Médecins**/*Doctors – 24h house calls*: 01 47 07 77 77
**SOS Dentaire**/*Dental emergency*: 01 43 37 51 00

If you come from the UK, remember to take form E111 with you, which you obtain from any post office. It will enable you to obtain a refund after receiving medical and/or dental treatment. All you need to do is send the form E111 (keep a photocopy) to the local social security office with your **ordonnance** (*prescription*) and **feuille de soins** (*the signed statement of treatment given*).

## Activity 3

Here are a few French words which appear on the **feuille de soins** and which you may need to recognize in order to fill it in correctly. Match the words in the left column with their equivalent in the right column, then check your answers at the back of the book.

a  la facturation du pharmacien
b  le remboursement
c  les honoraires perçus
d  le médecin traitant
e  la feuille de soins
f  conserver l'original de l'ordonnance
g  coller les vignettes
h  l'organisme d'assurance maladie

i    *the social security office*
ii   *signed statement of treatment given*
iii  *the GP*
iv   *keep the original prescription*
v    *refund*
vi   *the chemist's bill*
vii  *the received fee (by the GP)*
viii *stick on the (detachable) labels*

# ▶ Dialogue 2: *Chez le docteur* At the doctor's

*Mrs Jones phones Dr Leroux's surgery to make an appointment. Why does Mrs Jones phone? Who is the patient? Has the patient got a temperature? What other symptom?*

**Réceptionniste**  Allô, le cabinet du docteur Leroux, j'écoute.

**Mrs Jones**  Je voudrais prendre rendez-vous, s'il vous plaît.

**Réceptionniste**  Bon, c'est pour une consultation ou une visite?

**Mrs Jones**  Je ne comprends pas, vous pouvez expliquer?

**Réceptionniste**  Pour une consultation vous venez ici, pour une visite le médecin va chez vous. Vous êtes la patiente?

**Mrs Jones**  Non, c'est ma fille. Elle a beaucoup de fièvre …

**Réceptionniste**  Alors, vous voulez une visite… Ecoutez, le docteur est pris toute la journée mais il pourrait passer voir votre fille dans la soirée vers … peut-être 19h.30. Qu'est-ce qu'elle a, votre fille?

**Mrs Jones**  Je ne sais pas, peut-être la grippe. Elle a très mal à la tête.

**Réceptionniste**  Vous pouvez me donner votre nom et adresse?

**Mrs Jones**  Jones. J-O-N-E-S et j'habite appartement 2, 10 rue Legrand, à côté de la piscine.

| Réceptionniste | Bon, eh bien Mme Jones, le docteur Leroux passera voir votre fille vers 19h30. |
| --- | --- |
| **Mrs Jones** | Merci beaucoup. Au revoir, Madame. |

> **est pris** *is busy* (lit. is taken)   **la grippe** *flu*
> **passer voir** *come (go) and see*

## Activity 4

It's your turn to make an appointment at the dentist's. Say your part.

| Réceptionniste | Allô, allô. |
| --- | --- |
| **a You** | *Say: I would like to make an appointment.* |
| Réceptionniste | Oui, très bien; c'est pour vous? |
| **b You** | *Say: no, it's for my son. We are English, on holiday here and he has had toothache since Tuesday.* |
| Réceptionniste | Il a quel âge votre fils? |
| **c You** | *Say: he's 12.* |
| Réceptionniste | Oui, je vois. Et quand peut-il venir? |
| **d You** | *Say: today, this morning or this afternoon.* |
| Réceptionniste | Bon; eh bien cet après-midi, à 3h.45. Ça vous va? |
| **e You** | *Ask her to repeat the time.* |
| Réceptionniste | À 3h.45. Votre nom s'il vous plaît? |
| **f You** | *Say your name and spell it.* |
| Réceptionniste | Merci, nous attendons donc votre fils à 3h.45. Au revoir Monsieur/Madame. |

# Le téléphone et l'Internet en France
# Phoning and using the Internet in France

France Telecom: **www.francetelecom.fr**

La Poste: **www.laposte.fr**

ℹ️ La plupart des cabines téléphoniques s'utilisent avec des télécartes (50 unités = 6,19€ ou 120 unités = 14,86€); elles sont en vente dans les bureaux de poste, dans les principales stations de métro et de RER, dans les bureaux de tabac et aux caisses des supermarchés. Les cabines téléphoniques ont un numéro d'appel qui permet de vous faire appeler. Dans les gares, les aéroports, de nombreuses cabines acceptent le paiement par carte bancaire.

Pour téléphoner depuis la France, faites les dix chiffres indiqués. Pour téléphoner à l'étranger, composez le 00 avant l'indicatif du pays de votre choix puis celui de la région sans le 0 initial et le numéro de votre correspondant.

## *L'Internet* The Internet

Pour avoir accès à l'Internet, essayez la Poste ou renseignez-vous auprès de France Télécom qui sponsorise des centres Internet un peu partout en France. Si vous êtes internaute (*an Internet addict*), sachez que vous pouvez prendre un verre ou un repas léger tout en vous connectant sur les réseaux multimédias, dans un de ces cafés 'branchés' (*connected cafés*) à Paris:

| | |
|---|---|
| **CAFÉ ORBITAL** | **CYBERPORT** |
| *13, rue de Médicis* | *Forum des Halles* |
| *75006 Paris* | *Porte Saint-Eustache* |
| tél.: 01 43 25 76 77 | *75001 Paris* |
| www.cafeorbital.com | tél.: 01 44 76 63 99 |
| info@orbital.fr | www.forumdesimages.net |
| | |
| **C@AFÉ CA&RI TÉLÉMATION** | **JARDIN DE L'INTERNET** |
| *72–74, passage de Choiseul* | *79, boulevard Saint-Michel* |
| *75002 Paris* | *75005 Paris* |
| tél.: 01 47 03 36 12 | tél./fax: 01 44 07 22 20 |
| www.cari.com/internet | www.jardin-internet.net |
| cafe@cari.com | cybercafe@jardin-internet.net |

## Activity 5

Look at the call charges below and fill in the blanks, using the correct word from the box.

Pour la France, l'Australie, le Royaume-Uni et les USA, les heures pleines sont de **a** _____ à **b** _____ tous les jours de la c _____. Le week-end et jours d _____ les heures sont creuses. Le tarif est le même que l'on téléphone au Royaume-Uni ou aux e _____. Pour f _____, le tarif est de 0,49 €/min. pendant les heures g _____ et de 0,24 €/min. pendant les heures h _____.

---

férié  semaine  l'Australie  8h  creuses  USA  19h  pleines

---

| Jours | h. | PRIX DES COMMUNICATIONS PAR MIN. | | | |
|---|---|---|---|---|---|
| | | France | UK | Australie | USA |
| lundi au vendredi | 0 | 0,061€ | 0,12€ | 0,24€ | 0,12€ |
| | 8 | | | | |
| | 19 | 0,091€ | 0,23€ | 0,49€ | 0,23 € |
| | 24 | | | | |
| samedi, dimanche et jours fériés | | 0,061€ | 0,12€ | 0,24€ | 0,12€ |

heures creuses          heures pleines

## Activity 6

Here are some instructions you might see in a **cabine téléphonique** when using a **télécarte**. Can you find for each French instruction its English equivalent?

a décrochez
b introduisez la carte ou faites numéro libre
c patientez SVP
d crédit
e numéro appelé
f retirez votre carte

i  *credit*
ii  *number being connected*
iii  *remove card*
iv  *insert card or dial free number*
v  *wait*
vi  *lift receiver*

**i** Using the phone in France may seem like a daunting experience but it doesn't need to be. Here are two useful tips when speaking on the phone.

• Speak clearly and open your mouth wide, particularly when pronouncing the vowels **i**, **o**, **u**, **é**.

• If you don't understand what is being said, don't be afraid to ask the person at the other end to repeat using one of the following expressions:

> **Vous pouvez répéter, s'il vous plaît?**
> **Vous pouvez parler plus lentement?**
> **Je ne comprends pas.**
> **Vous pouvez expliquer?**

## ▶ Activity 7

To practise the first tip given above, listen to Cloé and repeat after her some of the following sentences: (if you don't have the recording, find out how to pronounce them by looking at the **Pronunciation guide** at the front of the book)

• J'ai pris un rendez-vous avec la réceptionniste du Docteur Mireau.
• Vous avez un médicament pour le mal de tête?
• Vous avez quelque chose d'autre?
• J'ai perdu mes clefs.
• Mes lunettes sont cassées.

## *Au commissariat de police* At the police station

ℹ️ Pour tout papier d'identité perdu ou volé, vous devez faire **une déclaration** (*statement*) au **commissariat de police** (*police station*) le plus proche. Vous pouvez aussi informer votre consulat. Pour un objet personnel perdu à Paris, contactez le **Bureau des objets trouvés** (*lost property office*), tél: 01 55 76 20 20. Pour une carte de crédit, faites une déclaration au commissariat de police après avoir téléphoné au service d'urgence de votre carte.

## ▶ Activity 8

To familiarize yourself with some of the vocabulary you need to describe the kind of problems you may experience in France, listen to Michel's various mishaps and fill in the blanks using the correct items from the box. Even without the recording, you may be able to work out what goes where.

**a** Hier matin, dans le métro, j'ai perdu mes ....... d'appartement.

b Après ça, à la banque, j'ai oublié mon ....... en or et mes .......
c A midi on m'a volé au restaurant mon ....... avec tout mon ....... et mes .......
d Au commissariat de police, hier soir, j'ai oublié mon ....... et ma .......
e Ce matin, je voulais téléphoner au commissariat de police mais mon ....... est cassé.
f Alors j'ai pris la voiture, mais je ne comprends pas, l'....... arrière ne fonctionne plus et les ....... ne marchent pas. Mais qu'est-ce que je vais faire?

| | | | |
|---|---|---|---|
| cartes de crédit | téléphone | freins | clés |
| lunettes | argent | parapluie | stylo |
| carte d'identité | portefeuille | essuie-glace | |

## ▶ Dialogue 3

*A man is at the police station reporting the theft of his car. Can you give the make, colour and number plate of his car?*

**Agent** Monsieur?
**Homme** Je suis anglais, en vacances avec ma famille ... On m'a volé ma voiture.
**Agent** Quand ça?
**Homme** La nuit dernière.
**Agent** Où **était** votre véhicule?
**Homme** Ma voiture? Dans la rue Gambetta devant l'hôtel du Lion d'Or.
**Agent** Elle est comment votre voiture?
**Homme** C'est une Volvo S70 rouge.
**Agent** Quel est le numéro d'immatriculation?
**Homme** Euh ... R546 YAP
**Agent** Bon, nous allons essayer de la retrouver. **En attendant**, il faut faire une déclaration par écrit. Vous pouvez remplir cet imprimé?
**Homme** Euh ... maintenant?
**Agent** Oui, tout de suite car vous en avez besoin pour vos assurances en Angleterre; mais c'est facile ... c'est traduit en anglais.

| | | |
|---|---|---|
| **était** *was* | | **en attendant** *in the meantime* |

## Activity 9

Read the dialogue again and try to spot the French version of the following phrases then write them out:

a  my car was stolen .................................................................
b  what make of car is it? .....................................................
c  what's the registration number? .......................................
d  write a statement .............................................................
e  fill in this printed form ...................................................
f  you need it for your insurance .......................................

## Activity 10

In this last exercise, following the examples given, practise saying who lost what, where, and what it looked like. Revise how to say my, your, his, etc. (see Unit 4).

**J'ai perdu ma montre en or dans le train.**
*I have lost my gold watch on the train.*

**Mon amie a perdu son sac à main en cuir marron dans le bus.**
*My friend has lost her brown, leather handbag on the bus.*

|   | Who | What | Description | Where |
|---|-----|------|-------------|-------|
| a | you | your pen | gold | office |
| b | my brother | his suitcase | brown | airport |
| c | your sister | her purse | leather white | park |
| d | his father | his passport | British | street |
| e | my friend | her scarf | in silk | bus |

# Mini-test on Unit 19

How would you say:

1  I would like something for headaches.
2  I would like to make an appointment.
3  I've got a sore throat.
4  My handbag was stolen in the cinema.
5  My glasses are broken.

**Congratulations!** You have completed *Teach Yourself Beginner's French* and are now a competent speaker of basic French. You should be able to handle most everyday situations on a visit to France and to communicate with French people sufficiently to make friends. If you would like to extend your ability so that you can develop your confidence, fluency and scope in the language, whether for social or business purposes, why not take your French a step further with the full *Teach Yourself French* course?

To find out more about France itself you might like to read *Teach Yourself World Cultures: France*.

I hope that working your way through *Teach Yourself Beginner's French* has been both a learning and enjoyable experience. If the course has provided you with what you wanted why don't you contact me and let me know what has worked well for you. If you think that the course could be improved I shall also be pleased to hear from you. All constructive comments and suggestions will be carefully looked at, and incorporated if possible into later editions.

You can contact me through the publishers at: Teach Yourself Books, Hodder Headline Ltd, 338 Euston Road, London NW1 3BH, UK.

**Bonne chance!**
Catrine Carpenter

**taking it further**

In the **Introduction** and **Unit 4** we emphasize how important it is for language learners to create every opportunity to speak the language with other learners or French speakers, listen to some French regularly and read French material. If the idea at first seems a little daunting we give some tips in Unit 7 to help you get the gist of what you read or listen to, or make the most of your conversations in French. Ideally you should find a 'study buddy' with whom you could work through the course and try your French out. Learning French would then become more meaningful and fun as speaking a language is about communicating with others. Going to France or one of the francophone countries would also be a most valuable experience to try the language out whilst getting direct feedback from the people you talk to. Anyhow if this is not possible you can still get a real flavour of French in your own home by using the following:

- Newspapers (*Libération*; *Le Parisien* – found in Paris and easy to read; *Le Figaro* – the weekend issue is particularly interesting).

- Magazines (*Paris-Match*, *Marie-Claire*, *Elle*, *Cosmopolitan*).

- Satellite and/or cable TV channels (e.g. **TV5 Europe, Canal +, La 5ème**. For news: CNN and Euronews).

- Radio stations on long wave (France Inter 162, RTL, Europe 1), or via satellite.

- Websites:
  **a** to find out information relating to France:
  **www.yahoo.fr** or **www.wanadoo.fr** or **www.google.fr**

**b** to keep up with French news and familiarize yourself with French society and institutions:

   **www.diplomatie.fr** (a site prepared by **Le Ministère des Affaires Etrangères**)

**c** to read the French press on-line:
   **www.lemonde.fr, www.lefigaro.fr, www.liberation.fr, www.leparisien.fr**

**d** to listen to French radio stations online:
   **www.radiofrance.fr**

* In London you can also get information and activities at l'Institut Français, 17 Queensberry Place, London SW7 2DT (telephone 020 7073 1350 or visit **www.institut-francais.org.uk**).

# self-assessment tests

To help you monitor your overall progress with *Teach Yourself Beginner's French* we have prepared two **Self-assessment tests** covering Units 1–10 and 11–19. Each **Self-assessment test** includes a series of short self-assessment tasks after every third or fourth unit with points allocated to the answers. You will find the answers to the test questions in the **Key to the exercises.** When the questions require individual responses, we usually give you model answers to guide you.

We indicate the number of points allocated to each answer, so that you can keep your own score (out of a total of 50 points per test). Here are a few guidelines to help you grade your performance:

| | |
|---|---|
| 40–50 points | Congratulations! You are ready to start the next units. |
| 30–40 points | Very good. You have mastered most of the points covered in the last units. Try to identify the areas which still need some work and go over them again. |
| 20–30 points | Well done, but it might be advisable to revise the areas where you are not quite so confident before moving on to the next units. |
| Below 20 points | Not bad, but we would strongly advise you to go back over the last units. When you have done so, take the test again and see how much you have improved. |

Always remember that learning a new language may take more time than you think. If you feel that it seems a bit difficult, don't be discouraged. Look back at the tips in the section **Be successful at learning languages** on page ix as well as those marked with the ⓘ symbol, and try to put them into practice. They do work!

**Bon courage!**

# Self-assessment test 1

## Units 1–3   Points: _____/50

This test covers the main vocabulary and phrases, skills and language points in Units 1–3. For how to read your score, refer back to page 200. You can check your answers in the **Key to the exercises. Bonne chance!** *Good luck!*

**1**   Can you do the following? Say the answers out loud and write them down. Three points for each correct answer. Check your pronunciation with the **Pronunciation guide.**

**a**   Introduce yourself and ask someone to introduce themselves.
**b**   Ask someone for their name using the formal way.
**c**   Ask someone how things are.
**d**   Answer the previous question and return the question (formally).
**e**   Tell someone what you do in life.
**f**   Ask someone what their job is.
**g**   Say where you live (town and country).
**h**   Say what nationality you are and what language(s) you speak.
**i**   Say whether you are married or single and whether you have children.
**j**   Say that you don't understand.
**k**   Ask someone if they speak English.
**l**   Ask someone to speak more slowly.

Points _____ /36

**2**   Fill in the blanks with the right endings of the verbs *to have* or *to be*. One point for each correct answer:.

Je **a** ....... anglais mais ma mère **b** ...... française. Mon père et ma mère **c** ...... mariés depuis 50 ans. J'**d**..... trois frères qui ne **e** ....... pas mariés et une soeur qui **f** ..... deux enfants. Ils **g** ....... quinze et dix ans. Ma soeur et moi **h** .....un mari anglais et nous **i** ....... professeures de français en Angleterre. Je n' **j** .... pas d'enfants.

Points _____ /10

3 Verb endings. Do you remember which endings go where?
Half a point for each correct answer. Choose the correct
ending from the box below.

a Tu parl____ français? b oui, je parl___ français. c Et lui, il
parl___ anglais? d Nous parl___ italien. e Et vous qu'est-ce
que vous parl__? f Mes parents parl___ espagnol g En
Allemagne, on parl___ allemand. h Ma soeur, elle parl___
japonais.

Points: _____ /4

- e   -e   -es   -e   -e   -ons   -ent   -ez

## Units 4–7   Points: _____/50

This test covers the main vocabulary and phrases, skills and
language points in Units 4–7. For how to read your score, refer
back to page 200. You can check your answers in the **Key to the
exercises. Bonne chance!**

4 Can you ask and say the following? Say the answers out
loud and write them down. Two points for each correct
answer.

a Is it far?
b No it is not far.
c Is there a bank nearby?
d No, there is not a bank nearby.
e Have you a stamp?
f No I haven't any.
g What is the film like?
h Where is the bus stop?
i It is ten minutes away on foot.
j When does the shop open?

Points: _____ /20

5 Complete the questions by selecting the appropriate
endings. One point for each correct answer.

a Il y a                    i c'est?
b Quel âge                  ii vous appelez-vous?
c Qu'est-ce que             iii commencez-vous le matin?
d A quelle heure            iv ont-ils?
e Comment                   v une cabine téléphonique
                               près d'ici?

Points: _____ /5

6 Using the example as a model, say these dates out loud in French, then write them out in full for practice. One point for each correct answer.

Tuesday, the 9th of November: **le mardi neuf novembre**

a Sunday the 31st of March
b Wednesday the 2nd of June
c Friday the 18th of January
d Tuesday the 24th of October
e Saturday the 11th of May
f Monday the 23rd of August
g Thursday the 19th of September

Points: ____/7

7 Fill in the blanks with the appropriate verbs from the box below. One point for each correct answer.

a Je ...... le petit-déjeuner à huit heures du matin.
b Ma mère ........ la cuisine tous les jours.
c Mon mari et moi......... le train pour aller travailler.
d Qu'est-ce que vous ...... pendant le week-end?
e Pour aller à Paris on peut ........ le train ou la voiture.
f Elle ....... le français mais ne le ...... pas.
g Nous ....... le travail à cinq heures de l'après-midi.
h Où est-ce que tu ............? Dans une compagnie d'aviation.
i J'adore ...... la télévision.

prendre  comprend  regarder  faites  finissons  prenons  parle
fait  travailles  prends

Points: ____/10

8 Can you say the following? Say the answers out loud and write them down. One point for each correct answer.

a I live in England.
b She works in the USA.
c We like Germany a lot.
d We spend our holidays in Australia.
e I know Portugal well.
f Do you speak French?
g She is English.
h Bordeaux is a French town.

Points: ____/8

## Units 8–10    Points: _____/50

This test covers the main vocabulary and phrases, skills and language points in Units 8–10. For how to read your score, refer back to page 200. You can check your answers in the **Key to the exercises**. **Bonne chance!**

9 Look at the box below and say out loud the likes and dislikes of Sophie and Mohamed. Then write down your own hobbies. Three points for each correct answer.

|   |   | Sophie | Mohamed | Yourself |
|---|---|---|---|---|
| a | playing football | 1 | 3 | |
| b | cooking | 3 | 1 | |
| c | watching TV | 3 | 2 | |
| d | listening to music | 4 | 3 | |
| e | swimming | 2 | 4 | |
| f | skiing | 4 | 1 | |
| g | going to restaurants | 2 | 3 | |
| h | playing tennis | 1 | 4 | |

| Adore | Aime beaucoup | N'aime pas | Déteste |
|---|---|---|---|
| 4 | 3 | 2 | 1 |

Points: _____/24

10 Fill in the part of the reflexive verbs which is missing. One point for each correct ending.

a je ..... lève
b tu ..... habilles
c il ..... lave
d nous ..... baignons
e vous ..... reposez
f elles ..... couchent

Points: _____/6

11 Talk about the weather in France, incorporating each icon into a full sentence:

e.g. **chaud → il fait chaud.**

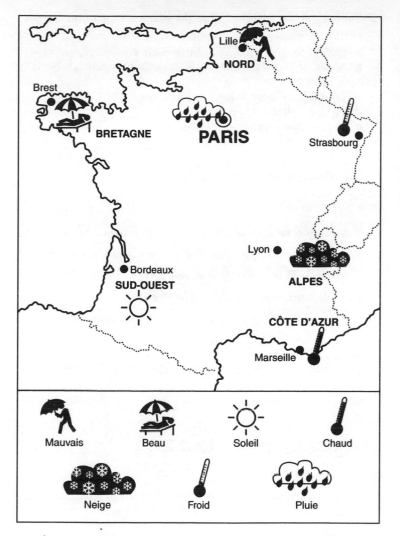

a  À Lille, ....................................................

b  En Bretagne, ......................................

c  Dans le Sud-Ouest ...........................

d  Sur la Côte d'Azur ..........................

e  Dans les Alpes.....................................

f  À Strasbourg  ......................................

g  À Paris ..................................................

**Points: _____/7**

**12** Talk about the future. Fill in the blanks. One point for each correct ending.

  **a** Qu'est-ce que vous ...... faire pour vos vacances?
  **b** Nous ...... passer deux semaines de vacances au bord de la mer.
  **c** Jane ...... visiter le sud de la France
  **d** Tu ...... aller voir le film ce soir?
  **e** Je ...... me reposer chez moi.
  **f** Les Durand ...... se baigner tous les jours

Points: _____/6

**13** Translate the following letter into French.

*Dear Amélie,*

*I am going to spend three weeks in France this summer with my sister Ruth. I am going to learn French in Paris. Ruth is going to visit old buildings and do some shopping. In the evening we are going to see friends. Are you going to see us (**nous voir**)?*
*See you soon.*

*Caroline*

Points: _____/7

# Self-assessment test 2

## Units 11–13   Points: _____/50

This test covers the main vocabulary and phrases, skills and language points in Units 11–13. For how to read your score, refer back to page 200. You can check your answers in the **Key to the exercises. Bonne chance!**

**1** Can you do the following? Say the answers out loud and write them down. Three points for each correct answer.

  **a** Say that you are looking for a cotton dress.
  **b** Give the English translation for **Vous faites quelle taille?**
  **c** Ask whether you can try it on.
  **d** Say that it is a bit too expensive/big/small
  **e** Ask: Do you have anything else?

Points: _____/15

**2** Say the following out loud and write them down. Three points for each correct answer.

   **a** Say good evening and ask if they have a double room with bathroom.
   **b** Say that it is for two nights.
   **c** Ask for the price.
   **d** Ask if breakfast is included.
   **e** Ask whether there is a restaurant in the hotel.
   **f** Say that the television does not work.

                                                         **Points:** _____/18

**3** Say the following out loud and write them down. Three points for each correct answer (answer **e** = 2 points).

   **a** You are hungry. Enter a bar/restaurant and ask what sandwiches are on offer.
   **b** What would you say to have one item of the menu explained?
   **c** Ask for a well done, medium and rare steak
   **d** Say 'I'll take .....'
   **e** Ask for the bill.
   **f** Ask what they have to drink.

                                                          **Points:** _____/17

## Units 14–16   **Points:** \_\_\_\_\_/50

This test covers the main vocabulary and phrases, skills and language points in Units 14–16. For how to read your score, refer back to page 200. You can check your answers in the **Key to the exercises. Bonne chance!**

**4** You are in the **Office de Tourisme** in Paris. Can you do the following? Say the answers out loud and write them down. Three points for each correct answer.

   **a** Find out whether they can book a room for you.
   **b** Ask for a town map.
   **c** Find out how to go to the Eiffel tower.
   **d** Ask what they've got in the way of excursions.
   **e** Ask what there is to do for the children.
   **f** Ask for a list of restaurants.
   **g** Ask the attendant to show you the **grands magasins** on the map.

                                                          **Points :** \_\_\_\_\_/21

5 Look at the following timetable and take part in the conversation. Say the answers out loud and write them down. Three points for each correct answer.

## BORDEAUX-DAX-PAU-(Tarbes)

| | ○ TER | ● TER | TER | ◉ TER | ● CAR | TGV | ● TER | ● | TGV | ● TER |
|---|---|---|---|---|---|---|---|---|---|---|
| Bordeaux-St-Jean | 6.43 | 7.04 | 8.20 | 8.31 | | 10.33 | | | 11.53 | 12.17 |
| Pessac | | | | 8.39 | | | | | | |
| Facture-Biganos | 7.05 | | | 9.02 | 9.08 | | | | | |
| Sanguinet | | | | | 9.32 | | | | | |
| Biscarrosse (Gare Routière) | | | | | 9.47 | | | | | |
| Parentis-en-Born | | | | | 9.57 | | | | | |
| Ychoux | 7.22 | | | | 10.09 | | | | | 12.55 |
| Labouheyre | 7.30 | | | | 10.31 | | | | | 13.04 |
| Morcenx | 7.41 | | | | 11.06 | | | | | 13.15 |
| Rion-des-Landes | | | | | | | | | | |
| Laluque | | | | | | | | | | |
| Dax | 8.02 | 8.11 | 9.25 | | | 11.40 | | | 12.59 | |
| Dax | 8.07 | | 9.27 | | | 11.46 | 12.10 | | | |
| Puyoo | 8.24 | | | | | | 12.30 | 13.04 | | |
| Orthez | 8.35 | | 9.56 | | | | 12.41 | 13.16 | | |
| Artix (SNCF) | 8.46 | | | | | | 12.54 | 13.29 | | |
| Pau | 8.58 | | 10.17 | | | 12.35 | 13.07 | 13.41 | | |
| Pau | 9.04 | | | | | 12.37 | | 13.43 | | |
| Coarraze-Nay | 9.15 | | | | | | | 13.56 | | |
| Lourdes | 9.33 | | | | | | 13.05 | 14.13 | | |
| Tarbes | 9.50 | | | | | | 13.20 | 14.27 | | |
| Vélo autorisé | x | x | x | | | | x | | | |

● du lundi au vendredi
◉ le samedi
○ du lundi au samedi

CAR : Desserte assurée par autocar. Tarification SNCF.
TER : Transport express régional
TGV : réservation obligatoire.
*horaires en italiques: train soumis à des conditions d'emprunt, ou à supplément; renseignements dans le gares.*

**a Vous** *Ask for a single to Tarbes.*
**Employé** Oui … c'est pour quel jour?
**b Vous** *Say on 16th April, in the morning around 10 o'clock.*
**Employé** Il y a un TGV qui quitte Bordeaux à 10.33. Ça vous va?
**c Vous** *Ask what time it arrives?*
**Employé** A 13.20.
**d Vous** *Ask if you need to reserve a seat?*
**Employé** Oui bien sûr, et il faut payer un supplément. Vous avez une réduction?
**e Vous** *Answer no. Find out the price.*
**Employé** Alors en seconde classe, c'est …

**Points: _____/15**

6 Read the text below describing Cauterets, a tourist town. Then answer the questions. Two points for each correct answer :

Cauterets (935–3298 m), village authentique et prestigieux, est situé au coeur des Pyrénées. Sa station thermale aux 11 sources attirent de nombreux touristes qui bénéficient de ses eaux et y admirent ses paysages grandioses. Joie de découvrir, l'été, lors des randonnées vers les sommets, sa montagne douce, cascades, lacs et plateaux fleuris. En hiver, ses pistes de ski alpin et de fond, merveilleusement enneigées, font le plaisir de tous les skieurs, des débutants aux experts.

a Where is Cauterets situated?
b What is the main attraction for the tourists?
c What is special about its landscapes?
d What sport can one do in summer?
e Why are the summits attractive?
f What sports can one do in winter?
g Does Cauterets cater for all levels of skiers?

Points: _____/14

## Units 17–19  Points: _____/50

This test covers the main vocabulary and phrases, skills and language points in Units 17–19. For how to read your score, refer back to page 200. You can check your answers in the **Key to the exercises. Bonne chance!**

7  You are staying in 'Les Edelweiss', 7, Boulevard Latapie-Flurin in the centre of Cauterets. Some French friends from Paris phone you and want to go hiking with you. Can you do the following? Look at the information below and say the answers out loud. Three points for each correct answer.

a Ask whether they are coming by car or train (translate: *take the car or train*).
b Give directions if they choose to come by train.
c Give directions if they choose to come by car and tell them that they can park the car opposite the hotel.
d Give them your address and say that the hotel is in the centre of Cauterets.
e Fix a date and time: Friday 22nd April around seven o'clock in the evening.

Points : _____/15

---

**CAUTERETS**

Hautes-Pyrénées (65) - Midi-Pyrénées – Altitude 932 m. –
1336 habitants - Paris 899 km – Capacité d'accueil: 22 000 lits

Accès par avion: Aéroport de Tarbes: 35 km de Cauterets
Accès par train: Gare SNCF à Lourdes puis bus jusqu'à
Cauterets (30 km)
Accès par voiture: Autoroute jusqu'à Tarbes, puis la N21 et la D921

---

8   Match up the words in the left-hand column with the correct English translation in the right-hand column. One point for each correct answer.

a  la monnaie                       i    *banknote*
b  un changeur de monnaie           ii   *banker's card*
c  un distributeur automatique      iii  *bill (drinks, snacks)*
d  une carte bancaire               iv   *exchange rate*
e  la pièce                         v    *coin changing machine*
f  la télécarte                     vi   *a cashpoint machine*
g  un billet                        vii  *means of identification*
h  le cours du change               viii *bill (hotel)*
i  l'addition                       ix   *telephone card*
j  la note                          x    *coin*
k  la pièce d'identité              xi   *small change*

**Points:** _____/11

9   You have damaged your knee after two days of skiing in Cauterets. As you need to see the doctor you speak to the hotel receptionist. Say the answers out loud and write them down. Three points for each correct answer.

a  Tell the receptionist that you need to see a doctor.
b  Ask for his/her address.
c  Ring the doctor and say that you want an appointment.
d  Explain that your knee (**le genou**) is sore.
e  Say that you have been suffering for three days.
f  Say that you cannot walk.
g  Tell the receptionist that you can come tomorrow morning at ten o'clock.
h  Say your name and spell it.

**Points:** _____/24

key to the exercises and tests

## Unit 1

**Activities: 1 a** Bonjour Madame/Mademoiselle **b** Bonjour
Monsieur **c** Bonsoir Madame/Mademoiselle **d** Bonjour
Messieurs-dames **e** Bonne nuit, Monsieur **f** Bonsoir Messieurs-
dames **2** Bonsoir Monsieur **3 c 4** Bonne nuit **5** Comment ça
va? Très bien merci. **6 a** s'il vous plaît **b** ça va **c** au revoir **d**
madame **e** bonsoir **f** non merci **7 a** iii, **b** ii, **c** iii, **d** iii
**Mini-test: 1** Bonjour, comment ça va? **2** Parlez plus
lentement, s'il vous plaît **3** Pardon **4** D'accord

## Unit 2

**Have a go!:** Bonjour Madame. Je voudrais une baguette, s'il
vous plaît.
**Dialogue:** Beer, wine and two bottles of mineral water; no,
she doesn't get any beer
**Activities: 1 a** un café **b** une bière **c** un journal **d** des
bouteilles **e** un euro **f** un timbre **2** une chambre, un café, un
journal **3 a** Je voudrais quatre cartes, s'il vous plaît **b** Vous
avez quatre timbres? **c** Et de l'aspirine, s'il vous plaît? **d** C'est
combien? **4** trois **5 a** ii, **b** iv, **c** iii, **d** i **6 a** Messieurs-dames **b**
café **c** bière **d** voudrais **e** addition **7 a** cinq **b** neuf **c** dix **d**
neuf **e** deux **f** quatre **g** neuf **h** huit
**Mini-test: 1** Très bien merci **2** Speak more slowly **3** Vous
avez de l'aspirine, s'il vous plaît? Merci, au revoir **4** la gare

## Unit 3

**Have a go!:** Je voudrais deux bouteilles d'eau minérale et un
kilo d'oranges.
**Dialogue:** Yes, as a secretary; 3 children – a girl and 2 boys;
Jane is not married, she has a boyfriend.

**Practise!:** travaille, travailles, travaille, travaillons, travaillez, travaillent

**Activities:** 1 a 13 b 18 c 4 d 12 e 7 f 19 g 5 h 15 i 11 j 9 2 a treize b quinze c vingt d treize e dix-neuf f onze g cinq h six i quatre j douze 3 a est b ont c Elles d enfants, un e n'a pas f n'est pas g dix h a, ans 4 a n'ai pas de timbres b n'a pas de café c n'est pas marié d n'est pas secrétaire e n'ai pas de chambre f n'ont pas d'enfants g n'est pas dans le nord de l'Angleterre h ne parle pas français i n'a pas 18 ans
5 a Je m'appelle Anne b Non, je suis mariée c Oui, j'ai deux enfants d Une fille et un garçon e Ils ont douze et dix ans f J'habite Chaville g Oui, je suis secrétaire 6 a Vous êtes marié? b Vous avez des enfants? c Vous travaillez? d Vous habitez Paris? e Vous avez des frères et soeurs? f Ils ont quel âge? g Vous êtes français? h Vous parlez anglais?

**Mini-test:** 1 Parlez plus lentement, s'il vous plaît 2 b 3 I don't understand 4 Je voudrais une bouteille de vin, s'il vous plaît 5 C'est combien? 6 a Je m'appelle b Je ne suis pas marié(e) c J'habite (à) Brighton

## Unit 4

**Have a go!:** Vous êtes français(e)? Vous êtes marié(e)? Je m'appelle … et vous? Vous travaillez?

**Dialogue:** Yes; Yes; Yes; 3 children

**Activities:** 1 a v b i c vii d viii e iii f ii g vi h iv 2 (*Note that there are alternative ways of asking these questions*) a Il y a un restaurant dans l'hôtel? b Il y a une pharmacie près d'ici? c Il y a des magasins près d'ici? d La banque est ouverte? e Il y a un train direct pour Paris? f C'est loin la gare? g Où sont les toilettes? 3 a Il y a une pharmacie mais il n'y a pas d'aspirine b Il y a une pâtisserie mais il n'y a pas de croissants c Il y a une gare mais il n'y a pas de trains d Il y a un arrêt d'autobus mais il n'y a pas de bus e Il y a un bar mais il n'y a pas de bière f Il y a une cabine téléphonique mais il n'y a pas de téléphone 4 a Vous êtes en vacances? b Vous êtes mariée? c Vous avez des enfants? d Vous habitez Londres? e Vous travaillez? 5 a combien b où c quand d où e où f comment 6 a 49,50 € b 3,75 € c 8,60 € d 56,15 € e 68 €

**Mini-test:** 1 Vous vous appelez comment? 2 Vous travaillez? 3 Vous habitez où? J'habite dans la banlieue de Londres 4 J'ai … ans 5 Il y a une banque près d'ici au bout de la rue

## Unit 5

**Have a go!:** Vous avez un plan, s'il vous plaît? Il y a une banque et une cabine téléphonique près d'ici? *You can find more questions to ask in* **Key words and phrases** *of Unit 4.*
**Dialogue:** 8.30 a.m. and 5.30 p.m.; school canteen
**Activities: 2 a** prends **b** commencent **c** arrive **d** apprend **e** déjeune **f** prenez **g** fais **h** est **i** finit **j** faites **k** attendons **l** comprennent **3 a** iii, **b** vii, **c** v, **d** i, **e** ii, **f** iv, **g** vi **4** f, e, a, c, g, d, h, b **5 a** prends **b** prennent **c** commence **d** travaille **e** déjeune **f** finit **g** fait **h** regardent **6** le 1er mai, le 10 juin, le 3 février, le 13 octobre, le 21 mars, le 30 septembre, le 15 juillet, le 6 août **7 a** mercredi **b** vendredi **c** dimanche **d** lundi **e** jeudi **f** samedi **g** mardi **8 a** il est neuf heures dix (du matin) **b** midi moins vingt **c** une heure et demie (de l'après-midi) **d** six heures vingt-cinq (du soir) **h** minuit moins dix **9 a** 2.35 p.m. **b** 12.15 p.m. **c** 9.10 a.m. **d** 11.45 p.m. **e** 4.25 a.m. **f** 6.30 p.m.
**Mini-test: 1** dimanche, samedi, vendredi, jeudi, mercredi, mardi, lundi **2** Quand est-ce que la banque ferme? **3** Il y a un train pour Lille? **4** Est-ce que je peux prendre le petit-déjeuner à l'hôtel? **5** (Nous sommes le ...) Aujourd'hui c'est le ... Il est ...

## Unit 6

**Have a go!: 1** Vous pouvez parler plus lentement? Vous pouvez répéter, s'il vous plaît? **2** *Use the dialogue and* **Key words and phrases** *of Unit 5*
**Dialogue:** As you leave the house turn left, go to the end of rue Vaugirard, turn right into rue Vincennes and the park is 200 metres on your left. It takes approximately 25 minutes.
**Activities: 1 a** Pour aller à la piscine? **b** Pour aller à la gare? **c** Pour aller à l'église St. Paul? **d** Pour aller au musée? **e** Pour aller à l'office du tourisme? **2 a** C **b** E **c** A **d** D **e** B **4** à Brighton, en France, l'Allemagne, à Berlin, à Bonn, au Danemark, aux Etats-Unis, au Japon, à Londres **5 a** en face du **b** à côté de la **c** au coin de **d** entre **e** au bout de **f** grands magasins **g** bar **h** pâtisserie **i** dans la rue **j** sur la place

## Unit 7

**Have a go!: 1** dans **2** sur **3** entre **4** à côté du **5** sous **6** devant **7** derrière
**Dialogue:** a silk scarf; 46 € , 53 € et 68,50 €; small with a scene of the Champs-Elysées
**Activities: 1** cet, ces, ce, ces, ce, cet, cette, cette **2** Mme Durand a 35 ans. Elle a les cheveux blonds et longs. Elle a les yeux verts. Elle fait 1,70 mètre et pèse 65 kg. Elle porte des lunettes

rondes. Elle porte un ensemble vert uni, des chaussures légères et une chemise blanche. Jane a 23 ans. Elle a les cheveux bruns et courts. Ses yeux sont bleus (Elle a les yeux bleus). Elle fait 1,62 mètre et pèse 55 kg. Elle porte un jean bleu pâle et un pull-over blanc. Elle a (porte) des bottes noires. **3 a** une boîte de petits pois français **b** une tarte aux pommes **c** un baba au rhum **d** une glace à la vanille **e** un sorbet au citron **f** un grand verre de vin rouge **g** un café au lait sans sucre **h** un poulet à 6,80 € **i** un petit café noir **j** un sandwich au fromage **k** une bouteille de lait **4 a** Chère **b** famille **c** tout **d** sympathique **e** bonnes **f** confortable **g** grande **h** longues **i** jours **j** meilleure **k** anglaise **l** mieux **m** prochaine **5 a** un grand café noir **b** deux pressions **c** et un petit crème **d** non, deux pressions, un petit crème et un grand café noir **e** Vous avez des croissants? **f** J'en voudrais quatre

**Mini-test: 1 a** au bout de la rue **b** Prenez la route pour Lille **2 b 3 a 4** Vous avez autre chose? C'est de quelle couleur? Je vais prendre le plus petit

## Unit 8

**Have a go!:** Je cherche quelque chose pour ouvrir les bouteilles de vin.

**Dialogue:** Cooking French dishes; squash, swimming, wind-surfing; beef stew with wine and chicken in wine; twice a week

**Activities: 1 a** Comment vous appelez-vous? Je m'appelle Roger Burru. **b** Quel âge avez-vous? J'ai 35 ans. **c** Vous êtes marié? Oui, je suis marié? **d** Vous avez des enfants? Non, je n'ai pas d'enfants. **e** Qu'est-ce que vous faites dans la vie? Je suis professeur. **f** Depuis quand? Depuis 10 ans. **g** Où habitez-vous? J'habite Lille. **h** Qu'est-ce que vous faites comme sport? Je fais de la natation. **i** Qu'est-ce que vous faites pendant vos loisirs? J'aime beaucoup faire la cuisine. **2** e, c, a adore, d, g aime beaucoup, f, h n'aime pas, b déteste **3 b** le prends **c** le connaissez **d** les a **e** l'ai **f** l'aiment **g** la fais **h** l'attendons **i** la regarde **j** les écoutons **4 a** viii, **b** vii, **c** iv, **d** ii, **e** ix, **f** x, **g** iii, **h** vi, **i** v, **j** i, **5 a** F **b** F **c** V **d** V **e** V **f** F **g** V **h** V **i** F **j** F **k** V **l** F

**Mini-test: 1** Je joue au squash mieux que Fabrice **2** La France est plus grande que l'Angleterre **3** Elle a des lunettes et des cheveux longs **4** Je cherche quelque chose pour réparer ma voiture **5** J'aime le squash mais je préfère jouer au tennis **6** J'aime beaucoup la cuisine française.

## Unit 9

**Have a go!:** 1 a Vous pouvez répéter, s'il vous plaît? b Vous pouvez parler plus lentement s'il vous plaît?

**Activities:** 1 a v, b vii, c ix, d vi, e iii, f viii, g ii, h iv, i i 2 a iv, b v, c i, d vi, e ii, f iii 3 a C b F c B d D e A f E; i 7 ii add pepper and salt iii 30 g of butter iv when the butter is hot v a fork

**Practise!:** It is strictly forbidden to take photographs using a tripod or flash; to damage the sculptures or the vases; to pick flowers or fruit; to climb on the sculptures; to walk on the lawn or to climb on the seats; to lunch outside the area reserved for the cafeteria; to bring animals into the museum's grounds; to ride a bicycle; to play ball games; to drop rubbish except in the litter baskets.

**Mini-test:** 1 Aujourd'hui il fait froid mais il ne pleut pas. 2 Qu'est-ce qu'il faut faire? 3 Il me faut une télécarte pour téléphoner. 4 a la direction de la gare? b où est la station de métro la plus proche? c l'adresse du docteur?

## Unit 10

**Have a go!:** 1 Out of order 2 Qu'est-ce qu'il faut faire pour utiliser l'Internet?

**Dialogue:** 4 weeks; to the seaside and to the mountains; swimming, play tennis, go for long walks and see regional historic monuments. No, she prefers to stay at home or go out with friends.

**Practise!:** Je m'habille, tu t'habilles, il/elle/on s'habille, nous nous habillons, vous vous habillez, ils s'habillent

**Activities:** *Activities 1, 2, 3, 4, 5, could have alternative answers to the ones given below:* 1 a D'abord je me lève à 7 heures b puis je me lave c ensuite je prends le petit-déjeuner avec les enfants d À 8h30 j'emmène les enfants à l'école e ensuite je fais des courses f À midi je prépare le déjeuner g L'après-midi, je joue au tennis h ou je vais chez mes amis i ou je vais au cinéma j Le soir, je regarde la télévision k ou j'écoute la radio l enfin je me couche à 23 heures. 2 a …il/elle se lève … b …il/elle se lave … c …il/elle prend … d il/elle emmène … e …il/elle va … f …il/elle rentre, prépare … g il/elle joue … h …il/elle va chez ses amis … i il/elle va … j il/elle regarde … k il/elle écoute … l il/elle se couche … 3 *Robert:* a en août b 3 semaines c à Oxford en Angleterre d Je vais apprendre l'anglais, visiter des monuments historiques, voir des amis, sortir le soir, jouer au tennis. *Jeanine:* a le 21 juin b 10 jours c à Anglet près de Biarritz dans le sud de la France d Je vais me baigner, lire beaucoup, regarder un peu la télévision, faire de longues promenades, me coucher tôt. **4 a** Vous allez partir quand en vacances? **b** Où allez-vous aller? **c** Comment allez-vous passer vos vacances? **5 a** beaucoup **b** mari **c** Grande-Bretagne **d** finit **e** samedi **f** après-midi **g** rester **h** jours **i** visiter **j** habitent **k** besoin **l** prendre **6 a** téléphoner à Marc **b** aller chez le dentiste **c** aller à la banque **d** faire des courses et acheter 2 steaks, une bouteille de vin et une glace à la fraise **e** écrire une lettre à ma mère **f** poster la lettre **g** jouer au tennis **h** faire la cuisine **i** inviter Anne à dîner

**Mini-test: 1 a** Vous pouvez m'aider s'il vous plaît? **b** Je ne comprends pas. Vous pouvez répéter s'il vous plaît? **2 a** il a besoin d'un jus de fruit/d'un verre d'eau/de boire **b** avons besoin d'une banque/d'un distributeur automatique **c** ont besoin de manger/de sandwiches **d** ai besoin d'un docteur/d'aller chez le docteur **3 a** vont **b** va **c** vont **d** vas **e** vais **f** allons

## Unit 11

**Activities: 1 a** 7/8 p.m. **b** shut **c** Monday **d** pâtisseries, charcuteries **3 a, c** boucherie, **d, e, g** épicerie, **b** boulangerie, **f** charcuterie **4 c, f, h, a, e, d, g, i, b 5 b, d, g, l 7 a** Confiserie **b** Fleuriste **c** Confection **d** Pressings **e** Généraliste **f** Librairie **g** Coiffeur-Esthéticienne **h** Informatique **i** Bijouterie **j** Kinésithérapeute **8 a** Je cherche une jupe noire **b** Vous faites quelle taille? **c** quelque chose de moins cher **d** Je vais essayer **e** la jupe à 50 euros **f** Elle vous va bien? **9 a** Je voudrais un journal, s'il vous plaît. Qu'est-ce que vous avez comme journaux anglais? **b** Je vais prendre le *Times* et ces trois cartes postales. C'est combien un timbre pour l'Angleterre? **c** Je vais prendre huit timbres **d** Je vais aussi acheter le magazine 'Elle' pour ma femme **10 a** a pullover **b** white/pale yellow **c** it's too big **d** he doesn't like the colour **e** 68,50 €

**Mini-test: 1** J'ai besoin de kleenex **2** Je voudrais quelque chose de plus grand, s'il vous plaît **3** Vous avez autre chose? **4** C'est tout **5** Vous acceptez les cartes de crédit?

## Unit 12

**Activities: 1 a** yes **b** no **c** book your accommodation **d** no **2 a** F, **b** F – up to 4 stars, **c** T, **d** T, **e** T, **f** F – usually but not always, **g** F, **h** T **3 a** Vous avez une liste d'hôtels? **b** Pouvez-vous me réserver une chambre? **c** Vous choisissez quel hôtel? **d** dans le 16ème arrondissement **e** J'espère que l'hôtel n'est pas complet **f** Il y aura de la place **4 a** F – au deuxième **b** F – c'est

en plus **c** V **d** V **e** F – au fond du couloir à droite **f** V **g** V **5**
Bonsoir, vous avez une chambre, s'il vous plaît? Non, une
chambre double à deux lits et avec salle de bains. C'est pour
trois nuits. C'est combien? Est-ce que le petit-déjeuner est
compris? À quelle heure servez-vous le petit-déjeuner? On peut
prendre un repas dans l'hôtel? Haussman c'est qui? **6 a** Le
radiateur ne marche pas **b** Il n'y a pas de savon **c** Il n'y a pas
d'eau chaude **d** La lampe ne marche pas **e** Il n'y a pas de
serviettes **f** La douche ne marche pas **g** La télévision ne marche
pas **h** Il n'y a pas de couvertures **8 a** river, forest **b** mountains
**c** hot water **d** children, meeting place **e** advisable **9 a** yes **b** 172
€ **c** send an international cheque for 11€
**Mini-test: 1** Je cherche un hôtel à deux étoiles **2** Vous pouvez
me réserver une chambre, s'il vous plaît? **3** Le petit-déjeuner
est compris? **4** Il n'y a pas de téléphone dans la chambre **5** Il y
a un camping près d'ici?

## Unit 13

**Activities: 1 a** a variety of cuisines **b** can easily be found **c**
usually cheap **d** meat, vegetables or noodles **e** a limited range
of dishes **f** today's special **g** a crêperie **h** le menu touristique **2 c**
**e b f d a 4 a** Je voudrais un croque-monsieur **b** Vous avez des
omelettes? **c** Qu'est-ce que c'est 'Parmentier'? **d** Je vais prendre
l'omelette Parmentier **e** Qu'est-ce que vous avez comme jus de
fruit? **f** Je voudrais un jus d'ananas et l'addition, s'il vous plaît
**5 a** Qu'est-ce que c'est une blanquette de veau? **b** Je n'aime pas
les viandes en sauce **c** Je préfère les grillades **d** Je voudrais mon
steak bien cuit **e** Comme légumes, je vais prendre des haricots
verts **f** Un demi-litre de vin rouge **g** Comme dessert, je vais
prendre une crème au caramel **6 a** Pour commencer je vais
prendre un filet de hareng **b** Je vais prendre un avocat à la
vinaigrette **c** Qu'est-ce que c'est le cassoulet? **d** Je n'aime pas
les haricots. Je vais prendre la grillade du jour avec frites
**e** A point. Je voudrais aussi une bouteille de Sauvignon
**f** Je voudrais du pain, s'il vous plaît **7** L'Auberge Au boin coin.
It provides special menus for children and offers a family type
atmosphere in the country.
**Mini-test: 1 a** Où est le restaurant le plus proche? **b** Je cherche
quelque chose de moins cher **c** Vous avez autre chose? **2 a 3 a**
Il n'y a plus de sandwiches au fromage **b** Comme dessert, je
vais prendre une glace à la vanille **c** Qu'est-ce que vous avez
comme boissons?

## Unit 14

**Activities: 1 a** V **b** F **c** F **d** F **e** V **f** V **2 a** direction **b** prenez **c** changer **d** Aéroport Charles de Gaulle **e** descendez **3** He needs to take direction La Défense, change at Châtelet Les Halles then take direction Orly and get off at la station Luxembourg **4 a** go up **b** crossroads **c** carry straight on **5 a** C'est quelle ligne pour aller au musée d'Orsay? **b** C'est direct? **c** C'est loin à pied? **d** Le bus part à quelle heure? **e** Où est-ce que je peux acheter un ticket? **f** Je voudrais acheter un aller-retour pour les Invalides **g** Je vais prendre un carnet **6 a** Je voudrais un aller-retour pour Paris. **b** le 24 juin, dans la matinée, vers 9 heures **c** Je vais prendre le premier à 9h.04. C'est combien, le billet en seconde classe? **d** Non **e** Il faut réserver la place?
**Mini-test: 1** Je voudrais un sandwich au fromage **2** Qu'est-ce que vous avez à boire? **3** Je voudrais un carnet (de tickets) **4** A quelle heure part le prochain train pour Paris?

## Unit 15

**Activities: 1 a** Je voudrais un plan de la ville **b** Qu'est-ce qu'il y a à voir? **c** Qu'est-ce qu'il y a à faire pour les enfants? **d** Il y a une piscine couverte? **e** Pour aller au Parc floral, il y a un bus? **2 a** Yes. There are animals, a children's play area, a miniature golf and a little train for a ride around the park. **b** Yes. There is a picnic area. **c** A butterfly glasshouse (*la serre*) and an exhibition on insects. **3 a** C'est combien l'entrée? **b** Qu'est-ce que c'est la serre? **c** douze ans; il faut payer pour le 'petit train' et le golf miniature? **d** On peut pique-niquer? **e** Merci Madame. A quelle heure ferme le parc? **4 a** B **b** A and C: on the 1st Sunday of a month, D on a Sunday **c** A: every evening except Tuesdays until 9pm + late-night openings with some exhibitions; C: late-night opening on Monday and Wednesday; D: late-night opening on Thursday; **d** B because of its dynamic approach in teaching sciences and techniques: interactive games, spectacles, etc. **5 a** 7.15 am. **b** one hour **c** have lunch, visit the Hospices, the wine museum and the wine cellar **d** 159€ **6 a** Nous voulons faire l'excursion de la route des vins de Bourgogne **b** Nous voulons deux places pour le 22 juillet **c** Le car part d'ici? **d** Vous pouvez répéter, s'il vous plaît? **e** Merci. A quelle heure part le car? **f** On peut acheter du vin dans la cave? **7 a** dimanche prochain **b** 9h.30 **c** 7 heures environ **d** 61 € **e** Les appartements du château le matin, les jardins à midi, et le Trianon et le petit village de la Reine Marie-Antoinette l'après-midi.

Mini-test: 1 Je voudrais un plan de ville, s'il vous plaît 2 Est-ce que le musée ferme entre midi et deux heures? 3 Il y a une visite guidée?

## Unit 16

Activities: 1 a F in the evenings b F they like to dance and eat well c F it is a restaurant with music, open all night d V e V f V 2 a E b D c C d B e A 3 a Monday b his wedding anniversary c dinner by candlelight d Spanish e 2 am f a dozen red roses 4 a Je voudrais des places pour dimanche prochain. b Ça finit à quelle heure le concert? c C'est combien la place? d C'est tarif réduit. e Ma soeur doit payer? 5 Those who are students, OAPs, from large families, servicemen, under 18. From 6 o'clock Monday to Friday except on public holidays and the days before. 6 a Où est-ce qu'on peut jouer au tennis? b Où est-ce qu'on réserve le court? c C'est combien l'heure? d On peut louer une raquette? e Vous pouvez me donner l'adresse du club, s'il vous plaît? 7 a i yes ii no; b i yes ii no; c i no ii yes d i yes ii no e i play table tennis ii board games
Mini-test: 1 a date-stamp b exit c connection d left luggage e platform f ticket office 2 a un carnet (de tickets), s'il vous plaît b un aller-retour svp c un horaire svp d l'arrêt d'autobus svp? e le bureau de renseignements svp? f un aller (simple) svp? 3 c 4 c 5 a 6 place, tarif, boîte de nuit, ambiance, spectacles

## Unit 17

Activities

1 a Yes b Yes, in wet conditions the speed limit is lowered to 110 km/h on motorways and 100km/h on dual carriageways c route nationale d a recommended alternative route
2 a mai, juin, b du 25 au 27 juillet c les weekends du 22 au 24 et 29 au 31 août 3 e, c, d, b, a 4 a Je voudrais passer une nuit dans votre hôtel. Quelles sont les directions pour Est-Artigues? b De Bayonne c Vous pouvez répétez s'il vous plaît? d Une fois sorti, il faut prendre aux feux à droite, sortie CourtePaille, et c'est à 500 mètres e Il y a un restaurant? f Je peux (on peut) arriver à quelle heure? 5 a v, b vi, c iv, d vii, e iii, f i, g ii 6 a F it is free from 1 to 2 pm, after 7 o'clock, on Sundays and bank holidays b T c F only 0,50€, 1€, 2€ d F e T f T 7 a iv, b vii, c i, d vi, e iii, f ii, g v 8 pompiste a, c, f; client b, d, e 9 a Bonjour, je voudrais de l'essence sans plomb, s'il vous plaît b Non, pour 38 € c Vous pouvez vérifier l'huile? d Un litre e Non, merci, ça va 10 a Vous pouvez m'aider, je suis en panne

b Je ne sais pas, le moteur ne marche pas c Je suis entre
Orléans et Blois sur l'autoroute A10 d direction/vers Tours
e C'est une voiture anglaise: une Ford Mondeo bleue. Vous
arrivez quand? 11 a B b A c D d C  e E f F g H h G 12 a le
pneu est crevé b la batterie est à plat c le pare-brise est cassé
d les freins ne marchent pas et le moteur chauffe

## Unit 18

**Activities: 1 a** not in the Paris region but outside Paris they do
**b** the side with the € is common, the other is not **c** each
country shows its national symbols  **2 a** Vous pouvez changer
10€, svp? **b** Il me faut des pièces de 1€ **c** No change given **3 a**
vous n'avez pas de carte bancaire? **b** il me faut cinq pièces de
1€ **c** elle n'accepte que … **d** vous pouvez changer … **e** je n'en
ai pas **f** je ne sais pas **g** ça vous va? **h** Vous avez de la chance. **i**
Je vais regarder. **4 a** Pardon Monsieur, vous avez de la
monnaie pour le téléphone, s'il vous plaît? **b** Je n'ai qu'un
billet de 5€ et il me faut des pièces de 1€ **c** Une télécarte,
qu'est-ce que c'est? **d** Où est-ce que je peux acheter une
télécarte? **5 a** changer **b** pièce **c** signer **d** écrire **e** combien
**f** payer **6 a** Je voudrais changer des dollars **b** des dollars
américains **c** des billets **d** 200 dollars; il est à combien le
dollar? **e** Vous êtes ouvert le dimanche? **7 a** 5,40 € **b** 7,22 €
**c** 19,75 € **d** 22 € **e** 89,56 € **f** 172 € **g** 315,40 €   **h** 632,15 €
**i** 918,30 € **8 a** after breakfast **b** 14 **c** no **d** drinks from the
mini-bar **e** yes
**Mini-test: 1** Il y a un parking près d'ici? **2** Il me faut quatre
pièces de 1€ pour le parcmètre **3** Vous pouvez m'aider, s'il
vous plaît? Je suis en panne **4** Il me faut un litre d'huile **5** Vous
avez de la monnaie? **6** Vous acceptez les cartes de crédit? **7** Je
voudrais régler ma note **8** Vous pouvez vérifier la pression des
pneus, s'il vous plaît? **9** Vous pouvez faire le plein, s'il vous
plaît? **10** Je voudrais changer cent cinquante livres en euros.

## Unit 19

**Activities: 1 a** ii, iv **b** No **c** iii, iv **d** iii two every four hours and
iv one when needed **2 a** Ma fille a mal aux dents. **b** Oui, un
peu. **c** Depuis hier. **d** Merci; vous avez quelque chose pour les
piqûres d'insectes? **d** Je vais la prendre; c'est combien? **3 a** vi, **b**
v, **c** vii, **d** iii, **e** ii, **f** iv, **g** viii, **h** i **4 a** Je voudrais prendre rendez-
vous **b** Non, c'est pour mon fils. Nous sommes anglais, en
vacances ici et il  a mal aux dents depuis mardi. **c** Il a 12 ans **d**
aujourd'hui, ce matin ou cet après-midi **e** À quelle heure, s'il
vous plaît? **f** Monsieur/ Madame … **5 a** 8h **b** 19h **c** semaine

d fériés e USA f l'Australie g pleines h creuses 6 a vi, b iv, c v,
d i, e ii, f iii 8 a clés b stylo, lunettes c portefeuille, argent,
cartes de crédit d parapluie, carte d'identité e téléphone f
essuie-glace, freins 9 a on m'a volé ma voiture b elle est
comment votre voiture? c quel est le numéro d'immatriculation
d faire une déclaration par écrit e remplir cet imprimé f vous
en avez besoin pour vos assurances 10 a J'ai perdu mon stylo
en or au bureau b mon frère a perdu sa valise marron à
l'aéroport c ma soeur a perdu son porte-monnaie en cuir blanc
au parc d son père a perdu son passeport britannique dans la
rue e mon amie a perdu son foulard en soie dans l'autobus
**Mini-test:** 1 Je voudrais quelque chose pour le mal de tête 2 Je
voudrais prendre rendez-vous 3 J'ai mal à la gorge 4 On m'a
volé mon sac au cinéma 5 Mes lunettes sont cassées

## Self-assessment test 1 (Units 1–10)

1a Je m'appelle .... et vous? b Vous vous appelez comment? /
Comment vous appelez-vous? / Quel est votre nom?
c Comment ça va? d Je vais très bien et vous? e Je suis
dentiste. / Je travaille pour Air France/dans une banque. f Vous
travaillez? / Qu'est-ce que vous faites dans la vie? g J'habite
Brighton en Angleterre (dans le Sud de l'Angleterre). h Je suis
anglais(e) et je parle anglais et allemand. i Je suis marié(e) et
j'ai trois enfants. / Je ne suis pas marié(e) et je n'ai pas
d'enfants. j Je ne comprends pas. k Vous parlez anglais? (*raise
the voice on the last syllable*) l Parlez plus lentement.  2 a suis
b est c sont d ai e sont f a g ont h avons i sommes j ai  3 a es
b e c e d ons e ez f ent g e h e  4 a C'est loin? b Non, ce n'est
pas loin. c Il y a une banque près d'ici? d Non, il n'y a pas de
banque près d'ici. e Avez-vous/Vous avez un timbre? f Non, je
n'en ai pas. g C'est comment le film? / Le film est comment? h
C'est où l'arrêt d'autobus? i C'est à dix minutes d'ici à pied. j
Le magasin ouvre quand? / Quand est-ce que le magasin
ouvre? 5 a v b iv c i d iii e ii  6 a le dimanche trente-et-un mars
b le mercredi deux juin c le vendredi dix-huit janvier, d le
mardi vingt-quatre octobre e le samedi onze mai f le lundi
vingt-trois août g le jeudi dix-neuf septembre.  7 a prends
b fait c prenons d faites  e prendre f comprend parle
g finissons h travailles  i regarder  8 a J'habite en Angleterre.
b Elle travaille aux USA. c Nous aimons beaucoup
l'Allemagne. d Nous passons nos vacances en Australie. e Je
connais bien le Portugal. f Tu parles /vous parlez français?
g Elle est anglaise. h Bordeaux est une ville française.  9 a
Sophie déteste, Mohamed aime beaucoup, je n'aime pas jouer

au football. **b** Sophie aime beaucoup, Mohamed déteste, j'adore faire la cuisine. **c** Sophie aime beaucoup, Mohamed n'aime pas, j'adore regarder la télévision. **d** Sophie adore, Mohamed aime beaucoup, j'adore écouter de la musique. **e** Sophie n'aime pas, Mohamed adore, j'aime beaucoup faire de la natation. **f** Sophie adore, Mohamed déteste, je n'aime pas faire du ski. **g** Sophie n'aime pas, Mohamed aime beaucoup, j'adore aller au restaurant. **h** Sophie déteste, Mohamed adore, et je n'aime pas jouer au tennis **10 a** me **b** t' **c** se **d** nous **e** vous **f** se **11 a** il fait mauvais **b** il fait beau **c** le soleil brille **d** il fait chaud **e** il neige **f** il fait froid **g** il pleut **12 a** allez **b** allons **c** va **d** vas **e** vais **f** vont **13** Chère Amélie, Je vais passer (1) trois semaines en France (1) cet été avec ma soeur Ruth. Je vais apprendre le français (1) à Paris. Ruth va visiter (1) les/des monuments historiques et faire des courses (1) Le soir, nous allons voir (1)des amis. Tu vas venir (1) nous voir? A bientôt. Caroline.

### Self-assessment test 2 (Units 11–19)

**1 a** Je cherche une robe en coton **b** What size are you? **c** Je peux essayer? **d** C'est un peu trop cher/grand/petit. **e** Vous avez autre chose? **2 a** Bonsoir. Vous avez une chambre double avec salle de bains? **b** C'est pour deux nuits. **c** C'est combien? **d** Le petit-déjeuner est compris? **e** Il y a un restaurant dans l'hôtel / On peut manger dans l'hôtel? **f** La télévision ne marche pas. **3 a** Qu'est-ce que vous avez comme sandwiches? **b** Qu'est-ce que c'est le…? **c** Je voudrais un steak bien cuit / à point / saignant *or* bleu. **d** Je vais prendre … **e** L'addition, s'il vous plaît. **f** Qu'est-ce que vous avez à boire? **4 a** Je voudrais un billet simple pour Tarbes. **b** Le 16 avril, le matin/dans la matinée vers dix heures. **c** Il arrive à quelle heure? **d** Il faut réserver une place? **e** Non. C'est combien? **5** These are only possible answers. **a** Vous pouvez (me/nous) réserver une chambre, s'il vous plaît? **b** Vous avez un plan de Paris? **c** Pour aller/Je voudrais aller à la Tour Eiffel. **d** Qu'est-ce que vous avez comme excursions? **e** Qu'est-ce qu'il y a à faire pour les enfants? **f** Vous avez une liste de restaurants? **g** Vous pouvez me montrer les grands magasins sur le plan? **6 a** in the heart of the Pyrenees **b** it is a spa with 11 hot springs **c** grandiose **d** hiking in the mountains **e** waterfalls, lakes, flower-laden plateaux **f** downhill and cross-country skiing **g** yes, from beginners to experts. **7 a** Vous prenez la voiture ou le train? **b** En train vous descendez à la gare de Lourdes, puis vous prenez

l'autobus jusqu'à Cauterets. Cauterets est à 30 km de Lourdes.
**e** En voiture, vous prenez l'autoroute jusqu'à Tarbes, puis la N
21 et la D 921. Vous pouvez garer la voiture en face de l'hôtel.
**d** 'L'Edelweiss' est situé au 7, Boulevard Latapie Flurin, au
centre de Cauterets. **e** le vendredi 22 avril vers sept heures du
soir. **8 a** xi **b** v **c** vi **d** ii **e** x **f** ix **g** i **h** iv **i** iii **j** viii **k** vii **9 a** J'ai
besoin d'un docteur / Il me faut (voir) un docteur. **b** Quelle est
son adresse? / Vous pouvez me donner son adresse? **c** Allô, je
voudrais prendre rendez-vous. **d** J'ai mal au genou. **e** J'ai
mal/Je souffre depuis trois jours. **f** Je ne peux pas marcher. **g** Je
peux venir demain matin à dix heures. **h** Check with the
**French alphabet** on page 118.

# numbers

| | | | | | |
|---|---|---|---|---|---|
| 0 | zéro | 21 | vingt et un | 70 | soixante-dix |
| 1 | un | 22 | vingt-deux | 71 | soixante et onze |
| 2 | deux | 23 | vingt-trois | 72 | soixante-douze, |
| 3 | trois | 24 | vingt-quatre | | etc. |
| 4 | quatre | 25 | vingt-cinq | 80 | quatre-vingts |
| 5 | cinq | 26 | vingt-six | 81 | quatre-vingt-un |
| 6 | six | 27 | vingt-sept | 82 | quatre-vingt-deux, |
| 7 | sept | 28 | vingt-huit | | etc. |
| 8 | huit | 29 | vingt-neuf | 90 | quatre-vingt-dix |
| 9 | neuf | 30 | trente | 91 | quatre-vingt-onze |
| 10 | dix | 31 | trente et un | 92 | quatre-vingt-douze, |
| 11 | onze | 32 | trente-deux, etc. | | etc. |
| 12 | douze | 40 | quarante | 100 | cent |
| 13 | treize | 41 | quarante et un | 101 | cent un |
| 14 | quatorze | 42 | quarante-deux, etc. | 102 | cent deux, etc. |
| 15 | quinze | 50 | cinquante | 200 | deux cents |
| 16 | seize | 51 | cinquante et un | 210 | deux cent dix |
| 17 | dix-sept | 52 | cinquante-deux, etc. | 300 | trois cents |
| 18 | dix-huit | 60 | soixante | 331 | trois cent trente |
| 19 | dix-neuf | 61 | soixante et un | | et un |
| 20 | vingt | 62 | soixante-deux, etc. | | |

1,000 mille        1,000,000 un million

2,000 deux mille     2,000,000 deux millions

à *to, in*
abord *see* d'abord
accord *see* d'accord
abricot (m) *apricot*
achat (m) *shopping*; faire des achats
  *to do some shopping*
acheter *to buy*
addition (f) *bill, sum*
adorer *to adore, to love*
adresse (f) *address*
affaires (f pl) *business*; homme
  d'affaires *businessman*
âge (m) *age*
agence de voyages (f) *travel agency*
aider *to help*
aimer *to like, to love*
aire (f) de pique-nique *picnic area*
alcool (m) *spirit*
alimentation (f) *grocer's shop*
aller *to go*
aller (m) simple *single ticket*
aller-retour (m) *return ticket*
allô *hello (on phone)*
alors *well, then*
ambiance (f) *atmosphere*
ami (m), amie (f) *friend*
amende (f) *fine*
an (m) *year*
ancien(ne) *ancient, former*
anglais(e) *English (often used for
  British)*
Angleterre (f) *England*
année (f) *year*
après *after*
après-midi (m) *afternoon*
apprécier *to appreciate*
août *August*
apparaître *to appear*

s'appeler *lit. to be called* je m'appelle
  *my name is*
apprendre *to learn*
argent (m) *money*
arrêt (m) *stop*
arrivée (f) *arrival*
arriver *to arrive*
arrondissement (m) *district in large
  towns*
ascenseur (m) *lift*
aspirine (f) effervescente *soluble
  aspirin*
assez *enough, fairly*
assiette (f) *plate*
attendre *to wait for*
aujourd'hui *today*
au revoir *goodbye*
aussi *also, too, as well*
autobus (m) *bus*; en autobus *by bus*
autocar (m) *coach*; en autocar *by
  coach*
automne (m) *autumn*; en automne
  *in autumn*
autoroute (f) *motorway*
autre *other*; autre chose *something
  else*
avec *with*
avion (m) *aeroplane*
avoir *to have*; avoir l'air *to seem*
avril *April*

se baigner *to go for a swim*
baguette (f) *'French stick' (bread)*
balle (f) *ball*
banlieue (f) *suburb*
banque (f) *bank*
bar (m) *bar*
bas(se) *low*

bas (m) *bottom, lower part*
bâtiment (m) *building*
battre *to beat*
beau (belle) *handsome, beautiful*
beaucoup (de) *much, a lot*
belle *see* beau
besoin (m) *need;* avoir besoin *to need*
beurre (m) *butter*
bien *well;* bien sûr *certainly*
bientôt *soon;* à bientôt *see you soon*
bière (f) *beer*
billet (m) *ticket, (bank) note*
blanc (blanche) *white*
bleu(e) *blue;* bleu marine *navy blue;*
   bleu pâle *pale blue*
blond(e) *blond*
boeuf (m) *beef, ox*
boire *to drink*
boîte (f) *box, can, tin*
boîte aux lettres *letter box*
boîte (f) (de nuit) *disco, nightclub*
boisson (f) *drink*
bol (m) *bowl*
bon(ne) *good;* bon marché *cheap*
bonjour *good day, hello*
bonsoir *good evening*
botte (f) *boot*
boucherie (f) *butcher's*
bouchon (m) *cork, bottleneck*
boulangerie (f) *baker's*
boulevard (m) *boulevard*
bout (m) *end;* au bout de *at the end of*
bouteille (f) *bottle*
brasserie (f) *pub-restaurant*
briller *to shine*
britannique *British*
brouillard (m) *fog*
bruit (m) *noise*
brun (brune) *brown (hair,*
   *complexion)*
bureau (m) de location *box office*
bureau (m) de renseignements
   *information office*
bureau (m) des réservations *booking*
   *office*
bus (m) *see* autobus

cabine téléphonique (f) *telephone box*
cabinet de toilette (m) *small room*
   *containing wash basin and bidet*
cadeau (m) *present*
café (m) *coffee, café;* café au lait (m)
   *white coffee;* café crème *coffee*
   *served with cream*

caisse (f) *cash desk, cashier's ticket*
   *office*
ça *that, it;* ça va? *how are things?;* ça
   va *things are OK*
cabine (f) d'essayage *fitting room*
campagne (f) *country;* à la campagne
   *in (to) the country*
camping (m) *camping, campsite*
car (m) *see* autocar
carnet (m) *book (of tickets), ten*
   *metro tickets*
carrefour (m) *crossroads*
carte (f) *map, card, menu;* carte
   bancaire *banker's card;* carte
   d'abonnement *season ticket;* carte
   de crédit *credit card;* carte
   d'identité *identity card;* carte
   postale (f) *postcard*
cassé(e) *broken*
ce, cet, cette *this, that (adjective)*
ceci *see* ce
célèbre *famous*
célibataire (m and f) *single, bachelor*
cent *a hundred*
centime (m) *centime*
centre (m) *centre;* au centre de *in the*
   *centre of;* centre ville *town centre*
centre commercial (m) *shopping*
   *centre*
certain(e) *certain*
certainement *certainly*
ces *these, those*
c'est *it is, this is*
c'est ça *that's it*
cet, cette *see* ce
chambre (f) *(bed)room*
champignon (m) *mushroom*
chance (f) *luck*
changer *to change*
changeur (m) de monnaie *coin*
   *changing machine*
chaque *each, every*
charcuterie (f) *selling cooked meats*
chaud(e) *hot;* avoir chaud *to be hot*
chauffer *to heat up*
chaussure (f) *shoe*
chemise (f) *shirt*
chèque de voyage (m) *see* traveller
cher (chère) *expensive, dear*
chercher *to look for;* aller chercher
   *to go and fetch*
cheveux (m pl) *hair*
chez *at the home of;* chez moi *at my*
   *house, at home*

choisir *to choose*
choix (m) *choice*
chose (f) *thing*
chocolat (m) *eating or drinking chocolate*
cinq *five*
cinquante *50*
circulation (f) *traffic*
citron (m) *lemon*
classe (f) *class*
classique *classical*
clé (f) *key*
coin (m) *corner*
combien (de)? *how much? how many?*
commander *to order*
comme *as, like, in the way of*
commencer *to start, to begin*
comment *how, how to, what*
complet(ète) *full*
composer *to dial (a telephone number)*
composter *to date-stamp (a ticket)*
comprendre *to understand*
comprimé (m) *tablet*
compris *understood, included*
connaître *to know (a person or a place)*
connu(e) *known*
conseiller *to advise*
consigne (f) *left luggage*; consigne automatique *luggage lockers*
content(e) *pleased*
continuer *to continue*
copain/copine *(boy, girl) friend*
correspondance (f) *connection*
côté (m) *side*; à coté de *next to*; de l'autre côté *on the other side*
costume (m) *suit for men*
couchette (f) *couchette*
se coucher *to go to bed*
couleur (f) *colour*
coup (m) de fil *telephone call*
cours (m) particulier *private lesson*
cours (m) de change *exchange rate*
courses (f pl) *shopping*
court(e) *short*
court (m) de tennis *tennis court*
coûter *to cost*
couverture (f) *blanket, cover*
cravate (f) *tie*
crème (f) *cream*
crêperie (f) *pancake house*
croire *to believe*

croissant (m) *croissant*
croque-monsieur (m) *toasted cheese sandwich with ham*
en cuir *in leather*
cuisine (f) *kitchen, cooking*
cuit (e) *cooked*

d'abord *firstly*
d'accord *OK, agreed*
dans *in, into*
danser *to dance*
date (f) *date*
de *of, from*
décembre *December*
décider *to decide*
décrocher l'appareil *to lift the receiver*
déjeuner *to lunch, lunch*; petit-déjeuner (m) *breakfast*
demain *tomorrow*
demi(e) *half*; demi-kilo (m) *half a kilogram*; demi-heure (f) *half an hour*
dent (f) *tooth*
dentifrice (m) *toothpaste*
dépannage: le service de dépannage *breakdown service*
dépendre de *to depend on*
depuis *since*; je suis marié depuis dix ans *I've been married for ten years*
déranger *to disturb, to inconvenience*; en dérangement *out of order*
dernier(ière) *last*
descendre *to go down*
désirer *to wish for*
desservir *to serve*
détester *to hate*
deux *two*
deuxième *second*
devoir *must, should, ought*
différent(e) *different*
dimanche *Sunday*
diminuer *to decrease*
dîner (m) *dinner, to have dinner*
dire *to say*
direct(e) *direct*
directement *directly*
direction (f) *direction*
disque (m) *record*
dix *ten*
dix-huit *18*
dix-neuf *19*
dix-sept *17*
doit, ça doit *see devoir*
donner *to give*

dormir *to sleep*
douche (f) *shower*
douze *12*
droit(e) *straight*; tout droit *straight on*
à droite *right (hand)*; avoir droit *to be entitled*

eau (f) *water*
  eau minérale (f) *mineral water*
école (f) *school*
écouter *to listen*
église (f) *church*
élève (m and f) *pupil*
écrire *to write*
par écrit *in writing*
émetteur(rice) *issuing*
emmener *to take (someone somewhere)*
emplacement (m) *pitch*
en *in, on, of it, of them*
enfant (m and f) *child*
ensemble *together*
ensemble (m) *outfit, suit (woman)*
ensuite *then*
entre *between*
entrée (f) *way in, admission charge*
environ *about*
environs (m pl) *surroundings*
envoyer *to send*
équitation (f) *riding*
erreur (f) *mistake*
espérer *to hope*
essayer *to try*
essence (f) *petrol*
essuie-glace (m) *windscreen wiper*
est (m) *east*
et *and*
étage (m) *floor*
été (m) *summer*; en été *in summer*
étoile (f) *star*
être *to be*
eux *them (people)*
éviter *to avoid*
excursion (f) *excursion, trip*; faire une excursion *to go on an excursion*
excuser *to excuse*
expliquer *explain*
en face (de) *facing*

facile *easy*
faim (f) *hunger*; avoir faim *to be hungry*
faire *to do, to make*

famille (f) *family*
il faut *it is necessary, one has to*
il faudra *it will be necessary*
faux (fausse) *false*
favori (favorite) *favourite*
femme (f) *wife, woman*
fenêtre (f) *window*
fermé(e) *closed*
fermer *to close*
fête (f) *feast-day, celebration*
feux (m pl) (rouges) *traffic lights*
février *February*
fièvre (f) *fever, temperature*
figurer *to appear*
fille (f) *daughter, girl*
fils (m) *son*
finalement *finally*
finir *to finish*
fleur (f) *flower*
fois (f) *time*; une fois *once*
fond (m) *back, far end*; au fond du couloir *at the far end of the corridor*
fondre *to melt*
forme (f) *shape*
formidable *great*
foulard (m) *scarf*
fourchette (f) *fork*
fraise (f) *strawberry*
franc (m) *franc*
français(e) *French*
France (f) *France*
frère (m) *brother*
frein (m) *brake*
frite (f) *chip*; *(adjective) fried*
froid(e) *cold*; avoir froid *to be cold*
fromage (m) *cheese*
fruit (m) *fruit*

garçon (m) *boy, waiter*
garder *to keep*
gare (f) *station*; gare routière (f) *bus, coach station*; gare SNCF (f) *railway station*
garer *to park*
garni(e) *served with vegetables, salads, etc.*
à gauche *left*
généralement *generally*
glace (f) *ice cream*
gonflage (m) des pneus *pumping up the tyres*
gorge (f) *throat*
gourmet (m) *gourmet*

grand (e) *big, tall*
Grande-Bretagne (f) *Great Britain*
gratuit (e) *free*
grillade (f) *grilled meat*
grippe (f) *flu*
gros (grosse) *fat, large*
guichet (m) *ticket office*

(s')habiller *to dress*
habiter *to live*
haricot (m) *bean*; haricot vert *green bean*
heure (f) *hour*; quelle heure est-il? *what time is it?*
hiver (m) *winter*; en hiver *in winter*
homme (m) *man*; homme d'affaires *businessman*
hôpital (m) *hospital*
horaire (m) *timetable*
hôtel (m) *hotel*; hôtel de ville (m) *town hall*
hors *outside*; hors-d'oeuvre *starter*; hors de service *out of service*
huile (f) *oil*
huit *eight*

ici *here*
île (f) *island*; Ile de France *Paris area*
indicatif (m) *dialling code*
indiquer *indicate*
ingénieur (m) *engineer*
intéressant(e) *interesting*
introduire *to insert*
inviter *to invite*
inscription (f) *enrolment*

jamais *never*
jambon (m) *ham*
janvier *January*
jardin (m) *garden*
jardinage (m) *gardening*
jaune *yellow*
jean (m) or jeans (m pl) *jeans*
jeu (m) *game*; jeu de société *parlour game*
jeudi *Thursday*
jeune *young*
joli(e) *pretty*
jouer *to play*
jour (m) *day*; jour férié *bank holiday*
journal (m) *newspaper*
journée (f) *day, day-time*
joyeux(se) *joyful, merry*
juillet *July*

juin *June*
jupe (f) *skirt*
jus (m) de fruit *fruit juice*
jusqu'à *until, as far as*

kilo(gramme) (m) *kilogram*

la *the, her, it*
là(-bas) *(over) there*
lait (m) *milk*
laisser *to leave*; laissé *left*
large *wide, big*
(se) laver *to wash*
le *the, him, it*
léger (légère) *light*
légume (m) *vegetable*
lentement *slowly*
lequel, laquelle *who, which*; sur laquelle *on which*
lettre (f) *letter*
leur(s) *their, to them*
se lever *to get up*
libre *free (but for free of charge use gratuit)*; libre service (m) *small supermarket*
ligne (f) *number (bus), line (métro)*
lire *to read*
lit (m) *bed*; à deux lits *twin-bedded*; le grand lit *double bed*
litre (m) *litre*
livre (m) *book*; (f) *pound*
location (f) *hire*
loin *far*
loisir (m) *hobby*
long (longue) *long*
louer *to let, to hire, to book*
lourd(e) *heavy*
lui *to him, to her, he, as for him*
lundi *Monday*
lunettes (f pl) *glasses*

Madame *Madam, Mrs*
Mademoiselle *Miss*
magasin (m) *shop*; grand magasin *department store*
mai *May*
maillot de bain (m) *swimming costume, swimsuit*
maintenant *now*
mais *but*
maison (f) *house*; à la maison *at home*
mal *badly*; avoir mal *to have a pain*; mal (m) de dos *backache*

malheureusement *unfortunately*
manger *to eat*
manquer *to be lacking, missing*
marché (m) *market*; bon marché
  *cheap*
marcher *to walk, to work (for a*
  *machine)*
mardi *Tuesday*
mari (m) *husband*
marié(e) *married*
marron *brown*
mars *March*
matin (m) *morning*
mauvais(e) *bad*
médecin (m) *doctor, physician*
médicament (m) *medicine*
meilleur(e) *better*
mélange (m) *mixture*, mélanger *to*
  *mix*
même *same, even*
menu (m) *set meal*
mer (f) *sea*; au bord de la mer *at the*
  *seaside, by the sea*
mère (f) *mother*
merci *thank you*
mercredi *Wednesday*
mesurer *to measure*
Messieurs-dames *ladies and*
  *gentlemen*
métro (m) *underground*
mettre *to put*
midi *midday, lunch time*
mieux *better*
milieu (m) *middle, milieu*
mille *a thousand*
mince *thin*
minuit *midnight*
moi *me, I*
moins *less*
mois (m) *month*
moitié (f) *half*
mon, ma, mes *my*
monument (m) *monument*
monde (m) *world*; tout le monde
  *everybody*
monnaie (f) *small change*
Monsieur *Sir, Mr*
montagne (f) *mountain*; à la
  montagne *in, to the mountains*
monter *to go up*
montre (f) *watch*
montrer *to show*
morceau (m) *piece*
moteur (m) *engine*

motif (m) *pattern, design*
moyen(ne) *medium, average*
musée (m) *museum*

natation (f) *swimming*
neiger *to snow*
neuf *nine*
neuf (neuve) *new*
niveau (m) *level*
nocturne *late-night opening*
Noël (m) *Christmas*
noir(e) *black*
nom (m) *name*
non *no*
nord (m) *north*
note (f) *bill (hotel, telephone)*
notre, nos *our*
nouveau (elle) *new*; à nouveau *again*
novembre *November*
nuit (f) *night*
numéro (m) *number*, numéro
  d'immatriculation *number plate*

occupé(e) *busy*
s'occuper *to deal with, to attend to*
octobre *October*
office du/de tourisme (m) *tourist office*
oeil (m) *eye*
oeuf *egg*
oéuvre (f) *work of art*
omelette (f) *omelette*
on *one (used also for 'we' and 'I')*
onze *11*
(en) or *(made of) gold*
ou *or*; ou ... ou *either ... or*
où *where*
ouest (m) *west*
oui *yes*
ouvert(e) *open*
ouvrir *to open*

pain (m) *bread*
panne (f) *breakdown*
panneau (m) *sign*
pantalon (m) *trousers*
paquet (m) *packet*
paquet-cadeau (m) *gift-package*
parcmètre (m) *parking meter*
pardon *pardon, sorry, excuse me*
parfum (m) *perfume, flavour (ice*
  *cream)*
parking (m) *car park*
parler *to speak*
en particulier *particularly*

partir *to go, to leave*
à partir de *from, as*
pas *not*; pas du tout *not at all*
passant(e) *passer-by*
passer *to pass*
pâté (m) *pâté*; pâté de campagne *country pâté*
pâtisserie (f) *a cake shop, pastry, cake*
payer *to pay*
pays (m) *country; area*
à péage *toll payable*
pendant *during*
penser *to think*
perdre *to lose*; perdu *lost*
père (m) *father*
personne (f) *person*; personne (+ ne) *nobody*
peser *to weigh*
pétanque (f) *petanque (kind of bowls)*
petit(e) *small*; petit-déjeuner *breakfast*
(un) peu *(a) little, few*
pharmacie (f) *chemist's*
pharmacien(ne) *chemist*
pied (m) *foot*; à pied *on foot*
pièce (f) *room, coin*; pièce d'identité *identification*
pique-nique (m) *picnic*
piscine (f) (couverte) *(indoor) swimming pool*
plan (m) (de la ville) *(town) map*
place (f) *square, space, seat*
plaisir (m) *pleasure*; faire plaisir *to please*; avec plaisir *with pleasure*
planche à voile (f) *windsurfing board*
plat (m) *dish, course*
plein(e) *full*; le plein, s'il vous plaît *(at the garage) fill it up, please*
il pleut *it is raining*
sans plomb (m) *lead-free petrol*
(la) plupart *most*
plus *more, plus*; plus ... que *more than*;
    en plus *in addition, extra*; ne ... pas *no longer, no more*
pneu (m) *tyre*
poêlle (f) *frying pan*
poids (m) *weight*
à point *medium done (meat)*
pois, petits pois (m pl) *peas*
poisson (m) *fish*
pointure (f) *size shoes*
poivre (m) *pepper*; poivrer *to pepper*
pomme (f) *apple*; pomme de terre (f)

*potato*; pommes frites (f pl) *chips*
pompiste (m) *pump attendant*
pont (m) *bridge*
portefeuille (m) *wallet*
porte-monnaie (m) *purse*
porter *to carry, to wear*
poste (f) *post, post office*
pourboire (m) *tip*
poulet (m) *chicken*
pour *for, in order to*
pouvoir *can, be able to*; vous pouvez *you can*
pratique *practical, convenient*
pratiquer *to practise, to do*
préférer *to prefer*
premier(ière) *first*
prendre *to take*; pris *taken*
près (de) *near*; près d'ici *near by*
pression (f) *pressure (tyre); draught (beer)*
presque *nearly*
printemps (m) *spring*; au printemps *in spring*
prix (m) *price*
prochain(e) *next*
proche *near*
professeur(e) *teacher*
profession (f) *profession*
promenade (f) (à pied) *walk*
se promener (à pied) *to go for a walk*
puis *then*
pull-over (m) *pullover*

quai (m) *platform*
quand? *when?*
quarante *40*
quatorze *14*
quatre *four*
quatre-vingts *80*
quatre-vingt-dix *90*
quel(le)? *which?, what?*
quelque(s) *some (a few)*; quelque chose *something*
quelqu'un *someone*
quelquefois *sometimes*
que *that, than*
(ne) ... que *only*
qu'est-ce que *what*
qui *who, which*
quinze *15*
quinzaine (f) *15 or so*
quitter *to leave*
quoi? *what?*

raide *straight (hair)*
randonnée (f) *hike*
rapide *rapid*
raquette (f) *racket*
régler *to settle (bill)*
regretter *to be sorry*
regarder *to watch*
remplir *to fill in*
rendez-vous (m) *appointment*
rendre *to give back*
rendre visite *to pay a visit*
renseignement (m) *(piece of) information*
se renseigner *to inquire*
rentrer *to go back, to go home*
réparer *to repair*
repas (m) *meal*
répéter *to repeat*
se reposer *to rest*
RER *fast extension of the underground in the suburbs*
restaurant (m) *restaurant*
réserver *to reserve, to book*
rester *to stay*
retourner *to go back, to return*
rien *nothing*; de rien *don't mention it*
robe (f) *dress*
rocade (f) *ring road, bypass*
rouge *red*
route (f) *road*
rue (f) *street*

sac à main (m) *handbag*
saignant(e) *bleeding, rare (meat)*
saison (f) *season*; hors saison *out of season*; en pleine saison *in high season*
saler *to salt*
salle (f) *hall, auditorium, room*; salle de bains *bathroom*; salle à manger *dining room*
sandwich (m) *sandwich*
sans *without*
saucisson (m) *kind of salami*
savoir *to know (a fact or how to do something e.g.* je sais faire la cuisine *I know how to cook)*
savon (m) *soap*
scène (f) *scene*
séance (f) *session*
secrétaire (m and f) *secretary*
seize *16*
sel (m) *salt*
selon *according to*

semaine (f) *week*
sept *seven*
septembre *September*
servir *to serve*
serviette (f) *towel, napkin*; serviette de toilette *hand towel*
shampooing (m) *shampoo*
s'il vous plaît *please*
situé(e) *situated*
six *six*
ski (m) *ski*; ski de fond *cross-country ski-ing*, de piste *downhill*
SNCF *French railways*
soeur (f) *sister*
soie (f) *silk*; en soie *made of silk*
soif (f) *thirst*; avoir soif *to be thirsty*
soir (m) *evening*
soirée (f) *evening, evening entertainment*
soixante *60*
soixante-dix *70*
en solde *in the sale*
soleil (m) *sun*
son, sa, ses *his, her, its*
sortie (f) *exit*
sortir *to go out*
souffrir *to suffer*
source (f) *spring*
souvenir (m) *souvenir, memory*
souvent *often*
spectacle (m) *show*
sport (m) *sport*
station (f) de métro *underground station*
station thermale (f) *spa*
station-service (f) *petrol station*
stationnement (m) (interdit) *(no) parking*
stationner *to park*
stylo (m) *pen*
sucre (m) *sugar*, sucreries (f pl) *sweet things*
sud (m) *south*
suivre *to follow*
supermarché (m) *supermarket*
sur *on*
surtout *mainly, especially*
svp (s'il vous plaît) *please*
sympathique *friendly, pleasant*
syndicat d'initiative (m) *tourist office*

tabac (m) *tobacconist's-cum-newsagent's*

taille (f) *size, waist*
tarif (m) *price list, rate;* tarif réduit *reduced rate*
tarte (f) *pie*
taxi (m) *taxi*
télécarte (f) *phone card*
téléphone (m) *telephone*
téléphoner (à) *to phone*
temps (m) *time, weather*
tête (f) *head*
T.G.V. *high speed train*
thé (m) *tea*
ticket (m) *ticket*
timbre (m) *stamp*
tir-à-l'arc (m) *archery*
tire-bouchon (m) *corkscrew*
toi *you (familiar)*
toilette (f), faire sa toilette *to wash and dress;* les toilettes *lavatory*
ton, ta, tes *your*
tonalité (f) *dialling tone*
toujours *always*
touriste (m and f) *tourist*
tourner *to turn*
tout(e) tous *all;* tout de suite *immediately;* tout droit *straight ahead;* tout le monde *everybody;* tous les deux *both of them;* tous les jours *every day*
train (m) *train;* en train *by train*
trajet (m) *journey*
tranche (f) *slice*
travail (m) *work, job*
travailler *to work*
traveller (m) *travellers' cheque*
traverser *to cross*
treize *13*
trente *30*
très *very*
trois *three*
troisième *third*
se tromper *to make a mistake*
trop *too, too much, too many*
trouver *to find;* se trouver *to be (situated)*
TTC *all taxes included*

un(e) *a, an, one*
uni(e) *plain*

va, vas *see* aller
vacances (f pl) *holiday(s)*
valise (f) *suitcase*
vanille (f) *vanilla*

vase (m) *vase*
il vaut *it costs, it is worth*
veau (m) *veal*
vélo (m) *bicycle*
vendeur (m), vendeuse (f) *sales assistant*
vendredi *Friday*
vent (m) *wind*
ventre (m) *stomach*
vérifier *to check*
verre (m) *glass*
vers *towards*
verser *to pour*
vert(e) *green*
vêtement (m) *garment*
viande (f) *meat*
vie (f) *life, cost of living*
vieux (vieil, vieille) *old*
ville (f) *town*
vin (m) *wine*
vingt *20*
vite *quickly*
vitesse (f) *speed*
visite (f) guidée *guided tour*
visiter *to visit (a place)*
voie (f) *track*
voilà *there is, here is, there you are*
voir *to see*
voiture (f) *car;* voiture-restaurant *restaurant-car;* en voiture *by car*
voler *to steal;* volé *stolen*
votre, vos *your*
je voudrais *I'd like*
vouloir *to want;* vous voulez *you want*
voyager *to travel*
vrai(e) *true*
V.T.T. *mountain biking*

WC (m) (pronounced vé-cé) *toilet*
week-end (m) *weekend*

y *there, to it*
yaourt (m) *yoghurt*
yeux *see* oeil

zéro *zero*

# English–French vocabulary

*a* un, une
*about* environ
*address* l'adresse (f)
*admission charge* l'entrée (f)
*after* après
*afternoon* après-midi (m)
*again* encore, de nouveau
*age* l'âge (m)
*agency* l'agence (f); *travel agency* l'agence (f) de voyages
*all* tout, toute, tous, toutes
*also* aussi
*always* toujours
*and* et
*appear* apparaître
*apple* la pomme
*appointment* le rendez-vous
*April* avril
*arrival* l'arrivée (f)
*arrive* arriver
*as* comme
*aspirin* l'aspirine (f)
*at* à, chez; *at the corner* au coin; *at home* à la maison
*August* août
*autumn* l'automne; *in autumn* en automne

*bad* mauvais(e); *badly* mal
*baker's* la boulangerie
*bank* la banque; *bank holiday* le jour férié
*bath* le bain; *to have a bath* prendre un bain; *bathroom* salle de bains
*be* être
*be able to* pouvoir
*bean* l'haricot (m)
*beautiful* beau, belle

*bed* le lit; *double bed* le grand lit; *twin-bedded* à deux lits
*beer* la bière; *draught (beer)* la pression
*before* avant
*behind* derrière
*believe* croire
*better* meilleur(e), mieux
*between* entre
*bicycle* le vélo
*big* grand(e)
*bill (food, drinks)* l'addition (f)
*bill (hotel)* la note
*black* noir(e)
*blue* bleu(e)
*book* le livre
*book* louer, réserver
*bottle* la bouteille
*box* la boîte; *box office* le bureau de location
*boy* le garçon
*bread* le pain
*break* casser; *broken* cassé(e)
*breakdown* la panne; *breakdown service* le service de dépannage
*breakfast* le petit-déjeuner
*bridge* le pont
*British* britannique
*brother* le frère
*brown* marron
*bus* l'autobus (m), le bus; *bus stop* l'arrêt (m) d'autobus
*busy* occupé(e)
*but* mais
*butcher's* la boucherie
*butter* le beurre
*buy* acheter

*cake, cake shop* une pâtisserie
*camping, campsite* le camping
*can* peux, peut, pouvez
*car park* le parking
*car* la voiture; *by car* en voiture
*carry* porter
*cash desk, cashier's* la caisse
*catch* prendre
*certainly* bien sûr
*change* changer
*change (small)* la monnaie
*cheap* bon marché; *cheaper* meilleur marché
*check* vérifier
*cheese* le fromage
*chemist* le pharmacien, la pharmacienne
*chemist's* la pharmacie
*chicken* le poulet
*child* l'enfant (m and f)
*chips* les frites
*choose* choisir
*church* l'église (f)
*close* fermer; *closed* fermé(e)
*clothes* les vêtements, la tenue
*coach* l'autocar (m), le car
*coffee (black)* le café
*coin* la pièce
*cold* froid(e); *to be cold* avoir froid
*colour* la couleur
*come* venir; *come home* rentrer
*cook* faire la cuisine
*cooking* la cuisine
*corkscrew* le tire-bouchon
*cost* coûter
*country* le pays
*course* le plat
*credit card* la carte de crédit
*cross* traverser

*dance* danser
*daughter* la fille
*day* le jour; *the whole day* toute la journée
*dear* cher, chère
*December* décembre
*dinner* le dîner
*dish* le plat
*do* faire
*doctor* le médecin
*dress* la robe; s'habiller
*drink* boire; la boisson
*during* pendant

*easy* facile
*eat* manger
*egg* l'oeuf (m)
*end* le bout; *at the end* au bout
*engine* le moteur
*England* l'Angleterre (f)
*English* anglais(e)
*Englishman* l'Anglais; *Englishwoman* l'Anglaise
*enough* assez
*evening* le soir, la soirée
*every* tout, toute
*everyday* tous les jours; *everybody* tout le monde
*everything* tout
*excuse me* pardon
*exit* la sortie
*expensive* cher, chère
*eye* l'oeil (m)

*false* faux, fausse
*family* la famille
*far* loin
*fat* gros(se)
*father* le père
*February* février
*fill in* remplir; *fill it up (with petrol)* faire le plein
*find* trouver
*finish* finir
*first* premier, première
*firstly* d'abord
*fish* le poisson
*floor* l'étage (m)
*follow* suivre
*foot* le pied; *on foot* à pied
*for* pour
*France* la France
*free (costing nothing)* gratuit(e)
*French* français(e)
*Frenchman* le Français, *Frenchwoman* la Française
*French railways* S.N.C.F.
*Friday* vendredi
*friend* l'ami (m), l'amie (f)
*friendly* sympathique
*from* de, à partir de
*fruit juice* le jus de fruit
*full* complet, complète, plein(e)

*gardening* le jardinage
*get up* se lever
*girl* la fille
*give* donner

*glasses* les lunettes (f pl)
*go* aller, partir, *to go up* monter; *to go down* descendre
*go and get* aller chercher
*go out* sortir; *go home* rentrer à la maison
*good* bon, bonne
*good evening* bonsoir
*goodbye* au revoir
*good night* bonne nuit
*Great Britain* la Grande-Bretagne
*green* vert(e)
*grocer's shop* l'alimentation (f)

*hair* les cheveux (m pl)
*half* demi(e); *half an hour* demi-heure
*ham* le jambon
*handbag* le sac à main
*hate* détester
*have* avoir
*head* la tête
*headache* le mal de tête
*hear* entendre
*heavy* lourd(e)
*hello* bonjour, allô *(on the phone)*
*help* aider
*here* ici
*here is* voilà
*hike* la randonnée
*hire, hiring* louer, la location
*hobby* le loisir
*holiday(s)* les vacances (f pl)
*home, at home* à la maison; *at my home* chez moi
*hope* espérer
*hospital* l'hôpital (m)
*hot* chaud(e); *to be hot* avoir chaud
*hotel* l'hôtel (m)
*hour* l'heure (f)
*house* la maison
*how* comment
*how much/how many* combien
*hundred (a)* cent
*hunger* la faim, *to be hungry* avoir faim
*husband* le mari

*I* je, moi
*ice cream* la glace
*identification* la pièce d'identité
*ill* malade
*immediately* tout de suite
*in, into* à, en, dans
*in front of* devant

*information (piece of)* le renseignement
*information office* le bureau de renseignements
*inquire* se renseigner
*insert* introduire
*interesting* intéressant(e)
*invite* inviter
*it's* c'est, il est, elle est

*January* janvier
*jeans* le jean, les jeans
*journey* le trajet
*July* juillet
*June* juin

*key* la clé
*know* savoir, connaître

*ladies and gentlemen* Messieurs-dames
*large* gros(se), grand(e)
*last* dernier, dernière
*late-night opening* le nocturne
*learn* apprendre
*leave* quitter
*left, on the left* à gauche
*left luggage* la consigne
*lemon* le citron
*less* moins
*letter box* la boîte aux lettres
*letter* la lettre
*lift* l'ascenseur (m)
*like* aimer
*like* comme
*line (underground)* la ligne
*listen* écouter
*litre* le litre
*little* petit(e); *(a) little* (un) peu
*live* habiter
*long* long, longue
*look for* chercher
*lose* perdre; *lost* perdu(e)
*lot, a lot (of)* beaucoup (de)
*love* aimer
*lunch* le déjeuner

*Madame, Mrs* Madame, Mme
*make* faire
*man* l'homme (m)
*many* beaucoup
*map* la carte; *map (town)* le plan (de la ville)
*March* mars

market le marché
married marié(e)
May mai
me moi
meal le repas
measure mesurer
meat la viande; *well done* bien
cuit(e); *medium* à point
medicine le médicament
menu à la carte
midday midi
middle milieu; *in the middle* au
milieu
midnight minuit
milk le lait
Miss Mademoiselle
Monday lundi
money l'argent (m)
month le mois
more plus; *no ... more* ne ... plus
morning le matin, la matinée
mother la mère
motorway l'autoroute (f)
mountain la montagne; *in/to the
mountains* à la montagne
much beaucoup
museum le musée
must; *one must* il faut + infinitive

name le nom
near près (de)
nearby près de; *near here* près d'ici
nearly presque
need avoir besoin
never jamais
new neuf, neuve, nouveau, nouvelle
newspaper le journal
next prochain(e)
next to à côté de
night la nuit
nightclub la boîte (de nuit)
no non
nothing rien
November novembre
now maintenant
number le numéro; *(bus) number* la
ligne

October octobre
of, off de
often souvent
oil l'huile (f)
OK d'accord
old vieux, vieil, vielle

omelet l'omelette (f)
on sur, à, en; *on foot* à pied
once une fois
one un, une, on
only seulement
open ouvrir; *opened* ouvert(e)
opposite en face de
or ou
order commander
other autre
out of hors de

packet le paquet
pain la douleur; *to have a pain* avoir
mal
park garer
parking meter le parcmètre
particularly particulièrement
passer-by passant(e)
pay payer
peas les petits pois
pepper le poivre
person la personne
petrol l'essence (f); *petrol station* la
station-service
petrol: lead-free le sans plomb
phone card télécarte (f)
picnic le pique-nique; *to have a picnic*
faire un pique-nique
pie la tarte
piece le morceau
platform le quai
play jouer
please s'il vous plaît
pleased content(e)
postcard la carte postale
post; post office la poste
potato la pomme de terre
pound (sterling) la livre (sterling)
prefer préférer
pressure (tyre) la pression
pretty joli(e)
price le prix
price list le tarif
pullover le pull-over
pump attendant le pompiste
purse le porte-monnaie
put mettre

quick rapide; *quickly* vite

rain la pluie; *it's raining* il pleut
rare (meat) saignant(e)
read lire

*record* le disque
*red* rouge
*repair* réparer
*repeat* répéter
*reserve* réserver
*rest* se reposer
*right, on the right* à droite
*road* la route
*room* la pièce, la salle; *bathroom* salle de bains; *dining room* la salle à manger

*sale (on)* en solde
*sales assistant* le vendeur, la vendeuse
*salt* le sel
*same* même
*sandwich* le sandwich
*Saturday* samedi
*say* dire
*school* l'école (f)
*sea* la mer; *by the sea* au bord de la mer
*season* la saison; *out of …* hors …; *in high …* en pleine …
*seat* la place
*secretary* le/la secrétaire
*see* voir
*send* envoyer
*September* septembre
*serve* servir
*serve (transport)* desservir
*shampoo* le shampooing
*shine* briller; *the sun shines* le soleil brille
*shirt* la chemise
*shoe* la chaussure; *shoe size* la pointure
*shop* le magasin
*shopping* les courses; *to do some shopping* faire les courses
*shopping centre* le centre commercial
*show* montrer
*show* le spectacle
*shower* la douche; *to have a shower* prendre une douche
*sign* le panneau
*since* depuis
*single/bachelor* célibataire
*Sir, Mr* Monsieur, M.
*sister* la soeur
*situated* situé(e)
*size* la taille
*skirt* la jupe
*sleep* dormir

*slice* la tranche
*slow* lent; *slowly* lentement
*small* petit(e)
*snow* neiger
*soap* le savon
*some* quelque(s)
*someone* quelqu'un
*something* quelque chose
*something else* quelque chose d'autre
*sometimes* quelquefois
*son* le fils
*soon* bientôt
*sorry* pardon
*speak* parler
*spend (time)* passer
*sport* le sport; *to do a sport* pratiquer un sport
*spring* le printemps; *in spring* au printemps
*square* la place
*stamp* le timbre
*star* l'étoile (f)
*start* commencer
*station (rail)* la gare (SNCF); *bus/coach station* la gare routière; *underground station* la station
*straight* raide, droit(e)
*straight on* tout droit
*street* la rue
*surburbs* la banlieue
*sugar* le sucre
*suitcase* la valise
*summer* l'été (m)
*sun* le soleil
*Sunday* dimanche
*supermarket* le supermarché
*surroundings* les environs (m pl)
*swim* nager
*swimming* la natation; *swimming pool* la piscine; *swimming costume, swimsuit* le maillot de bain

*take, taken* prendre, pris
*tall* grand(e)
*taxi* le taxi
*tea* le thé
*teacher* le professeur, la professeure
*tell* dire
*telephone* téléphoner, le téléphone
*telephone box* la cabine téléphonique
*than* que
*thank you* merci
*that's all* c'est tout
*the* le, la, les

*then* ensuite, puis, alors
*there* y
*these, those* ces
*thin* mince
*thing* la chose
*think* penser
*thirst* la soif; *to be thirsty* avoir soif
*this is* c'est
*this, that* ce, cet, cette
*thousand* mille
*throat* la gorge
*Thursday* jeudi
*ticket* le billet, le ticket
*ticket office* le guichet
*time* l'heure (f); *what time is it?* quelle heure est-il?
*time* le temps; *spend time* passer le temps
*timetable* l'horaire (m)
*tip* le pourboire
*to* à, en, pour, jusqu'à
*tobacconist's/newsagent's* le tabac
*today* aujourd'hui
*together* ensemble
*toilet* les toilettes (f pl)
*toll payable* à péage
*tomorrow* demain
*too; too much; too many* trop
*tooth* la dent; *toothpaste* le dentifrice
*tour* la visite; *guided tour* la visite guidée
*tourist* le/la touriste
*tourist office* l'office (m) du/de tourisme, le syndicat d'initiative
*towards* vers
*towel* la serviette
*town* la ville
*traffic* la circulation
*train* le train; *by train* en train; *on the train* dans le train
*travel* voyager, le voyage
*traveller's cheque* le traveller
*trip* l'excursion (f)
*trousers* le pantalon
*true* vrai
*try* essayer
*Tuesday* mardi
*turn* tourner
*tyre* le pneu

*underground* le métro
*understand* comprendre
*until* jusqu'à

*very* très
*visit* visiter

*wait* attendre
*walk* marcher; *a walk* une promenade; *to go for a walk* se promener
*wallet* le portefeuille
*wash (oneself)* (se) laver
*watch* regarder; la montre
*water (mineral)* eau minérale
*wear* porter
*weather* le temps
*Wednesday* mercredi
*week* la semaine
*weigh* peser
*well* bien
*what* que(le); qu'est-ce que; quoi
*when* quand
*where* où
*which* quel(le)
*white* blanc, blanche
*white coffee* le café crème
*who* qui
*wife* la femme
*windsurf board* la planche à voile
*wine* le vin
*winter* l'hiver (m); *in winter* en hiver
*wish* désirer
*with* avec
*without* sans
*woman* la femme
*work* travailler, marcher (machine)
*work* le travail
*write* écrire

*year* l'an (m), l'année (f)
*yellow* jaune
*yes* oui
*yoghurt* yaourt
*you* tu, toi
*young* jeune

# index